German PhraseFinder & Dictionary

2nd Edition

WILEY
John Wiley & Sons, Inc.

Published by:

John Wiley & Sons, Inc.

111 River St.
Hoboken, NJ 07030-5774

ISBN-13: 978-1-118-14362-9

Editor: Andrea Kahn
Photo Editor: Richard H. Fox
Illustrations by Maciek Albrecht

Translation, Copyediting, Proofreading, Production, and Layout by:
Language Line Translation Solutions, 15115 SW Sequoia Pkwy, Ste 200, Portland,
OR 97224

Front cover photo: Dining options written on a board outside Gasthaus
Hallerschlösschen in Nuschelberg, Bavaria, Germany.
©Helmut Meyer zur Capellen / Imagebroker / Alamy Images

For information on our other products and services or to obtain technical support,
please contact our Customer Care Department within the U.S. at 800/762-2974,
outside the U.S. at 317/572-3993 or fax 317/572-4002.
Wiley also publishes its books in a variety of electronic formats. Some content that
appears in print may not be available in electronic formats.

Manufactured in the United States of America

5 4 3 2 1

Contents

How to Contact Us

In putting together this book, we've chosen the sayings and terms we believe travelers in German-speaking countries will find most useful. We're sure you'll find others. Please tell us about them, so we can share the information with your fellow travelers in upcoming editions. If you were disappointed with any aspect of this book, we'd love to know that, too. Please write to:

Frommer's German PhraseFinder & Dictionary, 2nd Edition
John Wiley & Sons
111 River St. • Hoboken, NJ 07030-5774

Advisory & Disclaimer

Travel information can change quickly and unexpectedly, and we strongly advise you to confirm important details before traveling, including information on visas, health and safety, traffic and transport, accommodations, shopping, and eating out. We also encourage you to stay alert while traveling and to remain aware of your surroundings. Avoid civil disturbances, and keep a close eye on cameras, purses, wallets, and other valuables.

While we have endeavored to ensure that the information contained within this guide is accurate and up-to-date at the time of publication, we make no representations or warranties with respect to the accuracy or completeness of the contents of this work and specifically disclaim all warranties, including without limitation warranties of fitness for a particular purpose. We accept no responsibility or liability for any inaccuracy or errors or omissions, or for any inconvenience, loss, damage, costs, or expenses of any nature whatsoever incurred or suffered by anyone as a result of any advice or information contained in this guide.

Travel Resources at Frommers.com

Now that you have the language resources for your trip, visit our website, **www.frommers.com**, for travel information on more than 4,000 destinations. We update features regularly, giving you access to the most current trip-planning information and the best airfare, lodging, and car-rental bargains. You can also listen to podcasts, connect with other Frommers.com members through our active-reader forums, share your travel photos, read blogs from guidebook editors and fellow travelers, and much more.

INTRODUCTION: HOW TO USE THIS BOOK

An official language in Germany, Austria, Switzerland, Luxembourg, and Liechtenstein, German is spoken as a native language by over 90 million people. Tens of millions more speak it as a second language. German is the language of music, art, philosophy, science, and literature. Like English, German is a Germanic language, and the two languages share many cognates, or words that look alike with similar meanings.

Our intention is not to teach you German; a class or audio program is better for that. Our aim is to provide a portable travel tool that's easy to use. The problem with most phrasebooks is that you practically have to memorize the contents before you know where to look for the term you need on the spot. This phrasebook is designed for fingertip referencing, so you can whip it out and find the words you need fast.

Part of this book organizes terms by chapters, like the sections in a Frommer's guide—getting a room, getting a good meal, etc. Within those divisions, we tried to organize phrases intuitively, according to how frequently most readers are likely to use them. The most unique feature, however, is the two-way PhraseFinder dictionary in the back, which lists words as well as phrases organized by key word. Say a taxi driver hands you €5 instead of €10. Look up "change" in the dictionary and discover how to say: "Sorry, but this isn't the correct change."

To make best use of the content, we recommend that you spend some time flipping through it before you depart for your trip. Familiarize yourself with the order of the chapters. Read through the pronunciations section in chapter one and practice pronouncing random phrases throughout the book. Try looking up a few phrases in the phrasebook section as well as in the dictionary. This way, you'll be able to locate phrases faster and speak them more clearly when you need them.

What will make this book most practical? What will make it easiest to use? These are the questions we asked ourselves repeatedly as we assembled these travel terms. Our immediate goal was to create a phrasebook as indispensable as your passport. Our far-ranging goal, of course, is to enrich your experience of travel. And with that, we wish you *Viel Spaß!* (Have fun!)

CHAPTER ONE

SURVIVAL GERMAN

If you tire of toting around this phrasebook, tear out this chapter.
You should be able to navigate your destination with only the
terms found in the next 29 pages.

*For an explanation of pronunciations, please see "German
Grammar & Pronunciation Basics," later in this chapter.*

BASIC GREETINGS

For a full list of greetings, see p101.

Hello.	**Hallo.**
	Hah-LOH.
How are you?	**Wie geht es Ihnen?**
	Vee GAYT es EE-nen?
I'm fine, thanks.	**Mir geht es gut, danke.**
	Meer gayt es GOOT, DANK-ə.
And you?	**Und Ihnen?**
	Unt EE-nen?
My name is ____.	**Ich heiße ____.**
	I[ch] HEI-sə ____.
What's your name?	**Wie heißen Sie?**
	Vee HEI-sen zee?
It's a pleasure to meet you.	**Freut mich, Sie kennen zu lernen.**
	FROYT mi[ch], zee KEN-nen tsoo layr-nen.
Please.	**Bitte.**
	BIT-ə.
Thank you.	**Danke.**
	DANK-ə.
Yes.	**Ja.**
	Yah.
No.	**Nein.**
	Nein.

1

Okay.	**OK.**
	oh-KAY.
No problem.	**Kein Problem.**
	Kein proh-BLAYM.
I'm sorry, I don't understand.	**Entschuldigung, ich verstehe Sie nicht.**
	Ent-SHUL-dee-gung, i[ch] fer-SHTAY-ə zee ni[ch]t.
Would you speak slower please?	**Könnten Sie bitte etwas langsamer sprechen?**
	K[oe]n-ten zee bit-ə et-vas LANG-zah-mər shpre-[ch]en?
Would you speak louder please?	**Könnten Sie bitte etwas lauter sprechen?**
	K[oe]n-ten zee bit-ə et-vas LOW-tər shpre-[ch]en?
Do you speak English?	**Sprechen Sie Englisch?**
	Shpre-[ch]en zee ENG-lish?
Do you speak any other languages?	**Sprechen Sie irgendeine andere Sprache?**
	Shpre-[ch]en zee ir-gent-ei-nə AN-de-rə sprah-[kh]ə?
I speak ____ better than German.	**Ich spreche besser ____ als Deutsch.**
	I[ch] shpre-[ch]ə bes-sər ____ als DOYTSH.
Would you please spell that?	**Könnten Sie das bitte buchstabieren?**
	K[oe]n-ten zee das bit-ə boo[ch]-shtah-BEE-ren?
Would you please repeat that?	**Könnten Sie das bitte wiederholen?**
	K[oe]n-ten zee das bit-ə vee-dər-HOH-len?

| Would you please point that out in this dictionary? | **Könnten Sie mir das bitte in diesem Wörterbuch zeigen?** |
| | *K[oe]n-ten zee meer das bit-ə in dee-zem V[OE]r-tər-boo[ch] tsei-gen?* |

THE KEY QUESTIONS

With the right hand gestures, you can get a lot of mileage from the following list of single-word questions and answers.

Who?	**Wer?**
	Vayr?
What?	**Was?**
	Vas?
When?	**Wann?**
	Van?
Where?	**Wo?**
	Voh?
To where?	**Wohin?**
	Voh-HIN?
Why?	**Warum?**
	Vah-ROOM?
How?	**Wie?**
	Vee?
Which?	**Welcher (m) / Welche (f) / Welches (n)?**
	VEL-[ch]ər / VEL-[ch]ə / VEL-[ch]es?
How many? / How much?	**Wie viele?**
	Vee FEE-lə?

THE ANSWERS: WHO

For full coverage of pronouns, see p20.

I	**Ich**
	I[ch]
you	**Sie (formal, sing. + pl.) / du (informal, sing.) / ihr (informal, pl.)**
	zee / doo / eer
he	**er**
	ayr

she	**sie**
	zee
we	**wir**
	veer
they	**sie**
	zee

THE ANSWERS: WHEN

For full coverage of time, see p12. For days of the week, see p13.

now	**jetzt**
	yetst
later	**später**
	SHP[AY]-tər
afterwards	**danach**
	də-NAH[kh]
earlier	**früher**
	FR[UE]-ər
in a minute	**gleich**
	glei[ch]
today	**heute**
	HOY-tə
tomorrow	**morgen**
	MOR-gen
yesterday	**gestern**
	GES-tern
the day after tomorrow	**übermorgen**
	[UE]-bər-mor-gen
the day before yesterday	**vorgestern**
	FOHR-ges-tern
in a week	**in einer Woche**
	in ei-nər VO-[kh]ə
next week	**nächste Woche**
	neks-tə VO-[kh]ə
last week	**letzte Woche**
	lets-tə VO-[kh]ə
next month	**nächsten Monat**
	neks-ten MOH-nat

last month	**letzten Monat**
	lets-ten MOH-nat
At ____.	**Um ____.**
	Um ____.
ten o'clock this morning	**zehn Uhr heute Morgen**
	TSAYN oor hoy-tə MOR-gen
two o'clock this afternoon	**zwei Uhr heute Nachmittag**
	TSVEI oor hoy-tə NAH[KH]-mit-tahk
seven o'clock this evening	**sieben Uhr heute Abend**
	ZEE-ben oor hoy-tə AH-bent

For full coverage of numbers, see p8.

THE ANSWERS: WHERE

here	**hier**
	heer
there	**dort**
	dort
near ____	**in der Nähe von ____**
	in dayr NAY-ə fon ____
closer	**näher**
	NAY-ər
closest	**am nächsten**
	am NEKS-ten
far	**weit weg**
	VEIT vek
farther	**weiter weg**
	VEI-tər vek
farthest	**am weitesten weg**
	am VEI-tes-ten vek
across from ____	**gegenüber von ____**
	gə-gen-[UE]-bər fon ____
next to ____	**neben ____**
	NAY-ben ____
behind ____	**hinter ____**
	HIN-tər ____

straight ahead	**geradeaus**
	gə-rah-də-OWS
left	**links**
	links
right	**rechts**
	re[ch]ts
up	**aufwärts**
	OWF-vayrts
down	**abwärts**
	AP-vayrts
lower	**niedriger (height) / geringer (price)**
	NEE-drig-gər / gə-RING-ər
higher	**höher**
	H[OE]-ər
above ____	**über ____**
	[UE]-bər ____
below ____	**unter ____**
	UN-tər ____
forward	**vorwärts**
	FOHR-v[ae]rts
back	**zurück**
	tsu-R[UE]K
around	**herum**
	he-RUM
across the street	**auf der anderen Straßenseite**
	owf der an-de-ren SHTRAH-sen-zei-tə
down the street	**am Ende der Straße**
	am en-də dayr SHTRAH-sə
on the corner	**an der Ecke**
	an dayr EK-kə
kitty-corner	**schräg gegenüber**
	shr[ay]k gay-gen-[UE]-bər
____ blocks from here	**____ Straßen von hier**
	____ SHTRAH-sen fon heer

For a full list of numbers, see p8.

THE ANSWERS: WHICH

this one	**dieser (m) / diese (f) / dieses (n)**
	DEE-zər / DEE-zə / DEE-zes
that (that one, close by)	**dieser (m) / diese (f) / dieses (n)**
	DEE-zər / DEE-zə / DEE-zes
(that one, in the distance)	**jener (m) / jene (f) / jenes (n)**
	YAY-nər / YAY-nə / YAY-nes
these	**diese**
	DEE-zə
those (those there, close by)	**diese (pl.)**
	DEE-zə

HELP/EMERGENCIES

Can you help me?	**Können Sie mir helfen?**
	K[OE]-nen zee meer HEL-fen?
I'm lost.	**Ich habe mich verlaufen.**
	I[ch] hah-bə mi[ch] fer-LOW-fen.
Help!	**Hilfe!**
	HIL-fə!
Call the police!	**Rufen Sie die Polizei!**
	ROO-fen zee dee pohl-lee-TSEI!
I need a doctor.	**Ich brauche einen Arzt.**
	I[ch] brow-[kh]ə ei-nen ARTST.
Thief!	**Dieb!**
	Deep!
My child is missing.	**Mein Kind ist weg.**
	Mein KINT ist vek.
Call an ambulance.	**Rufen Sie einen Krankenwagen.**
	ROO-fen zee ei-nen KRANK-en-vah-gen.

NUMBERS & COUNTING

one	**Eins** *Eints*	eighteen	**Achtzehn** *A[KH]-tsayn*
two	**Zwei** *Tsvei*	nineteen	**Neunzehn** *NOYN-tsayn*
three	**Drei** *Drei*	twenty	**Zwanzig** *TSVAN-tsi[ch]*
four	**Vier** *Feer*	twenty-one	**Einundzwanzig** *EIN-unt-tsvan-tsi[ch]*
five	**Fünf** *F[ue]nf*	thirty	**Dreißig** *DREI-si[ch]*
six	**Sechs** *Zeks*	forty	**Vierzig** *FEER-tsi[ch]*
seven	**Sieben** *ZEE-ben*	fifty	**Fünfzig** *F[UE]NF-tsi[ch]*
eight	**Acht** *A[kh]t*	sixty	**Sechzig** *ZE[CH]-tsi[ch]*
nine	**Neun** *Noyn*	seventy	**Siebzig** *ZEEB-tsi[ch]*
ten	**Zehn** *Tsayn*	eighty	**Achtzig** *A[KH]-tsi[ch]*
eleven	**Elf** *Elf*	ninety	**Neunzig** *NOYN-tsi[ch]*
twelve	**Zwölf** *Tsv[oe]lf*	one hundred	**Einhundert** *EIN-hun-dert*
thirteen	**Dreizehn** *DREI-tsayn*	two hundred	**Zweihundert** *TSVEI-hun-dert*
fourteen	**Vierzehn** *FEER-tsayn*	one thousand	**Eintausend** *EIN-tow-zent*
fifteen	**Fünfzehn** *F[UE]NF-tsayn*		
sixteen	**Sechzehn** *ZE[CH]-tsayn*		
seventeen	**Siebzehn** *ZEEB-tsayn*		

FRACTIONS & DECIMALS

one eighth
ein Achtel
ein A[KH]-tel

one quarter
ein Viertel
ein FEER-tel

one third
ein Drittel
ein DRIT-tel

one half
die Hälfte
dee H[AE]LF-tə

two thirds
zwei Drittel
tsvei DRIT-tel

three quarters
drei Viertel
drei FEER-tel

double
doppelt
DOP-pelt

triple
dreifach
DREI-fa[kh]

one tenth
ein Zehntel
ein TSAYN-tel

one hundredth
ein Hundertstel
ein HUN-derts-tel

one thousandth
ein Tausendstel
ein TOW-sents-tel

MATH

addition
Addition
a-dits-YOHN

2 + 1
zwei plus eins
tsvei plus eins

subtraction
Subtraktion
zub-traks-YOHN

2 - 1
zwei minus eins
tsvei MEE-nus eins

multiplication
Multiplikation
mul-tee-plee-kats-YOHN

2 x 3	**zwei mal drei** *tsvei mahl drei*
division	**Division** *dee-vee-ZYOHN*
6 ÷ 3	**sechs geteilt durch drei** *zeks gə-TEILT dur[ch] drei*

ORDINAL NUMBERS

first	**erster (m) / erste (f) / erstes (n)** *AYRST-tər / AYRST-tə / AYRST-tes*
second	**zweiter (m) / zweite (f) / zweites (n)** *TSVEI-tər / TSVEI-tə / TSVEI-tes*
third	**dritter (m) / dritte (f) / drittes (n)** *DRIT-tər / DRIT-tə / DRIT-tes*
fourth	**vierter (m) / vierte (f) / viertes (n)** *FEER-tər / FEER-tə / FEER-tes*
fifth	**fünfter (m) / fünfte (f) / fünftes (n)** *F[UE]NF-tər / F[UE]NF-tə / F[UE]NF-tes*
sixth	**sechster (m) / sechste (f) / sechstes (n)** *ZEKS-tər / ZEKS-tə / ZEKS-tes*
seventh	**siebter (m) / siebte (f) / siebtes (n)** *ZEEB-tər / ZEEB-tə / ZEEB-tes*
eighth	**achter (m) / achte (f) / achtes (n)** *A[KH]-tər / A[KH]-tə / A[KH]-tes*
ninth	**neunter (m) / neunte (f) / neuntes (n)** *NOYN-tər / NOYN-tə / NOYN-tes*
tenth	**zehnter (m) / zehnte (f) / zehntes (n)** *TSAYN-tər / TSAYN-tə / TSAYN-tes*
last	**letzter (m) / letzte (f) / letztes (n)** *LETS-tər / LETS-tə / LETS-tes*

MEASUREMENTS

millimeter	**Millimeter**
	MIL-lee-may-tər
centimeter	**Zentimeter**
	TSEN-tee-may-tər
meter	**Meter**
	MAY-tər
kilometer	**Kilometer**
	KEE-loh-may-tər
squared	**quadriert**
	kvah-DREERT
milliliters	**Milliliter**
	MIL-lee-lee-tər
liter	**Liter**
	LEE-tər
kilo	**Kilo**
	KEE-loh
cup	**Tasse**
	TA-sə

QUANTITY

some	**etwas**
	ET-vas
none	**nichts**
	ni[ch]ts
all	**alles**
	AL-les
many / much	**viele / viel**
	FEE-lə / feel
a little bit	**ein bisschen**
	ein BIS-[ch]en
a dozen	**ein Dutzend**
	ein DUT-sent
too much	**zu viel**
	tsoo FEEL
not enough	**zu wenig**
	tsoo VAY-ni[ch]

SIZE

small	**klein**
	klein
the smallest	**der / die / das Kleinste**
	dayr / dee / das KLEIN-stə
medium	**mittel**
	MIT-el
big	**groß**
	grohs
the biggest	**der / die / das Größte**
	dayr / dee / das GR[OE]-stə
fat	**dick**
	dik
wide	**breit**
	breit
narrow	**schmal**
	shmahl
short	**kurz**
	kurts
long	**lang**
	lang

TIME

For full coverage of number terms, see p8.

HOURS OF THE DAY

What time is it?	**Wie spät ist es?**
	Vee SHP[AE]T ist es?
At what time?	**Um wie viel Uhr?**
	Um vee feel OOR?
For how long?	**Wie lange?**
	Vee LANG-ə?
It's one o'clock.	**Es ist ein Uhr.**
	Es ist EIN oor.
It's two o'clock.	**Es ist zwei Uhr.**
	Es ist TSVEI oor.
It's two thirty.	**Es ist halb drei.**
	Es ist halb DREI.

It's two fifteen.	**Es ist Viertel nach zwei.** *Es ist feer-tel na[kh] TSVEI.*
It's a quarter to three.	**Es ist Viertel vor drei.** *Es ist feer-tel fohr DREI.*
It's noon.	**Es ist Mittag.** *Es ist MIT-tahk.*
It's midnight.	**Es ist Mitternacht.** *Es ist MIT-tər-na[kh]t.*
It's early.	**Es ist früh.** *Es ist FR[UE].*
It's late.	**Es ist spät.** *Es ist SHP[AY]T.*
in the morning	**morgens** *MOR-gens*
in the afternoon	**nachmittags** *NA[KH]-mit-tahks*
at night	**nachts** *na[kh]ts*
at dawn	**bei Tagesanbruch** *bei TAH-ges-an-bru[ch]*

DAYS OF THE WEEK

Sunday	**Sonntag** *ZON-tahk*
Monday	**Montag** *MOHN-tahk*
Tuesday	**Dienstag** *DEENS-tahk*
Wednesday	**Mittwoch** *MIT-vo[kh]*
Thursday	**Donnerstag** *DON-ərs-tahk*
Friday	**Freitag** *FREI-tahk*
Saturday	**Samstag** *ZAMS-tahk*

MONTHS OF THE YEAR

January	**Januar**
	YA-noo-ahr
February	**Februar**
	FAY-broo-ahr
March	**März**
	Mayrts
April	**April**
	a-PRIL
May	**Mai**
	Mei
June	**Juni**
	YOO-nee
July	**Juli**
	YOO-lee
August	**August**
	ow-GUST
September	**September**
	zep-TEM-bər
October	**Oktober**
	ok-TOH-bər
November	**November**
	noh-FEM-bər
December	**Dezember**
	deh-TSEM-bər

SEASONS OF THE YEAR

in spring	**im Frühling**
	im FR[UE]-ling
in summer	**im Sommer**
	im ZOM-mər
in autumn	**im Herbst**
	im HAYRPST
in winter	**im Winter**
	im VIN-tər

False Cognates

If you try winging it with Denglish, beware of false cognates, known as *"falsche Freunde"* (false friends)—German words that sound like English ones, but with different meanings. Here are some examples of false cognates.

bald	soon
kahl	bald
Menü	today's special
Speisekarte	menu
Gift	poison
Geschenk	gift
Billion	trillion
Milliarde	billion
Puff	bordello
Hauch / Zug	puff
konsequent	consistent(ly)
folglich	consequently
Dom	cathedral
Kuppel	dome
aktuell	current
eigentlich, wirklich	actual
eventuell	maybe
schließlich	eventually
also	thus, therefore
auch	also
Art	kind, type
Kunst	art
Bad	bath, spa
schlecht	bad
blenden	dazzle, blind
mischen	blend
brav	well behaved
tapfer	brave

GERMAN GRAMMAR & PRONUNCIATION BASICS

PRONUNCIATION GUIDE

Below we explain which symbols we use to represent certain German sounds, give examples of English words with the same or similar sounds, and give examples of common German words with these sounds so that you can familiarize yourself with spelling patterns.

Vowels

Symbol	English example	German example
a	no English equivalent; between vowel of "father" and "cut"	danke
ah	father	Straße
ay	gate (but pure; no diphthong)	leben, See
e	let	nett, hätte
ee	seen	ihr, diese
ei	sky	zwei
i	sit	mit, bitte
o	hot (but with rounded lips, as in British "hot")	Gott
oh	load (but pure; no diphthong)	Strom, Boot
oo	cool (but pure; no diphthong)	gut
oy	boy	Deutsch, Häuser
ow	cow	laut
u	put, foot	Stunde
ə	tuna	danke
[oe]	no English equivalent; round lips as if to say oh but say ay (if you can't do this, the u in English "burn" is a good approximation)	schön
[ue]	no English equivalent; round lips as if to say oo but say ee	über

Note: There are also short versions of these last two sounds, found in the words Götter and zurück, respectively. Because the difference between the short and long versions is subtle (beginning German speakers may hear the vowels as the same and you will be understood even if you pronounce them the same way), we do not distinguish between long and short ü in our pronunciations. Focus instead on hearing the difference between oo and [ue], as this can often mean saying/hearing a different word than is intended!

Consonants

Symbol	English example	German example
b	boy	Bett
ch	Charlie	tschüss
[ch]	like the initial **h** + **y** sound in English "human" (if you can't do this, English "sh" will be understood)	ich
[kh]	no English equivalent *Hold tongue as if to say English k, then allow air to pass harshly between the tongue and the roof of the mouth. If you can't do this, English k will be understood.*	Ba**ch**
d	day	diese
f	fun	von, Philosophie
g	got	geht
h	hard	heißen
k	king	kosten, weg
l	log	lernen
m	man	mich
n	not	nicht
ng	hanger	gega**ng**en
p	pay	Post, taub
r	no English equivalent *German "r" is formed at the back of the mouth and is very similar to a French "r." American "r" is incorrect, but you will be understood if you pronounce it this way.*	Rose
s	sand	Fenster, Kreis
sh	should	Scheck, stehen, spät
t	ten	Tasche, Bad
v	villain	wie, etwas
y	yet	ja
z	zebra	sie, Rose
zh	rouge	Genie

The Alphabet

The German alphabet contains the same 26 letters as the
English alphabet. In addition, three vowels (**a**, **o**, and **u**)
can be written with an umlaut (**ä**, **ö**, and **ü**), which changes
the pronunciation of the vowel. The German alphabet also
contains an additional letter, the eszett (**ß**). In case you find
yourself in a situation in which you have to spell something,
here is how the letters of the alphabet are pronounced in
German.

a	*ah*	o	*oh*
ä	*e, as in 'led'*	ö	*[oe]*
b	*bay*	p	*pay*
c	*tsay*	q	*koo*
d	*day*	r	*er*
e	*ay*	s	*es*
f	*ef*	ß	*ess-tsett*
g	*gay*	t	*tay*
h	*hah*	u	*oo*
i	*ee*	ü	*[ue]*
j	*yot*	v	*fow*
k	*kah*	w	*vay*
l	*el*	x	*iks*
m	*em*	y	*[ue]p-sil-lon*
n	*en*	z	*tset*

WORD PRONUNCIATION

Syllables in words are also accented in a standard pattern. Generally, in words with two syllables the first syllable is stressed. For longer words, an accent mark is shown to indicate the stress.

Ending in -ieren

studieren   *shtoo-DEE-ren*

Loan word

Computer   *kom-PYOO-tər*

Compound adjective with hin, her, da or wo

damit   *da-MIT*

GENDER, ADJECTIVES, MODIFIERS

Each noun takes a masculine, feminine or neutral gender and is most often accompanied by a masculine, feminine or neutral definite article, like the English "the" (*der*, *die* or *das*), or by an indefinite article, like the English "a" or "an" (*ein* or *eine*). Definite articles ("the"), indefinite articles ("a," "an"), and related adjectives change their endings depending on whether they are the subject, direct or indirect object, or possessive. For example, you would say, "*Der Mann sieht den Hund*" (The man sees the dog), but "*Ich sehe den Mann*" (I see the man), because "Mann" is the subject of the first sentence and the direct object of the second.

The Definite Article ("the")

	Masculine	Feminine	Neutral	Plural
Subject	*der* Hund (the dog)	*die* Katze (the cat)	*das* Tier (the animal)	*die* Hunde (the dogs)
Direct Object	*den* Hund (the dog)	*die* Katze (the cat)	*das* Tier (the animal)	*die* Hunde (the dogs)

The Indefinite Article ("a" or "an")

	Masculine	Feminine	Neutral
Subject	*ein* Hund (a dog)	*eine* Katze (a cat)	*ein* Tier (an animal)
Direct Object	*einen* Hund (a dog)	*eine* Katze (a cat)	*ein* Tier (an animal)

PERSONAL PRONOUNS
SUBJECTS

LIEBEN: "To Love"

I love.	*Ich* liebe.	i[ch]
You (singular familiar) love.	*Du* liebst.	doo
He / She / It loves.	*Er / Sie / Es* liebt.	er / zee / es
We love.	*Wir* lieben.	veer
You (plural familiar) love.	*Ihr* liebt.	eer
They / You (singular formal / plural formal) love.	*Sie / Sie* lieben.	zee / zee

DIRECT OBJECTS

KENNEN: "To Know" (someone)

He knows me.	Er kennt *mich.*	mi[ch]
He knows you. (singular familiar)	Er kennt *dich.*	di[ch]
He knows him/her.	Er kennt *ihn / sie.*	een / zee
He knows you. (singular formal)	Er kennt *Sie.*	zee
He knows us.	Er kennt *uns.*	uns
He knows you. (plural familiar)	Er kennt *euch.*	oy[ch]
He knows them/you. (plural formal)	Er kennt *sie / Sie.*	zee/zee

Hey, you!

German has two words for "you"— *du*, spoken among friends and familiars, and *Sie*, used among strangers or as a sign of respect toward authority figures. When speaking with a stranger, expect to use *Sie*, unless you are invited to do otherwise. The second-person familiar plural form (*ihr*) is used among friends and family. The second-person formal plural is the same as the second-person formal singular: *Sie*. Both the singular and plural forms of the second-person formal are always written with an upper-case S: "*Sie*."

REGULAR VERB CONJUGATIONS

Most German verbs end in "-en" (*lieben, gehen, kommen, etc.*). To conjugate regular verbs in the present tense, drop the -en of the infinitive and add the italicized endings below.

Present Tense

Regular verbs	GEHEN "To Go"	
I go.	Ich geh*e*.	GAY-ə
You (singular familiar) **go.**	Du geh*st*.	gayst
He / She / It goes.	Er / Sie (singular feminine) / Es geh*t*.	gayt
You (singular formal) **go.**	Sie (singular formal) geh*en*.	GAY-en
We go.	Wir geh*en*.	GAY-en
You (plural familiar) **go.**	Ihr geh*t*.	gayt
They / You (plural formal) **go.**	Sie / Sie geh*en*.	GAY-en

Simple Past Tense

To conjugate regular verbs in the simple past tense, drop the -en of the infinitive and add the italicized endings below.

Regular verbs	LEBEN "To Live"	
I lived.	**Ich leb*te*.**	**LAYP-tə**
You (singular familiar) **lived.**	**Du leb*test*.**	**LAYP-test**
He / She / It lived.	**Er / Sie / Es leb*te*.**	**LAYP-tə**
You lived. (singular formal)	**Sie leb*ten*.**	**LAYP-ten**
We lived.	**Wir leb*ten*.**	**LAYP-ten**
You (plural familiar) **lived.**	**Ihr leb*tet*.**	**LAYP-tet**
They / You (plural formal) **lived.**	**Sie / Sie leb*ten*.**	**LAYP-ten**

The Future

For novice German speakers, the easiest way to express future tense is to use the conjugated verb WERDEN (to go) followed by the infinitive of the verb to be expressed (see below). In speech, it is also perfectly acceptable to use present-tense conjugations to refer to events that will happen in the future, especially when time expressions make the meaning clear (e.g. "Ich gehe morgen ins Museum" or "I am going to the museum tomorrow").

I am going to speak.	**Ich *werde* reden.**	**VAYR-də**
You (singular familiar) **are going to speak.**	**Du *wirst* reden.**	**Virst**
He / She / It is going to speak.	**Er / Sie / Es *wird* reden.**	**Virt**

You (singular formal) are going to speak.	Sie *werden* reden.	VAYR-den
We are going to speak.	Wir *werden* reden.	VAYR-den
You (plural familiar) are going to speak.	Ihr *werdet* reden.	VAYR-det
They / You (plural formal) are going to speak.	Sie / Sie *werden* reden.	VAYR-den

TO BE OR NOT TO BE (SEIN)

The German verb for "to be," SEIN, is irregular. It is conjugated as follows:

Present Tense

SEIN "To Be"

I am.	Ich *bin*.	bin
You (singular, familiar) are.	Du *bist*.	bist
He / She / It is.	Er / Sie / Es *ist*.	ist
You (singular formal) are.	Sie *sind*.	zint
We are.	Wir *sind*.	zint
You (plural familiar) are.	Ihr *seid*.	zeit
They / You (plural formal) are.	Sie *sind*.	zint

Simple Past Tense

SEIN "To Be"

I was.	Ich *war.*	vahr
You were.	Du *warst.*	vahrst
He / She / It was.	Er / Sie / Es *war*	vahr
You (singular formal) **were.**	Sie *waren.*	VAHR-en
We were.	Wir *waren.*	VAHR-en
You were.	Ihr *wart.*	vahrt
They / You (plural formal) **were.**	Sie *waren.*	VAHR-en

IRREGULAR VERBS

German has numerous irregular verbs that stray from the standard -EN conjugations. Rather than bog you down with too much grammar, we're providing the present tense conjugations for the most commonly used irregular verbs.

HABEN "To Have"

I have.	Ich *habe.*	HAH-bə
You (singular familiar) **have.**	Du *hast.*	hast
He / She / It has.	Er / Sie / Es *hat.*	hat
You (singular formal) **have.**	Sie *haben.*	HAH-ben
We have.	Wir *haben.*	HAH-ben
You (plural familiar) **have.**	Ihr *habt.*	hahbt
They / You (plural formal) **have.**	Sie / Sie *haben.*	HAH-ben

Haben

Haben means "to have," but it's also used to describe conditions such as hunger and thirst. For example:

Ich habe Hunger. I'm hungry.
(Literally: I have hunger.)
Ich habe Durst. I'm thirsty.
(Literally: I have thirst.)

SPRECHEN "To Speak, To Talk"

I speak.	Ich spreche.	SHPRE-[ch]ə
You (singular familiar) **speak.**	Du spri*ch*st.	shpri[ch]st
He / She / It speaks.	Er / Sie / Es spri*ch*t.	shpri[ch]t
You (singular formal) **speak.**	Sie sprech*en.*	SHPRE-[ch]en
We speak.	Wir sprech*en.*	SHPRE-[ch]en
You (plural familiar) **speak.**	Ihr sprech*t.*	shpre[ch]t
They / You (plural formal) **speak.**	Sie / Sie sprech*en.*	SHPRE-[ch]en

WOLLEN "To Want"

I want.	Ich will.	vil
You (singular familiar) **want.**	Du will*st.*	vilst
He / She / It wants.	Er / Sie / Es will.	vil
You (singular formal) **want**	Sie woll*en.*	VOL-len
We want.	Wir woll*en.*	VOL-len
You (plural familiar) **want.**	Ihr woll*t.*	volt
They / You plural formal) **want.**	Sie / Sie woll*en.*	VOL-len

KÖNNEN "To Be Able"

I can.	Ich kann.	kan
You (singular familiar) **can**.	Du kann*st*.	kanst
He / She / It can.	Er / Sie / Es kann.	kan
You (singular formal) **can**.	Sie könn*en*.	K[OE]-nen
We can.	Wir könn*en*.	K[OE]-nen
You (plural familiar) **can**.	Ihr könn*t*.	k[oe]nt
They / You (plural formal) **can**.	Sie / Sie könn*en*.	K[OE]-nen

KENNEN vs. WISSEN: There are two ways to say "to know" in German: *kennen* and *wissen*. *Kennen* is to be familiar with someone or something, while *wissen* is to know a fact. For example, "*Ich kenne Peter*" (I know Peter) BUT "*Ich weiß, wo das Restaurant ist*" (I know where the restaurant is).

KENNEN "To Know" (to be familiar with)

I know.	Ich kenne.	KEN-nə
You (singular familiar) **know**.	Du kenn*st*.	kenst
He / She / It knows.	Er / Sie / Es kenn*t*.	kent
You (singular formal) **know**.	Sie kenn*en*.	KEN-nen
We know.	Wir kenn*en*.	KEN-nen
You (plural familiar) **know**.	Ihr kenn*t*.	kent
They / You (plural formal) **know**.	Sie / Sie kenn*en*.	KEN-nen

WISSEN "To Know" (something)

I know.	**Ich weiß.**	veis
You (singular familiar) **know.**	**Du weißt.**	veist
He / She / It knows.	**Er / Sie / Es weiß.**	veis
You (singular formal) **know.**	**Sie wissen.**	VIS-sen
We know.	**Wir wissen.**	VIS-sen
You (plural familiar) **know.**	**Ihr wisst.**	vist
They / You (plural formal) **know.**	**Sie / Sie wissen.**	VIS-sen

Stem-changing Verbs

Some irregular verbs change their stem in addition to their ending. For example:

ESSEN (To Eat)
Ich esse (I eat)
Du isst (You eat)
Er / Sie / Es isst (He / She / It eats)
Wir essen (We eat)
Ihr esst (You eat) (informal)
Sie / Sie essen (You eat / They eat) (formal / pl.)

Notice that the stem only changes in two conjugations (I, you, and he/she/it). The first person singular and plural forms are conjugated like regular verbs by adding the correct ending to the stem.

Gefallen

To say you like something, use the verb *gefallen*. *Gefallen* is different from other verbs because the person doing the liking is the subject of the sentence, not the object. For example, to say you like music, you would say:

Mir gefällt Musik. I like music.
(Literally: Music is pleasing to me.)

When what is liked is plural, the verb is plural:

Mir gefallen die Blumen. I like the flowers.
(Literally: The flowers are pleasing to me.)

The person doing the liking is represented by an indirect object pronoun placed in front of the verb, as illustrated below. Remember, gefallen can only be conjugated in two ways: *gefällt* (for singular things that are liked) and *gefallen* (for plural things that are liked). The pronoun changes to reflect who is doing the liking.

GEFALLEN "To Like"

I like Germany.	*Mir* gefällt Deutschland.	gə-FELT
You (informal singular) like Germany.	*Dir* gefällt Deutschland.	gə-FELT
He / She/ It likes Germany.	*Ihm / Ihr / Ihm* gefällt Deutschland.	gə-FELT
You (formal singular) like Germany.	*Ihnen* gefällt Deutschland.	gə-FELT
We like Germany.	*Uns* gefällt Deutschland.	gə-FELT
You (informal plural) like Germany.	*Euch* gefällt Deutschland.	gə-FELT
They / You (formal plural) like Germany.	*Ihnen* gefällt Deutschland.	gə-FELT

REFLEXIVE VERBS

German has many reflexive verbs (when the subject and object both refer to the same person or thing). The following common verbs are used reflexively: *sich anziehen* (to get dressed, literally to dress oneself), *sich rasieren* (to shave, literally to shave oneself), *sich duschen* (to shower, literally to shower oneself), and *sich treffen* (to meet, literally to meet one another).

SICH ANZIEHEN "To Dress"

I get dressed.	Ich ziehe mich an.	tsee-ə mi[ch] AN.
You (singular familiar) **get dressed.**	Du zieh*st* dich an.	tseest di[ch] AN.
He / She / It gets dressed.	Er / Sie / Es zieh*t* sich an.	tseet si[ch] AN.
You (singular formal) **get dressed.**	Sie zieh*en* sich an.	tsee-en si[ch] AN.
We get dressed.	Wir zieh*en* uns an.	tsee-en uns AN.
You (plural familiar) **get dressed.**	Ihr zieh*t* euch an.	tseet oy[ch] AN.
They / You (plural formal) **get dressed.**	Sie / Sie zieh*en* sich an.	tsee-en si[ch] AN.

CHAPTER TWO

GETTING THERE & GETTING AROUND

This section deals with every form of transportation. Whether you've just reached your destination by plane or you're renting a car to tour the countryside, you'll find the phrases you need in the next 30 pages.

BY PLANE

AT THE AIRPORT

I am looking for ____.	**Ich suche ____.**
	I[ch] zoo-[ch]ə ____.
a porter	**einen Träger für mein Gepäck**
	ei-nen TRE-gər f[ue]r mein gə-PEK
a bus / train to city center	**einen Bus / Zug ins Stadtzentrum**
	ei-nen BUS / TSOOK ins shtat-tsen-trum
the check-in counter	**den Abfertigungsschalter**
	dayn AP-fer-tee-gungs-shal-tər
the ticket counter	**den Kartenschalter**
	dayn KAR-ten-shal-tər
arrivals	**den Ankunftsbereich**
	dayn AN-kunfts-bə-rei[ch]
departures	**den Abreisebereich**
	dayn AP-rei-zə-bə-rei[ch]
security	**den Sicherheitsdienst**
	dayn ZI-[ch]ə-heits-deenst
passport inspection	**die Passkontrolle**
	die PAS-kon-trol-lə
customs	**das Zollamt**
	das TSOL-amt
gate number ____	**Gate ____**
	Gayt ____

For full coverage of numbers, see p8.

the waiting area	**den Wartebereich**
	dayn VAR-tə-bə-rei[ch]
the men's restroom	**die Herrentoilette**
	dee he-ren-twa-LET-tə
the women's restroom	**die Damentoilette**
	dee dah-men-twa-LET-tə
the police station	**die Polizeidienststelle**
	dee poh-lee-TSEI-deenst-shtel-lə
a security guard	**einen Sicherheitsbeamten**
	ei-nen ZI-[ch]ər-heits-bə-am-ten
the smoking area	**den Raucherbereich**
	dayn ROW-[kh]ər-bə-rei[ch]
the information booth	**den Informationsstand**
	dayn in-fohr-mah-tsee-OHNS-shtant
a public telephone	**ein öffentliches Telefon**
	ein [oe]-fent-li-[ch]es te-le-FOHN
an ATM	**einen Geldautomaten**
	ei-nen GELT-ow-toh-mah-ten
baggage claim	**die Gepäckausgabe**
	dee gə-PEK-ows-gah-bə
a luggage cart	**einen Gepäckwagen**
	ei-nen gə-PEK-vah-gen
a currency exchange	**eine Geldwechselstube**
	ei-nə GELT-vek-sel-shtoo-bə
a mobile phone rental	**einen Leihservice für Mobiltelefone**
	ei-nen LEI-zer-vis f[ue]r moh-beel-te-le-foh-nə
a café	**ein Café**
	ein ka-FAY
a restaurant	**ein Restaurant**
	ein res-toh-RONG
a bar	**eine Bar**
	ei-nə bahr

GETTING THERE & AROUND

a bookstore or newsstand	**eine Buchhandlung oder einen Zeitungsstand** *ei-nə BOO[CH]-hant-lung oh-dər ei-nen TSEI-tungs-shtant*
a duty-free shop	**einen Duty-Free-Shop** *ei-nen dyoo-tee-FREE shop*
Is there Wi-Fi here?	**gibt es hier WLAN-Zugang?** *GEEPT es heer VAY-lahn-tsoo-gang?*
I'd like to page someone.	**Ich möchte jemanden ausrufen lassen.** *I[ch] m[oe][ch]-tə yay-man-den OWS-roo-fen las-sen.*
Do you accept credit cards?	**Akzeptieren Sie Kreditkarten?** *Ak-tsep-TEE-ren zee kre-DEET-kar-ten?*

CHECKING IN

I would like a one-way ticket to ____.	**Ich hätte gern ein einfaches Ticket nach ____.** *I[ch] HET-tə gern ein EIN-fa-[kh]es tik-ket na[kh] ____.*
I would like a round-trip ticket to ____.	**Ich hätte gern ein Ticket nach ____ inklusive Rückreise.** *I[ch] HET-tə gern ein EIN-fa-[kh]es tik-ket na[kh] ____ in-kloo-see-fə R[UE]K-rei-zə.*
How much are the tickets?	**Wie viel kosten die Tickets?** *Vee feel kos-ten dee tik-kets?*
Do you have anything less expensive?	**Haben Sie auch etwas Günstigeres im Angebot?** *Hah-ben zee ow[kh] et-vas G[UE]NS-tee-ge-res im an-gə-BOHT?*
How long is the flight?	**Wie lange dauert der Flug?** *Vee lang-ə dow-ert dayr flook?*

Common Airport Signs

Ankunft	Arrivals
Abreise	Departures
Terminal	Terminal
Gate	Gate
Tickets	Ticketing
Zoll	Customs
Gepäckausgabe	Baggage Claim
Drücken	Push
Ziehen	Pull
Rauchen verboten	No Smoking
Eingang	Entrance
Ausgang	Exit
Herren	Men
Damen	Women
Pendelbusse	Shuttle Buses
Taxis	Taxis

What time does flight _____ leave?	**Welche Abflugzeit hat Flug Nummer _____?**
	VEL-[ch]ə AP-flook-tseit hat flook num-mər _____?
What time does flight _____ arrive?	**Welche Ankunftszeit hat Flug Nummer _____?**
	VEL-[ch]ə AN-kunfts-tseit hat flook num-mər _____?
Do I have a connecting flight?	**Gibt es einen Anschlussflug?**
	Geept es ei-nen AN-shlus-flook?
Do I need to change planes?	**Muss ich umsteigen?**
	Mus i[ch] UM-shtei-gen?
My flight leaves at _____.	**Mein Flug geht um _____.**
	Mein flook gayt um _____.

For full coverage of numbers, see p8.
For full coverage of time, see p12.

What time will the flight arrive?	**Welche Ankunftszeit hat der Flug?** *VEL-[ch]ə AN-kunfts-tseit hat dayr flook?*
Is the flight on time?	**Ist der Flug pünktlich?** *Ist dayr flook P[UE]NKT-lich?*
Is the flight delayed?	**Hat der Flug Verspätung?** *Hat dayr flook fer-SHP[AE]-tung?*
From which terminal is flight _____ leaving?	**Welches Abflugterminal hat Flug _____?** *VEL-[ch]es AP-flook-ter-mee-nel hat flook _____?*
From which gate is flight _____ leaving?	**Welches Abfluggate hat Flug _____?** *VEL-[ch]es AP-flook-gayt hat flook _____?*
How much time do I need for check-in?	**Wie lange dauert das Einchecken?** *Vee lang-ə dow-ert das EIN-tshek-ken?*
Is there an express check-in line?	**Gibt es einen schnelleren Check-in?** *Geept es ei-nen SHNEL-le-ren tshek-in?*
Is online check-in available?	**Gibt es einen Online-Check-in?** *Geept es ei-nen ON-lein-tshek-in?*
I would like _____ ticket(s) in _____.	**Ich hätte gern _____ Ticket(s) in _____.** *I[ch] HET-tə gern _____ tik-kets in _____.*
first class	**der ersten Klasse** *dayr AYRS-ten kla-sə*
business class	**Business-Klasse** *Biz-nes kla-sə*
economy class	**Economy-Klasse** *Ee-kon-nə-mee kla-sə*
I would like _____.	**Geben Sie mir bitte einen _____.** *Gay-ben zee meer bit-ə ei-nen _____.*
Please don't give me _____.	**Geben Sie mir bitte keinen _____.** *GAY-ben zee meer bit-ə kei-nen _____.*

a window seat	**Fensterplatz**
	FENS-tər-plats
an aisle seat	**Gangplatz**
	GANG-plats
an emergency exit row seat	**Platz an einem Notausgang**
	Plats an ei-nem NOHT-ows-gang
a bulkhead seat	**Sitz hinter der Trennwand**
	Zits hin-tər dayr TREN-vant
a seat by the restroom	**Platz in der Nähe der Toiletten**
	Plats in dayr NAY-ə dayr
	twa-LET-ten
a seat near the front	**Platz im vorderen Teil**
	Plats im FOR-de-ren teil
a seat near the middle	**Platz im mittleren Teil**
	Plats im MIT-le-ren teil
a seat near the back	**Platz im hinteren Teil**
	Plats im HIN-te-ren teil
Is there a meal on the flight?	**Gibt es Verpflegung während des Flugs?**
	Geept es fer-PFLAY-gung v[ae]-rent des flooks?
I'd like to order ____.	**Ich hätte gern ____.**
	I[ch] HET-tə gern ____.
a vegetarian meal	**ein vegetarisches Essen**
	ein ve-ge-TAH-ri-shes es-sen
a vegan meal	**ein veganes Gericht**
	ein ve-GAH-nes gə-ri[ch]t
a kosher meal	**ein koscheres Essen**
	ein KOH-she-res es-sen
a gluten-free meal	**ein glutenfreies Gericht**
	ein GLOO-ten-frei-es gə-ri[ch]t
a diabetic meal	**ein Essen für Diabetiker**
	ein es-sen f[ue]r dee-ah-BAY-tik-kər
I am traveling to ____.	**Ich bin auf dem Weg nach ____.**
	I[ch] bin owf daym vek na[kh] ____.

I am coming from ____.	**Ich komme gerade aus ____.**
	I[ch] kom-mə gə-rah-də ows ____.
I arrived from ____.	**Ich bin aus ____ angekommen.**
	I[ch] bin ows ____ AN-gə-kom-men.

For full coverage of country terms, see English / German dictionary.

I'd like to change / cancel / confirm my reservation.	**Ich möchte meine Reservierung ändern / stornieren / bestätigen.**
	I[ch] m[oe][ch]-tə mei-nə re-zer-VEE-rung en-dern / shtor-NEE-ren / bə-SHT[AE]-tee-gen.
I have ____ bags to check.	**Ich habe ____ Taschen aufzugeben.**
	I[ch] hah-bə ____ tash-en OWF-tsoo-GAY-ben.

For full coverage of numbers, see p8.

Listen Up: Questions You May Be Asked

Ihren Ausweis, bitte?	Your passport, please.
EE-ren OWS-veis, bit-ə?	
Was ist der Grund Ihres Aufenthalts?	What is the purpose of your visit?
VAS ist der grunt ee-res OWF-ent-halts?	
Wie lange möchten Sie bleiben?	How long will you be staying?
Vee lang-ə m[oe][ch]-ten zee BLEI-ben?	
Wo bleiben Sie?	Where are you staying?
Voh BLEI-ben zee?	
Haben Sie etwas zu verzollen?	Do you have anything to declare?
HAH-ben zee et-vas tsoo fer-TSO-len?	
Öffnen Sie bitte diese Tasche.	Open this bag, please.
[OE]F-nen zee bit-ə dee-zə tash-ə.	

Passengers with Special Needs

Is it wheelchair-accessible?	**Ist es mit dem Rollstuhl zu erreichen?**
	Ist es mit daym ROL-shtool tsoo er-REI-[ch]en?
May I have a wheelchair / walker please?	**Könnte ich bitte einen Rollstuhl / eine Gehhilfe bekommen?**
	K[oe]n-tə i[ch] bit-ə ei-nen ROL-shtool / ei-nə GAY-hil-fə bə-KOM-men?
I need some assistance boarding.	**Ich benötige Hilfe beim Einsteigen.**
	I[ch] bə-N[OE]-ti-gə HIL-fə beim EIN-shtei-gen.
I need to bring my service dog.	**Ich bin auf die Begleitung meines Blindenhundes angewiesen.**
	I[ch] bin owf dee bə-GLEI-tung mei-nes BLIN-den-hun-des an-gə-VEE-zen.
Do you have services for the hearing impaired?	**Haben Sie Angebote für Hörgeschädigte?**
	Hah-ben zee an-gə-BOH-tə f[ue]r H[OE]R-gə-SH[AE]-dik-tə?
Do you have services for the visually impaired?	**Haben Sie Angebote für Sehbehinderte?**
	Hah-ben zee an-gə-BOH-tə f[ue]r ZAY-bə-hin-der-tə?

Trouble at Check-In

How long is the delay?	**Wie viel beträgt die Verspätung?**
	Vee feel be-TR[AE]K dee fer-SHP[AE]-tung?
My flight was late.	**Mein Flug hatte Verspätung.**
	Mein flook hat-tə fer-SHP[AE]-tung.
I missed my flight.	**Ich habe meinen Flug verpasst.**
	I[ch] hah-bə mei-nen flook fer-PAST.

When is the next flight?	**Wann geht der nächste Flug?**
	Van gayt dayr NEKS-tə floog?
May I have a meal voucher?	**Bekomme ich einen Essensgutschein?**
	Bə-KOM-mə i[ch] ei-nen es-sens-goot-shein?
May I have a room voucher?	**Bekomme ich einen Zimmergutschein?**
	Bə-KOM-mə i[ch] ei-nen TSIM-mə-goot-shein?

AT CUSTOMS / SECURITY CHECKPOINTS

I'm traveling with a group.	**Ich bin Mitglied einer Reisegruppe.**
	I[ch] bin mit-GLEET ei-nər REI-zə-grup-pə.
I'm on my own.	**Ich reise allein.**
	I[ch] rei-zə al-LEIN.
I'm traveling on business.	**Ich befinde mich auf Geschäftsreise.**
	I[ch] bə-FIN-də mi[ch] owf gə-SHEFTS-rei-zə.
I'm on vacation.	**Ich mache Urlaub.**
	I[ch] ma-[kh]ə OOR-lowp.
I have nothing to declare.	**Ich habe nichts zu verzollen.**
	I[ch] hah-bə ni[ch]ts tsoo fer-TSOL-len.
I would like to declare ____.	**Ich habe ____ zu verzollen.**
	I[ch] hah-bə ____ tsoo fer-TSOL-len.
I have some liquor.	**Ich habe etwas Alkohol dabei.**
	I[ch] hah-bə ET-vas al-koh-hohl dah-bei.
I have some cigars.	**Ich habe ein paar Zigarren dabei.**
	I[ch] hah-bə ein pahr tsee-GAR-ren dah-bei.
They are gifts.	**Das sind Geschenke.**
	Das zint gə-SHENK-ə.

They are for personal use.	**Sie sind für den Privatgebrauch.** *Zee zint f[ue]r dayn pree-VAHT-gə-brow[kh].*
That is my medicine.	**Das ist meine Medizin.** *Das ist mei-nə may-dee-TSEEN.*
I have my prescription.	**Ich habe ein Rezept.** *I[ch] hah-bə ein ray-TSEPT.*
I'd like a male / female officer to conduct the search.	**Ich hätte gern, dass die Durchsuchung von einem Mann / einer Frau durchgeführt wird.** *I[ch] HET-tə gern, das dee dur[ch]-ZOO-[ch]ung fon ei-nem man / ei-nər frow dur[ch]-gə-f[ue]rt virt.*

Trouble at Security

Help me. I've lost ____.	**Könnten Sie mir bitte helfen? Ich habe ____ verloren.** *K[oe]n-ten zee meer bit-ə HEL-fen? I[ch] hah-bə ____ fer-loh-ren.*
my passport	**meinen Ausweis** *mei-nen OWS-veis*
my boarding pass	**meine Bordkarte** *mei-nə BORT-kar-tə*
my identification	**meine Papiere** *mei-nə pa-PEE-rə*
my wallet	**meine Geldbörse** *mei-nə GELT-b[oe]r-zə*
my purse	**meine Handtasche** *mei-nə HANT-tash-ə*
Someone stole my purse / wallet!	**Jemand hat meine Handtasche / meine Geldbörse gestohlen!** *YAY-mand hat mei-nə HANT-tash-ə / mei-nə GELT-b[oe]r-zə gə-SHTOH-len!*

Listen Up: Security Lingo

Bitte ziehen Sie Ihre Schuhe aus.	Please remove your shoes.
Bit-ə tseen zee ee-rə SHOO-ə ows.	
Ziehen Sie Ihre Jacke aus.	Remove your jacket / sweater.
Tseen zee ee-rə YAK-kə ows.	
Legen Sie Ihren Schmuck ab.	Remove your jewelry.
Lay-gen zee ee-ren SHMUK ab.	
Legen Sie Ihre Taschen auf das Band.	Place your bags on the conveyor belt.
Lay-gen zee ee-rə TASH-ə owf das BAND.	
Treten Sie zur Seite.	Step to the side.
TRAY-ten zee tsoor ZEI-tə.	
Wir müssen Sie abtasten	We have to do a hand search.
Veer m[ue]s-sen zee AP-tas-ten.	

IN FLIGHT

It's unlikely you'll need much German on the plane, but these phrases will help if a bilingual flight attendant is unavailable or if you need to talk to a German-speaking neighbor.

I think that's my seat.	**Ich glaube, das ist mein Platz.**
	I[ch] GLOW-bə, das ist MEIN plats.
May I have ____?	**Ich hätte gern ____.**
	I[ch] HET-tə gern ____.
still water	**ein stilles Wasser**
	ein shtil-les vas-sər
sparkling water	**ein Wasser mit Kohlensäure**
	ein vas-sər mit KOH-len-zoy-rə
orange juice	**einen Orangensaft**
	ei-nen oh-RAN-shen-zaft

soda	**eine Limonade**
	ei-nə lim-moh-nah-də
diet soda	**eine Diätlimonade**
	ei-nə dee-AYT-lim-moh-NAH-də
a beer	**ein Bier**
	ein beer
a glass of wine	**ein Glas Wein**
	ein glahs vein

For a complete list of drinks, see p82.

a pillow	**ein Kissen**
	ein KIS-sen
a blanket	**eine Decke**
	ei-nə DAYK-kə
a hand wipe	**ein Tuch für die Hände**
	ein too[ch] f[ue]r dee H[AE]N-də
headphones	**Kopfhörer**
	KOPF-h[oe]rer
a magazine or newspaper	**eine Zeitschrift oder eine Zeitung**
	ei-nə TSEIT-shrift oh-dər ei-nə TSEI-tung
When will the meal be served?	**Wann wird das Essen serviert?**
	Van virt das ES-sen sayr-VEERT?
How long until we land?	**Wie lange noch bis zur Landung?**
	Vee lang-ə no[kh] bis tsoor LAN-dung?
May I move to another seat?	**Dürfte ich mich bitte woanders hinsetzen?**
	D[ue]rf-tə i[ch] mi[ch] bit-ə voh-AN-ders HIN-zet-sen?
How do I turn the light on / off?	**Wie kann ich das Licht einschalten / ausschalten?**
	Vee kan i[ch] das li[ch]t EIN-shal-ten / OWS-shal-ten?

Trouble in Flight

These headphones are broken.	**Dieser Kopfhörer funktioniert nicht.**
	DEE-zər KOPF-h[oe]-rər funk-tsee-oh-NEERT ni[ch]t.
I spilled something.	**Ich habe etwas verschüttet.**
	I[ch] hah-bə et-vas fer-SH[UE]T-tet.
My child spilled something.	**Mein Kind hat etwas verschüttet.**
	Mein kint hat et-vas fer-SH[UE]T-tet.
My child is sick.	**Meinem Kind ist schlecht.**
	Mei-nem kint ist SHLE[CH]T.
I need an airsickness bag.	**Ich brauche eine Spucktüte.**
	I[ch] BROW-[kh]ə ei-nə SHPUK-t[ue]-tə.
I smell something strange.	**Hier riecht etwas seltsam.**
	Heer ree[ch]t et-vas ZELT-zahm.
That passenger is behaving suspiciously.	**Dieser Passagier verhält sich verdächtig.**
	DEE-zər pas-sah-ZHEER fer-HELT zi[ch] fer-DE[CH]-ti[ch].

AT BAGGAGE CLAIM

Where is baggage claim for flight ____?	**Wo finde ich die Gepäckausgabe für Flug ____?**
	Voh fin-də i[ch] dee gə-PEK-ows-gah-bə f[ue]r flook ____?
Would you please help with my bags?	**Könnten Sie mir bitte mit meinem Gepäck behilflich sein?**
	K[oe]n-ten zee meer bit-ə mit mei-nem gə-PEK bə-hilf-li[ch] zein?
I am missing ____ bags.	**Mir fehlen ____ Taschen.**
	Meer FAY-len ____ ta-shen.

For full coverage of numbers, see p8.

My bag ____.	Meine Tasche ____.
	Mei-nə ta-shə ____.
was lost	**ist verschwunden**
	ist fer-shvun-den
was damaged	**wurde beschädigt**
	vur-də bə-SHAY-dikt
was stolen	**wurde gestohlen**
	vur-də gə-SHTOH-len
is a suitcase	**ist ein Koffer**
	ist ein KOF-fər
is a briefcase	**ist ein Aktenkoffer**
	ist ein AK-ten-kof-fər
is a carry-on	**ist eine Tragetasche**
	ist ei-nə TRAH-gə-tash-ə
is a suit bag	**ist ein Kleidersack**
	ist ein KLEI-dər-zak
is a trunk	**ist ein Schrankkoffer**
	ist ein SHRANK-kof-fər
contains golf clubs	**enthält Golfschläger**
	ent-HELT golf-shlay-gər

For full coverage of color terms, see English / German Dictionary.

is hard	**ist hart**
	ist hart
is made out of ____	**ist aus ____**
	ist ows ____
canvas	**Stoff**
	shtoff
vinyl	**Vinyl**
	vee-N[UE]HL
leather	**Leder**
	LAY-dər
hard plastic	**Hartplastik**
	HART-plas-tik
aluminum	**Aluminium**
	ah-loo-MEE-nee-oom

BY CAR

RENTING A VEHICLE

Is there a car rental agency in the airport?

Gibt es am Flughafen eine Autovermietung?
Geept es am FLOOK-hah-fen ei-nə OW-toh-fer-mee-tung?

I have a reservation.

Ich habe eine Reservierung.
I[ch] hah-bə ei-nə re-zer-VEE-rung.

Vehicle Preferences

I would like to rent ____.

Ich möchte gern ____ mieten.
I[ch] m[oe][ch]-tə gern ____ mee-ten.

an economy car

    ein sparsames Auto
    ein SHPAHR-zah-mes OW-toh

a midsize car

    einen Mittelklassewagen
    ei-nen MIT-tel-klas-sə-vah-gen

a convertible

    ein Cabrio
    ein CAH-bree-oh

a van

    einen Van
    ei-nen VEN

a sports car

    einen Sportwagen
    ei-nen SHPORT-vah-gen

a 4-wheel-drive vehicle

    ein Auto mit Vierradantrieb
    ein ow-toh mit FEER-rat an-treep

a motorcycle

    ein Motorrad
    ein moh-TOH-rat

a scooter

    einen Roller
    ei-nen Rol-lər

Do you have one with ____?

Ist ein Fahrzeug mit ____ verfügbar?
Ist ein FAHR-tsoyk mit ____ fer-F[UE]K-bar?

air conditioning

    Klimaanlage
    KLEE-mah-an-lah-gə

a sunroof	**Sonnendach** *ZON-nen-da[kh]*
a CD player	**CD-Player** *TSAY-DAY-play-ər*
an iPod connection	**iPod-Anschluss** *EI-pot-an-shlus*
a GPS system	**GPS-System** *chee-pee-ES-zis-taym*
a DVD player	**DVD-Player** *day-fow-DAY play-ər*
child seats	**Kindersitzen** *KIN-dər-zit-sen*
Do you have a ____?	**Haben Sie ein ____?** *Hah-ben zee ein ____?*
smaller car	**kleineres Auto** *KLEI-ne-res ow-toh*
bigger car	**größeres Auto** *GR[OE]-se-res ow-toh*
cheaper car	**günstigeres Auto** *G[UE]NS-tee-gə-res ow-toh*
Do you have a non-smoking car?	**Haben Sie ein Nichtraucherauto?** *Hah-ben zee ein NI[CH]T-row-[kh]ər-ow-toh?*
I need an automatic transmission.	**Ich hätte gern ein Automatikgetriebe.** *I[ch] HET-tə gern ein ow-toh-MAH-tik-gə-tree-bə.*
A standard transmission is okay.	**Schaltgetriebe ist in Ordnung.** *Shalt-gə-tree-bə ist in ORT-nung.*
May I have an upgrade?	**Könnte ich bitte eine höhere Kategorie bekommen?** *K[oe]n-tə i[ch] bit-ə ei-nə H[OE]-her-ə kah-tay-goh-ree bə-KOM-men?*

Money Matters

What's the daily / weekly / monthly rate?	**Wie hoch sind die Kosten pro Tag / Woche / Monat?**
	Vee hoh[ch] zint dee KOS-ten proh TAHK / VO-[kh]ə / MOH-nat?
What is the mileage rate?	**Wie hoch sind die Kosten pro Kilometer?**
	Vee hoh[kh] zint dee KOS-ten proh KEE-loh-may-tər?
How much is insurance?	**Wie viel kostet die Versicherung?**
	Vee feel kos-tet dee fer-ZI-[ch]e-rung?
Are there other fees?	**Fallen weitere Kosten an?**
	FAL-len vei-te-rə KOS-ten an?
Is there a weekend rate?	**Gibt es einen Wochenendtarif?**
	Geept es ei-nen VO-[kh]en-ent-ta-reef?

Technical Questions

What kind of fuel does it take?	**Welche Kraftstoffart muss ich verwenden?**
	Vel-[ch]ə KRAFT-shtoff-art mus i[ch] fer-VEN-den?
Do you have the manual in English?	**Haben Sie ein englisches Handbuch?**
	Hah-ben zee ein ENG-li-shes hant-boo[ch]?
Do you have a booklet in English with the local traffic laws?	**Haben Sie eine englische Broschüre mit den örtlichen Verkehrsregeln?**
	Hah-ben zee ei-ne ENG-li-shə broh-SH[UE]-rə mit dayn [oe]rt-li-[ch]en fer-KAYRS-ray-geln?

CAR TROUBLE

It is already dented.	**Das Fahrzeug ist bereits beschädigt.** *Das FAHR-tsoyk ist bə-reits bə-SHAY-dikt.*
It is scratched.	**Das Fahrzeug hat einen Kratzer.** *Das FAHR-tsoyk hat ei-nen KRAT-sər.*
The windshield is cracked.	**Die Frontscheibe ist beschädigt.** *Dee FRONT-shei-bə ist bə-shay-dikt.*
The ____ doesn't work.	**Der / Die / Das ____ funktioniert nicht.** *Dayr / Dee / Das ____ funk-tsee-oh-NEERT ni[ch]t.*

See diagram on p48 for car parts.

The tires look low.	**Die Reifen scheinen wenig Druck zu haben.** *Dee REI-fen shei-nen vay-nig DRUK tsoo hah-ben.*
It has a flat tire.	**Das Fahrzeug hat einen Platten.** *Das FAHR-tsoyk hat ei-nen plat-ten.*
Whom do I call for service?	**Wo kann ich anrufen, wenn ich Hilfe benötige?** *Voh kan i[ch] an-roo-fen, ven i[ch] HIL-fə bə-N[OE]-ti-gə?*
It won't start.	**Der Motor springt nicht an.** *Dayr MOH-tohr shpringt ni[ch]t an.*
It's out of gas.	**Der Tank ist leer.** *Dayr tank ist layr.*
The Check Engine light is on.	**Das Lämpchen für ein Problem mit dem Motor leuchtet.** *Das LEMP-[ch]en f[ue]r ein proh-BLAYM mit daym MOH-tohr loy[ch]-tet.*

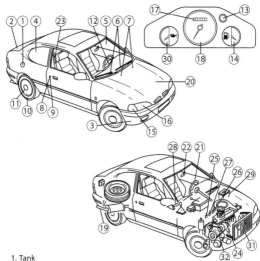

1. Tank
2. Kofferraum
3. Stoßstange
4. Fenster
5. Windschutzscheibe
6. Scheibenwischer
7. Scheibenwaschanlage
8. Tür
9. Schloss
10. Reifen
11. Radkappe
12. Lenkrad
13. Warnleuchte
14. Tankanzeige
15. Blinker
16. Scheinwerfer
17. Kilometerzähler

18. Tacho
19. Auspuff
20. Motorhaube
21. Lenkrad
22. Rückspiegel
23. Sicherheitsgurt
24. Motor
25. Gaspedal
26. Kupplung
27. Bremse
28. Handbremse
29. Batterie
30. Ölstandsanzeige
31. Kühler
32. Keilriemen

The oil light is on.	**Das Öllämpchen leuchtet.**
	Das [OE]L-lemp-[ch]en loy[ch]-tet.
The brake light is on.	**Die Bremsleuchte leuchtet.**
	Dee BREMS-loy[ch]-tə loy[ch]-tet.
It runs rough.	**Das Fahrzeug läuft unruhig.**
	Das FAHR-tsoyk loyft UN-rooi[ch].
The car is over heating.	**Das Fahrzeug überhitzt.**
	Das FAHR-tsoyk [ue]bər-HITST.

ASKING FOR DIRECTIONS

Excuse me, please.	**Verzeihung bitte.**
	Fer-TSEI-ung bit-ə.
How do I get to _____?	**Wie komme ich zum _____?**
	Vee KOM-mə i[ch] tsum _____?
Go straight.	**Gehen Sie geradeaus.**
	GAY-en zee gə-RAH-də-ows.
Turn left.	**Gehen Sie nach links.**
	Gay-en zee nah[kh] links.
Continue right.	**Gehen Sie nach rechts.**
	Gay-en zee nah[kh] re[ch]ts.
It's on the right.	**Das Ziel befindet sich auf der rechten Seite.**
	Das tseel bə-FIN-det zi[ch] owf der RE[CH]-ten ZEI-tə.
Can you show me on the map, please?	**Könnten Sie mir das bitte auf der Karte zeigen?**
	K[oe]n-ten zee meer das bit-ə owf dayr KAR-tə tsei-gen?
What are the GPS coordinates?	**Wie lauten die GPS-Koordinaten?**
	VEE low-ten dee chee-pee-ES-KOH-or-dee-nah-ten?
How far is it from here?	**Wie weit ist das von hier entfernt?**
	Vee veit ist das fon heer ent-FAYRNT?
Is this the right road for _____?	**Ist das die Straße nach _____?**
	Ist das dee shtrah-sə nah[kh] _____?

Road Signs

Geschwindigkeitsbegrenzung	Speed Limit
Stopp	Stop
Vorfahrt gewähren	Yield
Gefahr	Danger
Sackgasse	No Exit
Einbahnstraße	One Way
Einfahrt verboten	Do Not Enter
Straße gesperrt	Road Closed
Maut	Toll
Nur Bargeld	Cash Only
Parken verboten	No Parking
Parkgebühr	Parking Fee
Parkhaus	Parking Garage

I've lost my way.	**Ich habe mich verirrt.**
	I[ch] hah-bə mi[ch] fer-IRT.
Could you repeat that, please?	**Könnten Sie das bitte wiederholen?**
	K[oe]n-ten zee das bit-ə vee-dər-HOH-len?
Thanks for your help.	**Vielen Dank für Ihre Hilfe.**
	FEE-len dank f[ue]r ee-rə HIL-fə.

For full coverage of direction-related terms, see p5.

SORRY, OFFICER

What is the speed limit?	**Welche Geschwindigkeitsbegrenzung gilt hier?**
	Vel-[ch]ə gə-SHVIN-di[ch]-keits-bə-grent-sung gilt heer?
I wasn't going that fast.	**So schnell bin ich nicht gefahren.**
	Zoh shnel bin i[ch] ni[ch]t gə-FAH-ren.
How much is the fine?	**Wie hoch ist die Strafe?**
	Vee hoh[ch] ist dee SHTRAH-fə?

Where do I pay the fine?	**Wo muss ich die Strafe bezahlen?**
	Voh mus i[ch] dee shtrah-fə
	bə-TSAH-len?
Do I have to go to court?	**Komme ich vor Gericht?**
	Kom-mə i[ch] fohr gə-RI[CH]t?
I had an accident.	**Ich hatte einen Unfall.**
	I[ch] hat-tə ei-nen UN-fal.
The other driver hit me.	**Der andere Fahrer hat den Unfall verursacht.**
	Dayr an-de-rə FAH-rər hat dayn UN-fal fer-OOR-za[kh]t.
I'm at fault.	**Es war mein Fehler.**
	Es vahr MEIN fay-lər.

BY TAXI

Where is the taxi stand?	**Wo ist der Taxistand?**
	Voh ist der TAK-see-shtant?
Is there a limo / bus / van for my hotel?	**Fährt eine Limousine / ein Bus / ein Van zu meinem Hotel?**
	Fayrt ei-nə li-mo-ZEE-nə / ein bus / ein ven tsoo mei-nem hoh-TEL?
I need to get to _____.	**Bringen Sie mich bitte zum _____.**
	Bring-en zee mi[ch] bit-ə tsum _____.
How much will that cost?	**Wie viel wird das kosten?**
	Vee feel virt das kos-ten?
How long will it take?	**Wie lange dauert die Fahrt?**
	Vee lang-ə dow-ert dee fahrt?
Can you take me / us to the train / bus station?	**Können Sie mich / uns bitte zum Bahnhof / Busbahnhof bringen?**
	K[oe]n-nen zee mi[ch] / uns bit-ə tsum BAHN-hohf / BUS-bahn-hohf bring-en?
I am in a hurry.	**Ich bin in Eile.**
	I[ch] bin in EI-lə.
Slow down.	**Fahren Sie bitte langsamer.**
	Fah-ren zee bit-ə LANG-zah-mər.

Am I close enough to walk? **Kann ich von hier aus zu Fuß gehen?**

Kan i[ch] fon heer ows tsoo FOOS gay-en?

Please let me out here. **Lassen Sie mich hier bitte aussteigen.**

Las-sen zee mi[ch] heer bit-ə OWS-shtei-gen.

That's not the correct change. **Das Wechselgeld stimmt leider nicht.**

Das VEK-sel-gelt shtimt lei-dər ni[ch]t.

Listen Up: Taxi Lingo

Steigen Sie ein! *Shtei-gen zee ein!*	Get in!
Lassen Sie Ihr Gepäck stehen. Ich kümmere mich darum. *LAS-sen zee eer gə-pek STAY-en. I[ch] K[UE]M-me-rə mi[ch] dah-rum.*	Leave your luggage. I got it.
Das kostet sieben Euro pro Tasche. *Das kos-tet ZEE-ben OY-roh proh tash-ə.*	It's seven Euros for each bag.
Wie viele Fahrgäste? *Vee fee-lə FAHR-ges-tə?*	How many passengers?
Sind Sie in Eile? *Zint zee in EI-lə?*	Are you in a hurry?

BY TRAIN

How do I get to the train station?	**Wie komme ich zum Bahnhof?** *Vee kom-mə i[ch] tsum BAHN-hohf?*
Would you take me to the train station?	**Könnten Sie mich bitte zum Bahnhof bringen?** *K[oe]n-ten zee mi[ch] bit-ə tsum BAHN-hohf bring-en?*
How long is the trip to ____?	**Wie lange dauert die Fahrt nach ____?** *Vee LANG-ə dow-ert dee fahrt na[kh] ____?*
When is the next train?	**Wann geht der nächste Zug?** *VAN gayt dayr NEKS-tə tsook?*
Do you have a schedule?	**Haben Sie einen Fahrplan?** *Hah-ben zee ei-nen FAHR-plahn?*
Do I have to change trains?	**Muss ich umsteigen?** *Mus i[ch] UM-shtei-gen?*
I'd like ____.	**Ich hätte gern ____.** *I[ch] HET-tə gern ____.*
a one-way ticket	**ein einfaches Ticket** *ein EIN-fa-[kh]es tik-ket*
a round-trip ticket	**ein Hin- und Rückreiseticket** *ein hin unt R[UE]K-rei-zə-tik-ket*
Which platform does it leave from?	**Von welchem Gleis fährt der Zug ab?** *Fon vel-[ch]em GLEIS fayrt dayr tsook ab?*
Is there a bar car?	**Gibt es einen Barwagen?** *Geept es ei-nen BAHR-vah-gen?*
Is there a dining car?	**Gibt es einen Speisewagen?** *Geept es ei-nen SHPEI-zə-vah-gen?*
Which car is my seat in?	**In welchem Wagen befindet sich mein Platz?** *In VEL-[ch]em VAH-gen bə-FIN-det zi[ch] mein PLATS?*

Is this seat taken?	**Ist dieser Platz besetzt?** *Ist DEE-zər plats bə-ZETST?*
Where is the next stop?	**Wo ist der nächste Halt?** *Voh ist dayr neks-tə HALT?*
How many stops to ____?	**Wie viele Haltestellen noch bis ____?** *Vee fee-lə HAL-tə-shtel-len no[kh] bis ____?*
What's the train number and destination?	**Welche Zugnummer und welchen Zielort hat dieser Zug?** *Vel-[ch]ə TSOOK-num-mər unt vel-[ch]en TSEEL-ort hat dee-zər tsook?*

BY BUS

How do I get to the bus station?	**Wie komme ich zum Busbahnhof?** *Vee KOM-mə i[ch] tsum BUS-bahn-hohf?*
Would you take me to the bus station?	**Könnten Sie mich bitte zum Busbahnhof bringen?** *K[oe]n-ten zee mi[ch] bit-ə tsum BUS-bahn-hohf bring-en?*
May I have a bus schedule?	**Könnte ich bitte einen Busfahrplan bekommen?** *K[oe]n-tə i[ch] bit-ə ei-nen BUS-fahr-plahn bə-KOM-men?*
Which bus goes to ____?	**Welcher Bus fährt nach ____?** *Vel-[ch]ər bus fayrt nah[kh] ____?*
Where does it leave from?	**Von wo fährt er ab?** *Fon VOH fayrt ayr ap?*

English	German
How long does the bus take?	**Wie lange dauert die Fahrt?** *Vee LANG-ə dow-ert dee fahrt?*
How much is it?	**Wie viel kostet das?** *Vee feel KOS-tet das?*
Is there an express bus?	**Gibt es einen Expressbus?** *Geept es ei-nen eks-PRES-bus?*
Does it make local stops?	**Hält der Bus unterwegs?** *Helt dayr bus un-ter-VAYKS?*
Does it run at night?	**Fährt der Bus nachts?** *Fayrt dayr bus NA[KH]TS?*
When does the next bus leave?	**Wann geht der nächste Bus?** *Van gayt dayr nayks-tə BUS?*
I'd like ____.	**Ich hätte gern ____.** *I[ch] HET-tə gern ____.*
a one-way ticket	**ein einfaches Ticket** *ein EIN-fa-[kh]es tik-ket*
a round-trip ticket	**ein Hin- und Rückreiseticket** *ein hin unt R[UE]K-rei-zə tik-ket*
How long will the bus be stopped?	**Wie lange steht der Bus?** *Vee lang-ə SHTAYT dayr bus?*
Is there an air-conditioned bus?	**Gibt es einen klimatisierten Bus?** *Geept es ei-nen klee-mah-tee-ZEER-ten bus?*
Is this seat taken?	**Ist dieser Platz besetzt?** *Ist DEE-zər plats bə-ZETST?*
Where is the next stop?	**Wo ist der nächste Halt?** *Voh ist dayr neks-tə HALT?*
Could you please tell me when we reach ____?	**Könnten Sie mir bitte sagen, wann wir ____ erreichen?** *K[oe]n-ten zee meer bit-ə ZAH-gen, van veer ____ er-REI-[ch]en?*
Let me off here please.	**Lassen Sie mich hier bitte aussteigen.** *Las-sen zee mi[ch] heer bit-ə OWS-shtei-gen.*

BY SUBWAY

Where's the subway station?	**Wo finde ich die U-Bahn-Haltestelle?** *Voh fin-də i[ch] dee OOH-bahn-halt-ə-shtel-ə?*
Where can I buy a ticket?	**Wo kann ich ein Ticket kaufen?** *Voh kan i[ch] ein tik-ket kow-fen?*
Could I have a map of the subway?	**Könnte ich bitte einen Plan des U-Bahn-Netzes bekommen?** *K[oe]n-tə i[ch] bit-ə ei-nen plahn des OO-bahn-net-ses bə-KOM-men?*
Which line should I take for ____?	**Welche Linie fährt nach ____?** *Vel-[ch]ə LEE-nee-ə fayrt nah[kh] ____?*
Is this the right line for ____?	**Ist das die Linie nach ____?** *Ist das dee LEE-nee-ə nah[kh] ____?*
Which stop is it for ____?	**An welcher Haltestelle muss ich für ____ aussteigen?** *An vel-[ch]ər HAL-tə-shtel-lə mus i[ch] f[ue]r ____ OWS-shtei-gen?*
How many stops is it to ____?	**Wie viele Haltestellen noch bis ____?** *Vee fee-lə HAL-tə-shtel-len no[kh] bis ____?*
Is the next stop ____?	**Ist ____ die nächste Haltestelle?** *Ist ____ dee neks-tə HAL-tə-shtel-lə?*
Where are we?	**Wo befinden wir uns gerade?** *Voh bə-FIN-den veer uns gə-rah-də?*

Where do I change to ____?

Wo muss ich nach ____ umsteigen?

Voh mus i[ch] nah[kh] ____ UM-shtei-gen?

What time is the last train to ____?

Wann geht der letzte Zug nach ____?

Van gayt dayr LETS-tə tsook nah[kh] ____?

SUBWAY TICKETS

U-Bahn-Fahrkarten

(One-way)	1 Einfache Fahrt	5 Zone 1 — (Zone 1)
(Round-trip)	2 Hin- und Rückfahrt	6 Zone 2 — (Zone 2)
(10 trips)	3 10 Fahrten	20 Fahrten — (20 trips)

Press 3 – 10 trips (€1.10/ride) — **3 - 10 Fahrten drücken (1,10 €/Fahrt)**

Press 4 – 20 trips (€1.05/ride) — **4 - 20 Fahrten drücken (1,05 €/Fahrt)**

Wechselgeld, Fahrkarten und Quittung entnehmen

(Take change, tickets, receipt)

Angezeigten Betrag einwerfen — Insert amount shown.

Geldscheine hier einführen — Insert bills here.

Kreditkarte einführen — Insert credit card.

Münzen einwerfen — Insert coins.

CONSIDERATIONS FOR TRAVELERS WITH SPECIAL NEEDS

Do you have wheelchair access?

Ist der Zugang behindertengerecht?
Ist dayr TSOO-gang bə-HIN-der-ten-gə-re[ch]t?

Do you have elevators? Where?

Gibt es Aufzüge? Wo?
Geept es OWF-ts[ue]-gə? Voh?

Do you have ramps? Where?

Haben Sie Rampen? Wo?
Hah-ben zee RAM-pen? Voh?

Are the restrooms wheelchair-accessible?

Sind die Toiletten behindertengerecht?
Zint dee twa-LET-ten bə-HIN-der-ten-gə-re[ch]t?

Do you have audio assistance for the hearing impaired?

Haben Sie Audioinformationen für Hörgeschädigte?
Hah-ben zee OW-dee-oh-in-fohr-mah-tsee-oh-nen f[ue]r H[OE]R-gə-shay-dik-tə?

I am deaf / hearing impaired.

Ich bin taub / schwerhörig.
I[ch] bin towb / shvayr-h[oe]-ri[ch].

May I bring my service dog?

Kann ich meinen Blindenhund mitnehmen?
Kan i[ch] mei-nen BLIN-den-hunt mit-nay-men?

I am blind / visually impaired.

Ich bin blind / sehbehindert.
I[ch] bin blint / zay-bə-hin-dert.

I need to charge my power chair.

Ich muss meinen elektrisch betriebenen Rollstuhl aufladen.
I[ch] mus mei-nen ay-LEK-trish bə-TREE-be-nen ROL-shtool owfladen.

CHAPTER THREE

LODGING

This chapter will help you find the right accommodations, at the right price, and the amenities you might need during your stay.

FINDING A HOTEL

Please recommend ____.	**Bitte empfehlen Sie mir ____.** *Bit-ə em-PFAY-len zee meer ____.*
a clean hostel	**eine saubere Jugendherberge** *ei-nə zow-be-rə YOO-gent-her-bayr-gə*
a moderately priced hotel	**ein Hotel der mittleren Preiskategorie** *ein hoh-TEL dayr MIT-lay-ren PREIS-kah-tay-goh-ree*
a moderately priced B&B	**eine Pension der mittleren Preiskategorie** *ei-nə pen-SEE-ohn dayr MIT-lay-ren PREIS-kah-tay-goh-ree*
a good hotel / motel	**ein gutes Hotel / Motel** *ein GOO-tes hoh-TEL / moh-TEL*
Does the hotel have ____?	**Verfügt das Hotel über ____?** *Fer-F[UE]KT das hoh-TEL [ue]-bər ____?*
an indoor / outdoor pool	**ein Hallenbad / Freibad** *ein HAL-len baht / FREI-baht*
a casino	**ein Kasino** *ein kah-ZEE-noh*
suites	**Suiten** *SWEE-ten*
balconies	**Balkone** *BAL-koh-nə*
a fitness center	**ein Fitness-Center** *ein FIT-nes-sen-tər*

a spa	**ein Heilbad**
	ein HEIL-baht
a tennis court	**einen Tennisplatz**
	ei-nen TEN-nis-plats
air-conditioned rooms	**Räume mit Klimaanlage**
	ROY-mə mit KLEE-mah-an-lah-gə
free Wi-Fi	**kostenlosen WLAN-Zugang**
	KOS-ten-loh-zen WAY-lahn-tsoo-gang

ROOM PREFERENCES

I would like a room for _____.　**Ich hätte gern ein Zimmer für _____.**
I[ch] HET-tə gern ein TSIM-mər f[ue]r _____.

For full coverage of number terms, see p8.

I would like _____.	**Ich hätte gern _____.**
	I[ch] HET-tə gern _____.
a king-sized bed	**ein breites Doppelbett**
	ein brei-tes DOP-pel-bet
a double bed	**ein Doppelbett**
	ein DOP-pel-bet

Listen Up: Reservations Lingo

Wir haben nichts mehr frei. *Veer hah-ben ni[ch]ts mayr frei.*	We have no vacancies.
Wie lange möchten Sie bleiben? *Vee lang-ə m[oe][ch]-ten zee BLEI-ben?*	How long will you be staying?
Raucher oder Nichtraucher? *ROW-[kh]ər oh-dər NI[CH]T-row-[kh]ər*	Smoking or nonsmoking?

twin beds	**zwei Betten** *tsvei bet-ten*
adjoining rooms	**angrenzende Zimmer** *AN-grent-sen-de tsim-mər*
a smoking room	**ein Raucherzimmer** *ein ROW-[kh]ər-tsim-mər*
a non-smoking room	**ein Nichtraucherzimmer** *ein NI[CH]T-row-[kh]ər-tsim-mər*
a private bathroom	**ein eigenes Bad** *ein EI-ge-nes baht*
a shower	**eine Dusche** *ei-nə DOO-shə*
a bathtub	**eine Badewanne** *ei-nə BAH-də-van-nə*
air conditioning	**eine Klimaanlage** *ei-nə KLEE-mah-an-lah-gə*
television	**einen Fernseher** *ei-nen FAYRN-zay-ər*
cable	**Kabelfernsehen** *KAH-bel-fayrn-zayn*
satellite TV	**Satellitenfernsehen** *SAT-tə-LEE-ten-fayrn-zayn*
a telephone	**ein Telefon** *ein te-le-FOHN*
Internet access	**einen Internetzugang** *ei-nen IN-tər-net-tsoo-gang*
Wi-Fi	**WLAN** *VAY-lahn*
a refrigerator	**einen Kühlschrank** *ei-nen K[UE]HL-shrahnk*
a beach view	**Blick auf den Strand** *blik owf dayn SHTRANT*
a city view	**Blick auf die Stadt** *blik owf dee SHTAT*
a kitchenette	**eine Kochnische** *ei-nə KO[KH]-nee-shə*

LODGING

a balcony	**einen Balkon**
	ei-nen BAL-kohn
a suite	**eine Suite**
	ei-nə SWEET
a penthouse	**ein Penthhaus**
	ein PENT-hows
I would like a room _____.	**Ich hätte gern ein Zimmer _____.**
	I[ch] HET-tə gern ein tsim-mər _____.
on the ground floor	**im Erdgeschoß**
	in AYRT-gə-shos
near the elevator	**in Aufzugnähe**
	in OWF-tsook-nay-ə
near the stairs	**in der Nähe des Treppenhauses**
	in dayr NAY-ə des TREP-pen-how-ses
near the pool	**in Poolnähe**
	in POOL-nay-ə
away from the street	**das nicht in Richtung der Straße liegt**
	das ni[ch]t in RI[CH]-tung dayr SHTRAH-sə leekt
I would like a corner room.	**Ich hätte gern ein Eckzimmer.**
	I[ch] HET-tə gern ein EK-tsim-mər.
Do you have _____?	**Haben Sie _____?**
	Hah-ben zee _____?
a crib	**ein Kinderbett**
	ein KIN-dər-bet
a foldout bed	**ein ausklappbares Bett**
	ein OWS-klap-bah-res bet

FOR GUESTS WITH SPECIAL NEEDS

I need a room with ____.	**Ich benötige ein Zimmer mit ____.**
	I[ch] bə-n[oe]-ti-gə ein tsim-mər mit ____.
wheelchair access	**Zugang per Rollstuhl**
	TSOO-gang payr ROL-shtool
services for the visually impaired	**Hilfe für Sehbehinderte**
	HIL-fə f[ue]r ZAY-bə-hin-der-tə
services for the hearing impaired	**Hilfe für Hörgeschädigte**
	HIL-fə f[ue]r H[OE]R-gə-shay-dig-tə
I am traveling with a service dog.	**Ich reise mit einem Blindenhund.**
	I[ch] REI-zə mit ei-nem BLIN-den-hunt.

MONEY MATTERS

I would like to make a reservation.	**Ich möchte reservieren.**
	I[ch] m[oe][ch]-tə re-zer-VEE-ren.
How much per night?	**Wie viel pro Übernachtung?**
	Vee-feel proh [ue]behr-NA[KH]-toong?
Do you have a ____?	**Bieten Sie ____?**
	BEE-ten zee ____?
weekly / monthly rate	**einen Wochentarif / Monatstarif an**
	ei-nen VO-[kh]en-tah-reef / MOH-nats-tah-reef an
a weekend rate	**einen Wochenendtarif an**
	ei-nen VO-[kh]en-ent-tah-reef an
We will be staying for ____ days / weeks.	**Wir möchten ____ Tage / Wochen bleiben.**
	Veer m[oe][ch]-ten ____ TAH-gə / VO-[kh]en blei-ben.

For full coverage of number terms, see p8.

For full coverage of number terms, see p8.

LODGING

What is the checkout time?	**Wann wird ausgecheckt?** *Van virt OWS-gə-tshekt?*

For full coverage of time-related terms, see p12.

Do you accept credit cards?	**Akzeptieren Sie Kreditkarten?** *Ak-tsep-TEE-ren zee kray-DEET-kar-ten?*
May I see a room?	**Kann ich mir ein Zimmer ansehen?** *Kan i[ch] meer ein tsim-mər an-zay-en?*
How much are taxes?	**Wie viel Steuer muss ich bezahlen?** *Vee feel shtoy-ər muss i[ch] bə-tsah-len?*
Is there a service charge, or is it included?	**Gibt es eine Servicegebühr, oder ist sie inbegriffen?** *Geept es ei-nə ZER-vis gə-b[ue]r oh-dər ist zee in-bə-grif-fen?*

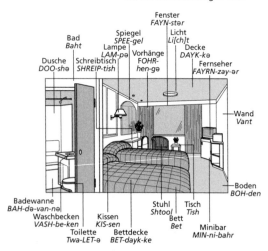

- Fenster *FAYN-stər*
- Spiegel *SPEE-gel*
- Licht *Li[ch]t*
- Lampe *LAM-pə*
- Vorhänge *FOHR-hen-gə*
- Decke *DAYK-kə*
- Bad *Baht*
- Dusche *DOO-shə*
- Schreibtisch *SHREIP-tish*
- Fernseher *FAYRN-zay-ər*
- Wand *Vant*
- Boden *BOH-den*
- Badewanne *BAH-də-van-nə*
- Waschbecken *VASH-be-ken*
- Toilette *Twa-LET-ə*
- Kissen *KIS-sen*
- Bettdecke *BET-dayk-ke*
- Stuhl *Shtool*
- Bett *Bet*
- Tisch *Tish*
- Minibar *MIN-ni-bahr*

Is breakfast included?	**Ist das Frühstück inbegriffen?** *Ist das FR[UE]-sht[ue]k IN-bə-grif-fen?*
I'd like to speak with the manager.	**Ich möchte den Manager sprechen.** *I[ch] m[oe][ch]-tə dayn ME-nay-tshər shpre-[ch]en.*

IN-ROOM AMENITIES

I'd like _____.	**Ich möchte _____.** *I[ch] m[oe][ch]-tə _____.*
to place an international call	**ein Auslandsgespräch führen** *ein OWS-lants-gə-shpre[ch] f[ue]-ren*
to place a long-distance call	**ein Ferngespräch führen** *ein FAYRN-gə-shpre[ch] f[ue]-ren*
directory assistance in English	**eine englischsprachige Telefonauskunft** *ei-nə ENG-lish-shprah-[kh]ig-gə te-le-FOHN-ows-kunft*

Instructions for Dialing from the Hotel Phone

Wählen Sie für einen Anruf auf einem anderen Zimmer die entsprechende Zimmernummer.	To call another room, dial the room number.
Wählen Sie für ein Ortsgespräch die 9 vor.	To make a local call, first dial 9.
Wählen Sie für einen Anruf bei der Vermittlung die 0.	To call the operator, dial 0.

LODGING

room service	**den Zimmerservice**
	dayn TSIM-mər-zer-vis
maid service	**den Raumpflegedienst**
	dayn ROWM-pflay-gə-deenst
the front desk operator	**die Vermittlung an der Rezeption**
	dee fer-MIT-lung an dayr ray-tsep-tsee-OHN

Do you have room service?	**Haben Sie Zimmerservice?**
	Hah-ben zee TSIM-mər-zer-vis?
When is the kitchen open?	**Ab wann ist die Küche geöffnet?**
	Ap van ist de k[ue]-[ch]ə gə-[oe]f-net?
When is breakfast served?	**Wann wird das Frühstück serviert?**
	Van virt das FR[UE]-sht[ue]k zayr-VEERT?

For full coverage of time-related terms, see p12.

Do you offer massages?	**Bieten Sie Massagen an?**
	Bee-ten zee ma-sah-shen an?
Do you have a lounge?	**Haben Sie ein Foyer?**
	Hah-ben zee ein fwa-YAY?
Do you have a business center?	**Haben Sie ein Geschäftscenter?**
	Hah-ben zee ein gə-SHEFTS-sen-tər?
Do you serve breakfast?	**Gibt es bei Ihnen Frühstück?**
	Geept es bei eenen FR[UE]H-sht[ue]ck?
Do you have Wi-Fi?	**Haben Sie WLAN?**
	Hah-ben zee VAY-lahn?
Is there Wi-Fi in the rooms, or in the lobby only?	**Gibt es in den Zimmern WLAN-Zugang oder nur in der Lobby?**
	Geept es in dayn tsim-mern VAY-lahn-tsoo-gang oh-dər noor in dayr lob-bee?

What is the Wi-Fi password?	**Wie lautet das WLAN-Kennwort?** *Vee low-tet das VAY-lahn-ken-vort?*
May I have a newspaper in the morning?	**Kann ich morgens bitte eine Zeitung bekommen?** *Kan i[ch] mor-gens bit-ə ei-nə TSEI-tung bə-kom-men?*
Do you offer a tailor service?	**Haben Sie eine Schneiderei?** *Hah-ben zee ei-nə shnei-de-REI?*
Do you offer laundry service?	**Haben Sie eine Wäscherei?** *Hah-ben zee ei-nə vesh-ay-REI?*
Do you offer dry cleaning?	**Haben Sie eine chemische Reinigung?** *Hah-ben zee ei-nə KAY-mi-shə REI-nee-gung?*
May we have ____?	**Könnten wir bitte ____?** *K[oe]n-ten veer bit-ə ____?*
clean sheets today	**frische Bettwäsche bekommen** *fri-shə BET-ve-shə bə-kom-men*
more towels	**mehr Handtücher bekommen** *mayr HANT-t[ue]-[ch]ər bə-kom-men*
more toilet paper	**mehr Toilettenpapier bekommen** *mayr twa-LET-ten-pah-peer bə-kom-men*
extra pillows	**zusätzliche Kissen bekommen** *TSOO-zets-li-[ch]ə kis-sen bə-kom-men*
shampoo	**Shampoo bekommen** *SHAM-poo bə-kom-men*
toothpaste	**Zahnpasta bekommen** *TSAHN-pas-tah bə-kom-men*
a toothbrush	**eine Zahnbürste bekommen** *ei-nə TSAHN-b[ue]rs-tə bə-kom-men*

an adapter	**einen Adapter bekommen** *ei-nen ah-DAP-tər bə-kom-men*
a bottle opener	**einen Flaschenöffner bekommen** *ei-nen FLASH-en-[oe]f-nər bə-kom-men*
Do you have an ice machine?	**Haben Sie eine Eismaschine?** *Hah-ben zee ei-nə EIS-mah-shee-nə?*
Did I receive any ____?	**Haben Sie ____?** *Hah-ben zee ____?*
messages	**Nachrichten für mich** *NA[KH]-ri[ch]-ten f[ue]r mi[ch]*
mail	**Post für mich** *POST f[ue]r mi[ch]*
A spare key, please.	**Geben Sie mir bitte einen Ersatzschlüssel.** *Gay-ben zee meer bit-ə ei-nen ayr-ZATS-shl[ue]s-sel.*
More hangers, please.	**Geben Sie mir bitte ein paar zusätzliche Kleiderbügel.** *Gay-ben zee meer bit-ə ein pahr TSOO-zets-li-[ch]ə KLEI-dər-b[ue]-gel.*
I am allergic to down pillows.	**Ich bin allergisch gegen Daunenkissen.** *I[ch] bin al-LAYR-gish gay-gen DOW-nen-kis-sen.*
I'd like a wake-up call.	**Ich hätte gern einen Weckruf.** *I[ch] HET-tə gern ei-nen VEK-roof.*

For full coverage of time-related terms, see p12.

Do you have alarm clocks?	**Haben Sie Wecker?** *Hah-ben zee VEK-kər?*

Is there a safe in the room?	**Verfügt das Zimmer über einen Tresor?**
	Fer-f[ue]kt das tsim-mər [ue]-bər ei-nen tray-ZOHR?
Does the room have a hair dryer?	**Gibt es auf dem Zimmer einen Haartrockner?**
	Geept es owf daym tsim-mər ei-nen HAHR-trok-nər?

HOTEL ROOM TROUBLE

May I speak with the manager?	**Könnte ich bitte den Manager sprechen?**
	K[oe]n-tə i[ch] bit-ə dayn ME-nay-tshər shpre-[ch]en?
The ___ does not work.	**___ funktioniert nicht.**
	___ funk-tsee-oh-NEERT ni[ch]t.
television	**Der Fernseher**
	Dayr FAYRN-zay-ər
telephone	**Das Telefon**
	Das te-le-FOHN
air conditioning	**Die Klimaanlage**
	Dee KLEE-mah-an-lah-gə
Internet	**Das Internet**
	Das IN-ter-net
Wi-Fi	**Das WLAN**
	Das VAY-lahn
cable TV	**Das Kabelfernsehen**
	Das KAH-bel-fayrn-zayn
The toilet is over flowing!	**Die Toilette läuft über!**
	Dee twa-LET-tə loyft [ue]-bər!

There is no hot water.	**Es kommt kein warmes Wasser.**
	Es komt kein var-mes VAS-sər.
This room is ____.	**Dieses Zimmer ist ____.**
	DEE-zes tsim-mər ist ____.
too noisy	**zu laut**
	tsoo lowt
too cold	**zu kalt**
	tsoo kalt
too warm	**zu warm**
	tsoo vahrm
dirty	**schmutzig**
	SHMUT-si[ch]
This room has ____.	**In diesem Zimmer gibt es ____.**
	In DEE-zem tsim-mər geept es ____.
bugs	**Ungeziefer**
	OON-gə-tsee-fər
mice	**Mäuse**
	MOY-zə
I'd like a different room.	**Ich möchte ein anderes Zimmer.**
	I[ch] m[oe][ch]-tə ein AN-day-res tsim-mər.
Do you have a bigger room?	**Haben Sie ein größeres Zimmer?**
	Hah-ben zee ein GR[OE]-say-res tsim-mər?
I locked myself out of my room.	**Ich habe mich aus meinem Zimmer ausgesperrt.**
	I[ch] hah-bə mi[ch] ows mei-nem TSIM-mər ows-gə-shpert.
I lost my key.	**Ich habe meinen Schlüssel verloren.**
	I[ch] hah-bə mei-nen shl[ue]s-sel fer-loh-ren.
Do you have a fan?	**Haben Sie einen Ventilator?**
	Hah-ben zee ei-nen ven-tee-LAH-tor?

The sheets are not clean.	**Die Bettwäsche ist schmutzig.** *Dee BET-vesh-ə ist shmut-si[ch].*
The towels are not clean.	**Die Handtücher sind schmutzig.** *Dee HANT-t[ue]-chər zint shmut-si[ch].*
The room is not clean.	**Das Zimmer ist schmutzig.** *Das tsim-mər ist shmut-si[ch].*
The guests next door / above / below are being very loud.	**Die Gäste nebenan / über dem Zimmer / unter dem Zimmer sind sehr laut.** *Dee ges-tə nay-ben-AN / [UE]-bər daym tsim-mər / UN-tə daym tsim-mər zint zayr lowt.*

CHECKING OUT

May I leave these bags?	**Kann ich diese Taschen hierlassen?** *Kan i[ch] DEE-zə tash-en HEER las-sen?*
I'm missing ____.	**Mir fehlt ____.** *Meer faylt ____.*
I've lost ____.	**Ich habe ____ verloren.** *I[ch] hah-bə ____ fer-loh-ren.*
I think this charge is a mistake.	**Ich glaube, diese Gebühr ist falsch.** *I[ch] glow-bə, dee-zə gə-B[UE]R ist falsh.*
Please explain this charge to me.	**Könnten Sie mir diese Gebühr bitte erklären?** *K[oe]n-ten zee meer dee-zə gə-b[ue]r bit-ə ayr-klay-ren?*
Thank you, we enjoyed our stay.	**Vielen Dank, es war schön bei Ihnen.** *Fee-len dank, es vahr SH[OE]N bei ee-nen.*
The service was excellent.	**Der Service war ausgezeichnet.** *Dayr ZER-vis vahr ows-gə-tsei[ch]-net.*

LODGING

The staff is very professional and courteous.	**Das Personal ist sehr professionell und zuvorkommend.** *Das payr-zoh-NAHL ist zayr proh-fess-yoh-NEL unt tsoo-VOHR-kom-ment.*
Please call a cab for me.	**Rufen Sie mir bitte ein Taxi.** *Roo-fen zee meer bit-ə ein TAK-see.*
Would someone please get my bags?	**Könnte sich bitte jemand um mein Gepäck kümmern?** *K[oe]n-tə zi[ch] bit-ə YAY-mant um mein gə-PEK k[ue]m-mern?*

HAPPY CAMPING

I'd like a site for ____.	**Ich hätte gern einen Platz für ____.** *I[ch] HET-tə gern ei-nen plats f[ue]r ____.*
a tent	**ein Zelt** *ein TSELT*
a camper	**einen Wohnwagen** *ei-nen VOHN-vah-gen*
Are there ____?	**Gibt es hier ____?** *Geept es heer ____?*
bathrooms	**Toiletten** *twa-LET-ten*
showers	**Duschen** *DOO-shen*
Is there running water?	**Gibt es fließendes Wasser?** *Geept es flee-send-es vas-sər?*
Is the water drinkable?	**Ist das Wasser trinkbar?** *Ist das vas-sər TRINK-bahr?*
Where is the electrical hookup?	**Wo finde ich den Elektroanschluss?** *Voh fin-də i[ch] dayn ay-LEK-troh-an-shlus?*

CHAPTER FOUR

DINING

This chapter includes a menu reader and the language you need to communicate in a range of dining establishments and food markets.

FINDING A RESTAURANT

Would you recommend a good ____?	**Können Sie mir ein gutes ____ empfehlen?** *K[oe]n-nen zee meer ein goo-tes ____ em-PFAY-len?*
local restaurant	**Restaurant mit lokaler Küche** *res-toh-RONG mit loh-KAH-lər k[ue]-[ch]ə*
Italian restaurant	**italienisches Restaurant** *ee-tahl-YAY-ni-shes res-toh-RONG*
French restaurant	**französisches Restaurant** *fran-TS[OE]-si-shes res-toh-RONG*
Turkish restaurant	**türkisches Restaurant** *T[UE]R-ki-shes res-toh-RONG*
Spanish restaurant	**spanisches Restaurant** *SHPAH-ni-shes res-toh-RONG*
Chinese restaurant	**chinesisches Restaurant** *kee-NAY-si-shes res-toh-RONG*
Japanese restaurant	**japanisches Restaurant** *yah-PAH-ni-shes res-toh-RONG*
Asian restaurant	**asiatisches Restaurant** *ah-zee-AH-ti-shes res-toh-RONG*
steakhouse	**Steakhaus** *STEAK-hows*
family restaurant	**Familienrestaurant** *fam-MEE-lee-en-res-toh-RONG*

seafood restaurant	**Fischrestaurant**
	FISH-res-toh-RONG
vegetarian restaurant	**vegetarisches Restaurant**
	vay-gay-TAH-ri-shes res-toh-RONG
buffet-style restaurant	**Selbstbedienungsrestaurant**
	ZELBST-bə-dee-nungs-res-toh-RONG
Greek restaurant	**griechisches Restaurant**
	GREE-[ch]i-shes res-toh-RONG
budget restaurant	**günstiges Restaurant**
	g[ue]ns-tee-ges res-toh-RONG
Would you recommend a good pizzeria?	**Können Sie mir eine gute Pizzeria?**
	K[oe]n-nen zee meer ei-nə goo-tə pitts-eh-REE-ah?
Which is the best restaurant in town?	**Welches Restaurant ist das beste der Stadt?**
	Vel-[ch]es res-toh-RONG ist das BES-tə dayr shtat?
Is there a late-night restaurant nearby?	**Gibt es in der Nähe ein Restaurant, das auch noch spät geöffnet hat?**
	Geept es in dayr nay-ə ein res-toh-RONG, das ow[kh] no[kh] shpayt gə-[oe]f-net hat?
Is there a restaurant that serves breakfast nearby?	**Gibt es in der Nähe ein Frühstückslokal?**
	Geept es in dayr nay-ə ein FR[UE]-sht[ue]ks-loh-kahl?
Is it very expensive?	**Ist es dort teuer?**
	Ist es dort TOY-ər?
Do I need a reservation?	**Benötige ich eine Reservierung?**
	Bə-n[oe]-ti-gə i[ch] ei-nə re-zer-VEE-rung?
Do I have to dress up?	**Muss ich mich herausputzen?**
	Mus i[ch] mi[ch] he-rows-put-sen?
Do they serve lunch?	**Gibt es dort Mittagessen?**
	Geept es dort MIT-tah-ges-sen?

What time do they open for dinner?	**Ab wann gibt es dort Abendessen?**
	Ab van geept es dort AH-bent-es-sen?
For lunch?	**Mittagessen?**
	MIT-tah-ges-sen?
What time do they close?	**Wie lange ist dort geöffnet?**
	Vee lang-ə ist dort gə-[oe]f-net?
Do you have a take out menu?	**Haben Sie Speisen zum Mitnehmen?**
	Hah-ben zee shpei-zen tsum MIT-nay-men?
Do you have a bar?	**Haben Sie eine Bar?**
	Hah-ben zee ei-nə BAHR?
Is there a café nearby?	**Gibt es ein Café in der Nähe?**
	Geept es ein kaf-FAY in dayr nay-ə?

GETTING SEATED

Are you still serving?	**Haben Sie noch geöffnet?**
	Hah-ben zee no[kh] gə-[OE]F-net?
How long is the wait?	**Wie lange muss ich warten? (sing.) / Wie lange müssen wir warten? (pl.)**
	Vee lang-ə mus i[ch] VAHR-ten? / Vee lang-ə m[ue]s-sen veer VAHR-ten?
May I see a menu?	**Darf ich die Speisekarte haben?**
	Darf i[ch] dee SHPEI-zə-kar-tə hah-ben?
Do you have a no-smoking section?	**Haben Sie einen Nichtraucherbereich?**
	Hah-ben zee ei-nen NI[CH]T-row-[kh]ər-bə-rei[ch]?
A table for ____, please.	**Einen Tisch für ____ Personen, bitte.**
	Ei-nen TISH f[ue]r ____ payr-zoh-nen, bit-ə.

For a full list of numbers, see p8.

Listen Up: Restaurant Lingo

Raucher oder Nichtraucher?	Smoking or
ROW-[kh]ər oh-dər NI[CH]T-row-[ch]ər?	nonsmoking?
Sie benötigen eine Krawatte und ein Jackett.	You'll need a tie and jacket.
Zee bə-n[oe]-ti-gen ei-nə krah-VAT-tə unt ein shah-KET.	
Es tut mir leid, aber kurze Hosen sind hier nicht erlaubt.	I'm sorry, no shorts are allowed.
Es toot meer LEIT, ah-bər kurt-sə HOH-sen zint heer ni[ch]t ayr-lowpt.	
Kann ich Ihnen etwas zu trinken bringen?	May I bring you something to drink?
Kan i[ch] ee-nen et-vas tsoo TRING-ken bring-en?	
Soll ich Ihnen die Weinkarte bringen?	Would you like to see a wine list?
Zol i[ch] ee-nen dee VEIN-kar-tə bring-en?	
Darf ich Ihnen unsere Spezialitäten vorstellen?	Would you like to hear our specials?
Darf i[ch] ee-nen un-zay-rə shpay-tsee-ah-lee-TAY-ten fohr-shtel-len?	
Möchten Sie jetzt bestellen?	Are you ready to order?
M[oe][ch]-ten zee yetst bə-SHTEL-len?	
Es tut mir leid, aber Ihre Kreditkarte wurde nicht akzeptiert.	I'm sorry, but your credit card was declined.
Es toot meer LEIT, ah-bər ee-rə kray-DEET-kar-tə vur-də ni[ch]t ak-tsep-TEERT.	

Do you have a quiet table?	**Haben Sie einen ruhigen Tisch?** *Hah-ben zee ei-nen ROOI-gen tish?*
Do you have highchairs?	**Haben Sie Hochstühle?** *Hah-ben zee HO[KH]-sht[ue]-lə?*
May we sit outside / inside please?	**Können wir draußen / drinnen sitzen?** *K[oe]n-nen veer DROW-sen / DRIN-nen zit-sen?*
May we sit at the counter?	**Können wir an der Theke sitzen?** *K[oe]n-nen veer an dayr TAY-kə zit-sen?*

ORDERING

Do you have a special tonight?	**Haben Sie heute Abend ein spezielles Angebot?** *Hah-ben zee hoy-tə ah-bent ein shpay-tsee-el-les AN-gə-boht?*
What do you recommend?	**Was können Sie empfehlen?** *Vas k[oe]n-nen zee em-PFAY-len?*
May I see a wine list?	**Könnte ich bitte die Weinkarte haben?** *K[oe]n-tə i[ch] bit-ə dee VEIN-kahr-tə hah-ben?*
Do you serve wine by the glass?	**Servieren Sie Wein im Glas?** *Zer-veer-en zee vein im GLAHS?*
May I see the drink list?	**Könnte ich bitte die Getränkekarte haben?** *K[oe]n-tə i[ch] bit-ə dee gə-TREN-kə-kar-tə hah-ben?*
I would like it cooked ____.	**Ich hätte es gern ____.** *I[ch] HET-tə es gern ____.*
rare	**blutig** *BLOO-ti[ch]*
medium rare	**halb gar** *HALP gahr*

DINING

medium	**medium**
	MEH-dee-oom
medium well	**halb durch**
	HALP dur[ch]
well	**gut durch**
	GOOT dur[ch]
charred	**verschmort**
	fer-SHMOHRT
Do you have a ____ menu?	**Haben Sie eine Karte mit ____ Speisen?**
	Hah-ben zee ei-nə kar-tə mit ____ shpei-zen?
diabetic	**diabetischen**
	dee-ah-BAY-ti-shen
kosher	**kosheren**
	KOH-sheh-ren
vegetarian	**vegetarischen**
	vay-gay-TAH-ri-shen
Do you have any ____ options?	**Haben Sie ____ Gerichte?**
	Hah-ben zee ____ gə-RI[CH]-tə?
vegan	**vegane**
	vay-GAH-nə
gluten-free	**glutenfreie**
	GLOO-ten-frei-ə
Do you have a children's menu?	**Haben Sie eine Karte für Kinder?**
	Hah-ben zee ei-nə kar-tə f[ue]r KIN-dər?
What is in this dish?	**Welche Zutaten enthält dieses Gericht?**
	Vel-[ch]ə TSOO-tah-ten ent-helt dee-zes-gə-RI[CH]T?
How is it prepared?	**Wie wird es zubereitet?**
	Vee virt es TSOO-bə-rei-tet?
What kind of oil is that cooked in?	**In welchem Öl wird dieses Gericht zubereitet?**
	In vel-[ch]em [OE]L virt dee-zes gə-ri[ch]t tsoo-bə-rei-tet?

I am allergic to ____.	**Ich bin allergisch gegen ____.**
	I[ch] bin al-LAYR-gish gay-gen ____.
seafood	**Meeresfrüchte**
	may-res-fr[ue]ch-tə
shellfish	**Schalentiere**
	shah-len-TEE-rə
nuts	**Nüsse**
	n[ue]-sə
peanuts	**Erdnüsse**
	ayrd-n[ue]-sə
I am lactose intolerant.	**Ich habe eine Laktoseunverträglichkeit.**
	I[ch] hah-bə ei-nə lak-TOH-zə-oon-fer-trayg-li[ch]-keit.
Would you recommend something without milk?	**Könnten Sie mir bitte etwas ohne Milch empfehlen?**
	K[oe]n-ten zee meer bit-ə et-vas oh-nə MIL[CH] em-PFAY-len?
Do you have any low-salt dishes?	**Haben Sie Gerichte mit wenig Salz?**
	Hah-ben zee gə-ri[ch]-tə mit vay-nig zalts?
On the side, please.	**Als Beilage, bitte.**
	Als BEI-lah-gə, bit-ə.
May I make a substitution?	**Kann ich die Zusammenstellung ändern?**
	Kan i[ch] dee tsoo-ZAM-men-shtel-lung en-dern?
I'd like to try that.	**Das würde ich gern probieren.**
	Das v[ue]r-də i[ch] gern proh-BEE-ren.
Is that fresh?	**Ist das frisch?**
	Ist das FRISH?
Extra butter, please.	**Könnte ich bitte noch etwas Butter haben?**
	K[oe]n-tə i[ch] bit-ə no[kh] et-vas BUT-tər hah-ben?

DINING

No butter, thanks.	**Keine Butter, danke.**
	Kei-nə BUT-tər, dank-ə.
No cream, thanks.	**Keine Sahne, danke.**
	Kei-nə ZAH-nə, dank-ə.
Dressing on the side, please.	**Dressing extra, bitte.**
	Dres-sing EKS-trah, bit-ə.
No salt, please.	**Kein Salz, bitte.**
	Kein ZALTS, bit-ə.
Water ____, please.	**Wasser ____, bitte.**
	VAS-sər ____, bit-ə.
with ice	**mit Eis**
	mit EIS
without ice	**ohne Eis**
	OH-nə eis

DURING THE MEAL

Waiter!	**Bedienung!**
	Bə-DEE-nung!
More water, please.	**Könnte ich bitte noch etwas Wasser haben?**
	K[oe]n-tə i[ch] bit-ə no[kh] et-vas VAS-sər hah-ben?
More bread, please.	**Könnte ich bitte noch etwas Brot haben?**
	K[oe]n-tə i[ch] bit-ə no[kh] et-vas BROHT hah-ben?
More butter, please.	**Könnte ich bitte noch etwas Butter haben?**
	K[oe]n-tə i[ch] bit-ə no[kh] et-vas BUT-tər hah-ben?
May I have some oil, please?	**Könnte ich bitte noch etwas Öl haben?**
	K[oe]n-tə i[ch] bit-ə no[kh] et-vas [OE]L hah-ben?

Could I have another _____ please?	**Könnte ich bitte noch _____ haben?**
	K[oe]n-tə i[ch] bit-ə no[kh] _____ hah-ben?
fork	**eine Gabel**
	ei-nə GAH-bel
knife	**ein Messer**
	ein MES-sər
spoon	**einen Löffel**
	ei-nen L[OE]F-fel
napkin	**eine Serviette**
	ei-nə zayr-VYET-tə
glass	**ein Glas**
	ein glahs
plate	**einen Teller**
	ei-nen TEL-lər
bowl	**eine Schüssel**
	ei-nə SH[UE]-sel
I'm sorry, I don't think this is what I ordered.	**Verzeihung, aber ich glaube, das habe ich nicht bestellt.**
	Fer-TSEI-ung, ah-bər i[ch] GLOW-bə, das hah-bə i[ch] ni[ch]t bə-SHTELT.
My meat is a little over / under cooked.	**Mein Fleisch ist etwas zu stark / zu wenig durch.**
	Mein fleish ist et-vas tsoo SHTAHRK / tsoo VAY-nig dur[kh].
My vegetables are a little over / under cooked.	**Mein Gemüse wurde etwas zu lang / zu kurz gekocht.**
	Mein gə-m[ue]-zə vur-də et-vas tsoo LANG / tsoo KURTS gə-ko[kh]t.
My food is cold.	**Mein Essen ist kalt.**
	Mein ES-sen ist kalt.
There's a bug in my food!	**Da ist ein Käfer in meinem Essen!**
	Da ist ein KAY-fər in mei-nem ES-sen!

DINING

May I have a refill?	**Würden Sie bitte nachschenken?** *V[ue]r-den zee bit-ə NAH[KH]- sheng-ken?*
A dessert menu, please.	**Die Dessertkarte, bitte.** *Dee des-SAYR-kar-tə, bit-ə.*

DRINKS

alcoholic drink	**alkoholisches Getränk** *al-koh-HOH-li-shes gə-TRENK*
cocktail	**cocktail** *KOK-tayl*
neat / straight	**pur** *poor*
on the rocks	**auf Eis** *owf EIS*
with (seltzer or soda) water	**mit (Selters- oder Soda-) Wasser** *mit (ZEL-ters oh-dər ZOH-da-) vas-sər*
beer	**Bier** *beer*
dark beer	**dunkles Bier** *DUNG-kləs beer*
light beer	**helles Bier** *HEL-les beer*
Kölsch	**Kölsch** *k[oe]lsh*
Weissbier	**Weißbier** *VEIS-beer*
pilsner	**Pils** *pils*
bock beer	**Bockbier** *BOCK-beer*
bottle	**Flasche** *FLASH-ə*
glass	**Glas** *glahs*

wine	**Wein**
	vein
house wine	**Hauswein**
	HOWS-vein
sweet wine	**lieblicher Wein**
	LEEB-li-[ch]ər vein
dry white wine	**trockener Weißwein**
	trok-ken-nər VEIS-vein
Gewürztraminer	**Gewürztraminer**
(a white, usually off-dry wine)	*Gə-v[ue]rts-trah-mee-nər*
Riesling	**Riesling**
	REES-ling
rosé	**Rosé**
	roh-ZAY
red wine	**Rotwein**
	ROHT-vein
champagne	**Sekt**
	zekt
hard cider	**Apfelmost**
	AP-fel-most
Scotch	**Scotch**
	skotsh
whiskey	**Whiskey**
	VIS-kee
liqueur	**Likör**
	lee-K[OE]HR
brandy	**Brandy**
	BREN-dee
cognac	**Kognak**
	KON-yak
Kirschwasser	**Kirschwasser**
(cherry-flavored liqueur)	*KIRSH-vas-sər*
gin	**Gin**
	zhin

DINING

vodka	**Wodka** *VOT-kah*
rum	**Rum** *rum*
radler / radlermass (beer mixed with lemonade or soda)	**Radler (0,5 L) / Radlermaß (1 L)** *RAHT-lər / RAHT-lər-mas*
nonalcoholic drink	**alkoholfreies Getränk** *al-koh-HOHL-frei-es gə-TRENK*
hot chocolate	**heiße Schokolade** *hei-sə shoh-koh-LAH-də*
lemonade	**Limonade** *lim-moh-NAH-də*
apple juice	**Apfelsaft** *AP-fel-zaft*
apple spritzer	**Apfelschorle** *AP-fel-shor-lə*
milkshake	**Milchshake** *MIL[CH]-shayk*
milk	**Milch** *mil[ch]*
tea	**Tee** *tay*
coffee	**Kaffee** *kah-FAY*
cappuccino	**Cappuccino** *kap-poo-CHEE-noh*
café au lait	**Milchkaffee** *MIL[CH]-kaf-fay*
espresso	**Espresso** *es-PRES-soh*
iced coffee	**Eiskaffee** *EIS-kaf-fay*
fruit juice	**Fruchtsaft** *FRU[CH]T-zaft*

For a full list of fruits, see p93.

SETTLING UP

I'm stuffed.	**Ich bin voll.**
	I[ch] bin FOL.
Could I have the check, please?	**Könnte ich bitte die Rechnung haben?**
	K[oe]n-tə i[ch] bit-ə dee RAY[CH]-nung hah-ben?
The meal was excellent.	**Das Essen war ausgezeichnet.**
	Das ES-sen vahr ows-gə-TSEI[CH]-net.
There's a problem with my bill.	**Es gibt da ein Problem mit meiner Rechnung.**
	Es geept dah ein proh-BLAYM mit mei-nər RAY[CH]-nung.
Is the tip included?	**Ist das inklusive Trinkgeld?**
	Ist das in-kloo-zee-və TRINK-gelt?
My compliments to the chef!	**Mein Kompliment an den Chefkoch!**
	Mein kom-plee-MENT an dayn SHEF-ko[kh]!

MENU READER

Each German-speaking country has its own regional and national specialties, but we've tried to make our list of classic dishes as broad as possible.

MENU TERMS

Frühstück	breakfast
FR[UE]-sht[ue]k	
Mittagessen	lunch
MIT-tah-ges-sen	
Abendessen	dinner
AH-bent-es-sen	
Vorspeisen	appetizers
FOHR-shpei-zen	
Hauptgerichte	entrees
HOWPT-gə-ri[ch]-tə	

Getränke	drinks
gə-TREN-kə	
Nachspeise	dessert
NAH[KH]-shpei-zə	
Menü	daily special
meh-N[UE]H	
Tagesgericht	dish of the day
TAH-ges-gə-ri[ch]t	

BREAKFAST

Eier	Eggs
EI-ər	
Brot	Bread
broht	
Roggenbrot	rye bread
rog-gen-BROHT	
Toastbrot	toast bread
TOHST-broht	
Vollkornbrot	whole-grain bread
FOL-korn-broht	
Weizenbrot	wheat bread
VEI-tsen-broht	
Weissbrot	white bread
VEIS-broht	
Mehrkornbrot	multigrain bread
MAYR-korn-broht	
Roggenmischbrot	rye-wheat bread
ROG-gen-mish-broht	
Zwiebelbrot	onion bread
TSVEE-bel-broht	
Semmel, Brötchen	bread rolls
ZEM-mel, BR[OE]T-[ch]en	
Wurst	Sausage
woorst	
Weisswurst	Weisswurst
VEIS-vurst	

Blutwurst *BLOOT-vurst*	Blutwurst
Würstchen *V[UE]RST-[ch]en*	Sausages
Kaffee *KAF-fay*	Coffee
Sahne *ZAH-nə*	Cream
Butter *BUT-tər*	Butter
Zucker *TSUK-kər*	Sugar
Salz *zalts*	Salt
Pfeffer *PFEF-fər*	Pepper
Jogurt *YOH-gurt*	Yogurt
Quark *kvahrk*	Quark (a creamy, savory spread eaten on bread)
Nutella *noo-TEL-ah*	Nutella (a chocolate-hazelnut spread)

GERMAN / SWISS / AUSTRIAN SPECIALTIES

Following are special dishes from different German-speaking regions and countries. Although many are available in most regions in one form or another, the names can vary.

Pfannkuchen *PFAN-koo-[ch]en*	potato pancakes
Sauerbraten *ZOW-ər-brah-ten*	marinated beef
Rösti *R[OE]S-tee*	fried potato dish (Switzerland)
Wiener Schnitzel *vee-nər SHNIT-sel*	breaded veal cutlets
Spätzle *SHPETS-lə*	heavy pasta served in place of potatoes

DINING

Knödel
KN[OE]-del
dumplings

Hasenpfeffer
HAH-zen-pfef-fər
rabbit stew

Jägerschnitzel
YAY-gər-shnit-sel
type of cutlet with mushrooms and peppers

Maultaschen
MOWL-tash-en
Swabian ravioli

Nockerln
NOK-kerln
dumplings in Austria and Bavaria

Ochsenschwanzsuppe
OK-sen-shvants-sup-pə
Oxtail soup

Schweinshaxe
SHVEINS-hak-sə
pork hock

Sauerkraut
SOW-ər-krowt
Sauerkraut

Spanferkel
SHPAHN-fayr-kel
whole-roasted suckling pig

Rote Grütze
roh-tə GR[UE]T-sə
red fruit pudding

Döner Kebab
d[oe]-nər KAY-bab
meat sandwich with lettuce, onions and a cream sauce; invented by Turkish immigrants to Germany in Berlin in 1971.

Currywurst
K[OE]R-ree-vurst
Sausage seasoned with curry powder, usually served with French fries

MEAT

Rindfleisch
RINT-fleish
Beef

Schweinefleisch
SHVEI-nə-fleish
Pork

Würstchen
V[UE]RST-[ch]en
Sausage

Hähnchen
HAYN-[ch]en
Chicken

Kalbfleisch *KALP-fleish*	Veal
Lammfleisch *LAM-fleish*	Lamb
Hasenfleisch *HAH-zen-fleish*	Rabbit

FISH AND SEAFOOD

Tunfisch *TOON-fish*	Tuna
Lachs *laks*	Salmon
Kabeljau *KAH-bel-yow*	Cod
Hering *HE-ring*	Herring
Forelle *foh-REL-lə*	Trout
Buntbarsch *BUNT-barsh*	Tilapia
Karpfen *KAHR-pfen*	Carp
Schwertfisch *SHVAYRT-fish*	Swordfish
Heilbutt *HEIL-but*	Halibut
Muscheln *MUSH-eln*	Mussels

CHEESE

Blauschimmelkäse *BLOW-shim-mel-kay-zə*	Blue cheese
Hüttenkäse *H[UE]T-ten-kay-zə*	Cottage cheese
Frischkäse *FRISH-kay-zə*	Cream cheese

Schweizer Käse	Swiss cheese
SHVEIT-sər kay-zə	
Gorgonzola	Gorgonzola
gor-gon-TSOH-lah	
Ziegenkäse	Goat cheese
TSEE-gen-kay-zə	

DESSERT

Sachertorte	Chocolate layered cake with
ZA-[kh]ər-tor-tə	apricot jam filling
Käsekuchen	Cheese cake
KAY-zə-koo-[ch]en	
Apfelstrudel	Apple strudel
AP-fel-shtroo-del	
Schokolade	Chocolate
shoh-koh-LAH-də	
Stollen	Loaf-shaped cake filled with
SHTOL-en	dried fruit and nuts (typically served at Christmas)
Marzipan	Marzipan (sweet ground almond
MAR-tsee-pahn	paste)
Eiscreme	Ice cream
EIS-kraym	
Kekse	Cookies / biscuits
KAYK-sə	

BUYING GROCERIES

Groceries can be purchased at supermarkets, neighborhood stores, or farmers' markets. Most cities and towns have farmers' markets that sell fruits, vegetables, cheeses, and other goods.

AT THE SUPERMARKET

Which aisle has ____?	**In welchem Regal finde ich ____?**
	In vel-[ch]em ray-GAHL fin-də i[ch] ____?
spices	**Gewürze**
	gə-V[UE]RT-sə

toiletries	**Hygieneartikel** *hee-GYAY-nə-ar-tik-kel*
paper plates and napkins	**Papierteller und Servietten** *pah-PEER-tel-lər unt zayr-VYET-ten*
canned goods	**Konserven** *kon-ZAYR-ven*
frozen food	**Tiefkühlprodukte** *TEEF-k[ue]hl-proh-duk-tə*
snack food	**Snacks** *sneks*
baby food	**Babynahrung** *BAY-bee-nah-rung*
water	**Wasser** *VAS-sər*
juice	**Säfte** *ZEF-tə*
bread	**Brot** *broht*
milk	**Milch** *Mil[ch]*
eggs	**Eier** *EI-ər*
cheese	**Käse** *KAY-zə*
fruit	**Obst** *ohbst*
vegetables	**Gemüse** *gə-M[UE]-zə*
cookies	**Kekse** *KAYK-sə*
Where is the checkout counter?	**Wo ist die Kasse?** *VOH ist dee KAS-sə?*

DINING

AT THE BUTCHER SHOP

Is the meat fresh?	**Ist das Fleisch frisch?**
	Ist das fleish FRISH?
Do you sell fresh ____?	**Verkaufen Sie frisches ____?**
	Fer-kow-fen zee frish-es ____?
beef	**Rindfleisch**
	RINT-fleish
pork	**Schweinefleisch**
	SHVEI-nə-fleish
lamb	**Lammfleisch**
	LAM-fleish
I would like a cut of ____.	**Ich hätte gern ____.**
	I[ch] HET-tə gern ____.
tenderloin	**ein Filetstück**
	ein fee-LAY-sht[ue]k
T-bone	**ein T-Bone-Steak**
	ein TEE-boan-shteak
brisket	**ein Bruststück**
	ein BRUST-sht[ue]k
rump roast	**ein Rumpsteak**
	ein RUMP-shteak
chops	**Koteletts**
	kot-LETS
filet	**ein Filet**
	ein fee-LAY.
Thin / Thick cuts please.	**Dünne / Dicke Scheiben, bitte.**
	D[UE]N-nə / DIK-kə shei-ben, bit-ə.
Please trim the fat.	**Entfernen Sie bitte das Fett.**
	Ent-fayr-nen zee bit-ə das FET.
Do you have any sausage?	**Haben Sie Würstchen?**
	Hah-ben zee V[UE]RST-[ch]en?
Is the ____ fresh?	**____ frisch?**
	____ FRISH?
fish	**Ist der Fisch**
	Ist dayr fish

seafood	**Sind die Meeresfrüchte**
	Zint dee may-res-fr[ue]ch-tə
shrimp	**Sind die Garnelen**
	Zint dee gahr-nay-len
trout	**Ist die Forelle**
	Ist dee foh-REL-lə
flounder	**Ist die Flunder**
	Ist dee FLUN-də
clams	**Sind die Muscheln**
	Zint dee MUSH-eln
oysters	**Sind die Austern**
	Zint dee OWS-tern
May I smell it?	**Dürfte ich bitte daran riechen?**
	D[ue]rf-tə i[ch] bit-ə dah-ran ree-[ch]en?
Would you please ____?	**Könnten Sie ____?**
	K[oe]nn-ten zee ____?
filet it	**das bitte filetieren**
	das bit-ə fee-lay-TEE-ren
debone it	**das bitte entbeinen**
	das bit-ə ent-BEI-nen
remove the head and tail	**bitte Kopf und Schwanz entfernen**
	bit-ə kopf unt SHVANTS ent-fayr-nen

AT THE PRODUCE STAND / MARKET

Fruits

banana	**Banane**
	bah-NAH-nə
apple	**Apfel**
	AP-fel
grapes (green, red)	**Trauben**
	TROW-ben
orange	**Orange**
	oh-RUN-shə

lime	**Limette**
	lee-MET-tə
lemon	**Zitrone**
	tsee-TROH-nə
mango	**Mango**
	MAN-goh
melon	**Melone**
	may-LOH-nə
cantaloupe	**Cantaloupe-Melone**
	kan-tah-loop-may-loh-nə
watermelon	**Wassermelone**
	VAS-sər-may-loh-nə
honeydew	**Honigmelone**
	HOH-nig-may-loh-nə
cranberry	**Cranberry**
	KRAHN-ber-ree
cherry	**Kirsche**
	KIR-shə
peach	**Pfirsich**
	PFIR-zi[ch]
apricot	**Aprikose**
	ap-ree-KOH-zə
strawberry	**Erdbeere**
	ERT-bay-rə
blueberry	**Heidelbeere**
	HEI-del-bay-rə
kiwi	**Kiwi**
	KEE-vee
pineapple	**Ananas**
	AN-nah-nas
blackberries	**Brombeeren**
	BROM-bay-ren
grapefruit	**Grapefruit**
	GREYP-froot
gooseberry	**Stachelbeere**
	SHTA[KH]-el-bay-rə

papaya	**Papaya**
	pah-PAH-yah
tamarind	**Tamarinde**
	tah-mah-RIN-də
tangerine	**Mandarine**
	man-dah-REE-nə
plum	**Pflaume**
	PFLOW-mə
pear	**Birne**
	BIR-nə
plantain	**Kochbanane**
	KOH[KH]-bah-nah-nə
regular	**normal**
	nor-MAHL
ripe	**reif**
	reif

Vegetables

lettuce	**Kopfsalat**
	KOPF-zah-laht
spinach	**Spinat**
	shpee-NAHT
avocado	**Avocado**
	ah-voh-KAH-doh
artichoke	**Artischocke**
	ar-tee-SHOK-kə
olives	**Oliven**
	oh-LEE-ven
beans	**Bohnen**
	BOH-nen
green beans	**grüne Bohnen**
	gr[ue]-nə BOH-nen
tomato	**Tomate**
	toh-MAH-tə
potato	**Kartoffel**
	kar-TOF-el

peppers	**Paprika**
	PAP-ree-kah
hot	**scharf**
	sharf
mild	**mild**
	milt
jalapeno	**Peperoni**
	pep-eh-ROH-nee
onion	**Zwiebel**
	TSVEE-bel
celery	**Sellerie**
	ZEL-eh-ree
broccoli	**Brokkoli**
	BROH-ko-lee
cauliflower	**Blumenkohl**
	BLOO-men-kohl
carrot	**Karrotte**
	kah-ROT-tə
corn	**Mais**
	meis
cucumber	**Gurke**
	GOOR-kə
bean sprouts	**Sojasprossen**
	ZOH-yah-shpros-en
sweet corn	**Mais**
	meis
eggplant	**Aubergine**
	oh-bayr-ZHEE-nə
sorrel	**Ampfer**
	AMPF-ər
yam	**Süßkartoffel**
	Z[UE]HS-kahr-tof-el
squash	**Kürbis**
	K[UE]R-bis

Fresh Herbs & Spices

cilantro / coriander	**Koriander**
	koh-ree-AN-dər
black pepper	**schwarzer Pfeffer**
	shvart-sər PFEF-fər
salt	**Salz**
	zalts
basil	**Basilikum**
	bah-ZEE-lee-koom
parsley	**Petersilie**
	pay-tər-ZEEL-yə
oregano	**Oregano**
	oh-RAY-gah-noh
sage	**Salbei**
	ZAL-bei
thyme	**Thymian**
	T[UE]H-mee-ahn
cumin	**Kreuzkümmel**
	KROYTS-k[ue]m-mel
paprika	**Paprika**
	PAP-ree-kah
garlic	**Knoblauch**
	KNOHB-low[kh]
clove	**Nelke**
	NEL-kə
allspice	**Piment**
	pee-MENT
saffron	**Safran**
	ZAF-rahn
rosemary	**Rosmarin**
	ROHS-mah-reen
anise	**Anis**
	AH-nis
sugar	**Zucker**
	TSUK-kər

marjoram	**Majoran**
	MAH-yoh-rahn
dill	**Dill**
	dil
caraway	**Kümmel**
	K[UE]M-mel
bay leaf	**Lorbeer**
	LOHR-bayr
cacao	**Kakao**
	kah-KOW
dried	**getrocknet**
	gə-TROK-net
fresh	**frisch**
	frish
seed	**Samen**
	ZAH-men

AT THE DELI

What kind of salad is that?	**Was für ein Salat ist das?**
	Vas f[ue]r ein zah-LAHT ist das?
What type of cheese is that?	**Was für ein Käse ist das?**
	Vas f[ue]r ein KAY-zə ist das?
What type of bread is that?	**Was für ein Brot ist das?**
	Vas f[ue]r ein BROHT ist das?
Some of that, please.	**Geben Sie mir etwas davon, bitte.**
	Gay-ben zee meer et-vas DAH-fon, bit-ə.
Is the salad fresh?	**Ist der Salat frisch?**
	Ist dayr zah-laht FRISH?
I'd like _____.	**Ich hätte gern _____.**
	I[ch] HET-tə gern _____.
a sandwich	**ein Sandwich**
	ein ZENT-vitsh
a salad	**einen Salat**
	ei-nen zah-LAHT

tuna salad	**einen Tunfischsalat**
	ei-nen TOON-fish-zah-laht
chicken salad	**einen Geflügelsalat**
	ei-nen gə-FL[UE]-gel-zah-laht
roast beef	**ein Roastbeef**
	ein ROHST-beef
ham	**einen Schinken**
	ei-nen SHING-ken
that cheese	**diesen Käse**
	dee-zen KAY-zə
cole slaw	**einen Krautsalat**
	ei-nen KROWT-zah-laht
mustard	**Senf**
	zenf
mayonaisse	**Majonäse**
	may-yoh-NAY-zə
a pickle	**eine Essiggurke**
	ei-nə ES-si[ch]-goor-kə
Is that smoked?	**Ist das geräuchert?**
	Ist das gə-ROY-[ch]ert?
a pound (0,5 kg)	**ein Pfund**
	ein PFUNT
a quarter-pound (0,125 kg)	**ein Viertelpfund**
	ein FEER-tel pfunt
a half-pound (0,25 kg)	**ein halbes Pfund**
	ein HAL-bes pfunt

CHAPTER FIVE

SOCIALIZING

Whether you're meeting people in a bar or a park, you'll find the language you need, in this chapter, to make new friends.

GREETINGS

Hello.	**Hallo.**
	Hah-LOH.
How are you?	**Wie geht es Ihnen?**
	VEE GAYT es ee-nen?
Fine, thanks.	**Gut, danke.**
	Goot, dankə.
And you?	**Und Ihnen?**
	Unt EE-nen?
I'm exhausted from the trip.	**Ich bin erschöpft von der Reise.**
	I[ch] bin ayr-sh[oe]pft fon dayr REI-zə.
I have a headache.	**Ich habe Kopfschmerzen.**
	I[ch] hah-bə KOPF-shmayrt-sen.
I'm terrible.	**Ich fühle mich schlecht.**
	I[ch] f[ue]-lə mi[ch] shle[ch]t.
I have a cold.	**Ich habe eine Erkältung.**
	I[ch] hah-bə ei-nə ayr-KEL-tung.
Good morning.	**Guten Morgen.**
	Goo-ten MOR-gen.
Good evening.	**Guten Abend.**
	Goo-ten AH-bent.
Good afternoon.	**Guten Tag.**
	Goo-ten TAHK.
Good night.	**Gute Nacht.**
	Goo-tə NA[KH]t.

Listen Up: Common Greetings

Freut mich.	It's a pleasure.
FROYT mi[ch].	
Sehr erfreut.	Delighted.
Zayr ayr-FROYT.	
Zu Ihren Diensten. / Ganz wie Sie wünschen.	At your service. / As you wish.
Tsoo ee-ren DEENS-ten. / Gants vee zee V[UE]n-shen.	
Guten Tag.	Good day.
Goo-ten TAHK.	
Hallo.	Hello.
Hah-LOH.	
Wie geht's?	How's it going?
Vee GAYTS?	
Was gibt's?	What's up?
Vas GEEPTS?	
Was ist los?	What's going on? / What's wrong?
Vas ist LOHS?	
Tschüss!	Bye!
Ch[ue]s!	
Auf Wiedersehen.	Goodbye.
Owf VEE-dər-zay-en.	
Bis später.	See you later.
Bis SHPAY-tər.	

OVERCOMING THE LANGUAGE BARRIER

I don't understand.	**Ich verstehe Sie nicht.** *I[ch] fer-SHTAY-ə zee ni[ch]t.*
Please speak more slowly.	**Könnten Sie bitte etwas langsamer sprechen?** *K[OE]N-ten zee bit-ə et-vas LANG-zah-mər shpre-[ch]en?*
Please speak louder.	**Könnten Sie bitte etwas lauter sprechen?** *K[oe]n-ten zee bit-ə et-vas LOW-tər shpre-[ch]en?*

Curse Words

Here are some common curse words used across German-speaking countries.

Scheiße *SHEIS-sə*	shit
Drecksau *DREK-zow*	son of a bitch (literally, dirty sow)
Vollidiot *FOL-ee-dee-oht*	jerk
Verdammt! *fer-DAMT!*	damn
Arsch *arsh*	ass
durchgeknallt *DUR[CH]-gə-knalt*	screwed up
Arschloch *ARSH-lo[kh]*	asshole
abgewichst *AP-gə-vikst*	fucked up

Do you speak English?	**Sprechen Sie Englisch?**
	Shpre-[ch]en zee ENG-lish?
I speak ____ better than German.	**Ich spreche besser ____ als Deutsch.**
	I[ch] shpre-[ch]ə bes-sər ____ als DOYTSH.
Could you please spell that?	**Könnten Sie das bitte buchstabieren?**
	K[oe]n-ten zee das bit-ə boo[ch]-shtah-BEE-ren?
Could you please repeat that?	**Könnten Sie das bitte wiederholen?**
	K[oe]n-ten zee das bit-ə vee-dayr-HOH-len?
How do you say ____?	**Wie sagt man ____?**
	Vee zahkt man ____?
Would you show me that in this dictionary?	**Könnten Sie mir das bitte in diesem Wörterbuch zeigen?**
	K[oe]n-ten zee meer das bit-ə in dee-zem V[OE]R-tər-boo[ch] tsei-gen?

GETTING PERSONAL

People in German-speaking countries are generally friendly, but more formal than Americans. Remember to use the *Sie* form of address until given permission to employ the more familiar *du*.

INTRODUCTIONS

What is your name?	**Wie heißen Sie?**
	Vee HEIS-sen zee?
My name is ____.	**Ich heiße ____.**
	I[ch] HEI-sə ____.
I'm very pleased to meet you.	**Freut mich, Sie kennen zu lernen.**
	Froyt mi[ch], zee KEN-nen tsoo layr-nen.

May I introduce my _____?	**Darf ich Sie meinem (male) / meiner (female) / meinen (plural) _____ bekannt machen?**
	Darf i[ch] zee mit mei-nem / mei-nər / mei-nem _____ bə-KANT ma-[kh]en?

How is / are _____?	**Wie geht es _____?**
	Ve gayt es _____?
your wife	**Ihrer Frau**
	ee-rər FROW
your husband	**Ihrem Mann**
	ee-rem MAN
your son / daughter	**Ihrem Sohn / Ihrer Tochter**
	ee-rem ZOHN / ee-rər TO[KH]-tər
your child	**Ihrem Kind**
	ee-rəm kint
your boyfriend / girlfriend	**Ihrem Freund / Ihrer Freundin**
	ee-rem FROYNT / ee-rər FROYN-din
your family	**Ihrer Familie**
	ee-rər fam-MEE-lee-ə
your mother / father	**Ihrer Mutter / Ihrem Vater**
	ee-rər MUT-tər / ee-rem FAH-tər
your parents	**Ihren Eltern**
	ee-ren EL-tern
your brother / sister	**Ihrem Bruder / Ihrer Schwester**
	ee-rem BROO-dər / ee-rər SHVES-tə
your friend	**Ihrem Freund**
	ee-rem FROYNT
your friends	**Ihren Freunden**
	ee-ren FROYN-den
your neighbor	**Ihrem Nachbarn**
	ee-rem NA[KH]-bahrn
your boss	**Ihrem Chef**
	ee-rem SHEF

your cousin	**Ihrem Cousin / Ihrer Cousine** *ee-rem coo-ZAHN / ee-rər coo-ZEE-nə*
your aunt / uncle	**Ihrer Tante / Ihrem Onkel** *ee-rər TAN-tə / ee-rem ONG-kel*
your fiancée / fiancé	**Ihrer / Ihrem Verlobten** *ee-rər/ ee-rem fer-LOHB-ten*
your partner	**Ihrem Partner** *ee-rem PART-ner*
your niece / nephew	**Ihrer Nichte / Ihrem Neffen** *ee-rər NI[CH]-tə / ee-rem NEF-fen*
your grandmother / grandfather	**Ihrer Großmutter / Ihrem Großvater** *ee-rər GROHS-mut-tər / ee-rem GROHS-fah-tər*
your grandparents	**Ihren Großeltern** *ee-ren GROHS-el-tern*
He / She is doing well, thanks.	**Es geht ihm / ihr gut, danke.** *Es gayt eem / eer GOOT, dank-ə.*
They are doing well, thanks.	**Es geht ihnen gut, danke.** *Es gayt EE-nen GOOT, dank-ə.*
Are you married / single?	**Sind Sie verheiratet / ledig?** *Zint zee fer-HEI-rah-tet / LAY-di[ch]?*
I'm married.	**Ich bin verheiratet.** *I[ch] bin fer-HEI-rah-tet.*
I'm single.	**Ich bin ledig.** *I[ch] bin LAY-di[ch].*
I'm divorced.	**Ich bin geschieden.** *I[ch] bin gə-SHEE-den.*
I'm a widow / widower.	**Ich bin Witwe / Witwer.** *I[ch] bin VIT-və / VIT-vər.*
We're separated.	**Wir leben getrennt.** *Veer lay-ben gə-TRENT.*

SOCIALIZING

I live with my boyfriend / girlfriend.	**Ich wohne mit meinem Freund / meiner Freundin zusammen.** *I[ch] voh-nə mit mei-nem FROYNT / mei-nər FROYN-din tsoo-zam-men.*
I live with a roommate.	**Ich habe einen Mitbewohner.** *I[ch] hah-bə ei-nen MIT-bə-voh-nər.*
How old are you?	**Wie alt sind Sie?** *Vee alt zint zee?*
How old is ____?	**Wie alt ist ____?** *Vee alt ist ____?*
your son	**Ihr Sohn** *Eer ZOHN*
your daughter	**Ihre Tochter** *Ee-rə TO[KH]-tər*
your child	**Ihr Kind** *Eer kint*
How old are your children?	**Wie alt sind Ihre Kinder?** *Vee alt zint ee-rə KIN-dər?*
I am ____ years old.	**Ich bin ____ Jahre alt.** *I[ch] bin ____ YAH-rə alt.*
He / She is ____ years old.	**Er / Sie ist ____ Jahre alt.** *Ayr / Zee ist ____ YAH-rə alt.*
They are ____ years old.	**Sie sind ____ Jahre alt.** *Zee zint ____ YAH-rə alt.*

For a complete list of numbers, see p8.

Wow! That's very young.	**Wow! Noch so jung?** *Wow! No[kh] zoh yung?*
What grade are they in?	**In welche Klasse gehen sie?** *In VEL-[ch]ə KLA-sə gay-en zee?*
No you're not! You're much younger.	**Das kann nicht stimmen! Sie sind doch viel jünger.** *Das kan ni[ch]t shtim-men! Zee zint do[kh] veel y[ue]ng-ər.*

Your wife / daughter is beautiful.	**Sie haben eine hübsche Frau / Tochter.** *Zee hah-ben ei-nə H[UE]B-shə frow / to[kh]-tər.*
Your husband / son is handsome.	**Sie haben einen gutaussehenden Mann / Sohn.** *Zee hah-ben ei-nen GOOT-ows-zay-en-den man / zohn.*
What a beautiful baby!	**Was für ein bezauberndes Baby!** *Vas f[ue]r ein bə-TSOW-bayrn-des bay-bee!*
Are you here on business?	**Sind Sie geschäftlich hier?** *Zint zee gə-SHEFT-li[ch] heer?*
I am vacationing.	**Ich mache Urlaub.** *I[ch] ma-[kh]ə OOR-lowp.*
I'm attending a conference.	**Ich nehme an einer Konferenz teil.** *I[ch] nay-mə an ei-nər kon-fay-RENTS teil.*
How long are you staying?	**Wie lange bleiben Sie?** *Vee lang-ə BLEI-ben zee?*
What are you studying?	**Was studieren Sie?** *Vahs shtoo-DEE-ren zee?*
I'm a student.	**Ich bin Student.** *I[ch] bin shtoo-DENT.*
Where are you from?	**Woher kommen Sie?** *Voh-her KOM-men zee?*

DISPOSITIONS AND MOODS

sad	**traurig** *TROU-ri[ch]*
happy	**fröhlich** *FR[OE]H-li[ch]*
angry	**verärgert** *fer-AYR-gayrt*
tired	**müde** *M[UE]-də*

Listen Up: Nationalities

German/Pronunciation	English
Ich bin Deutscher (m) / Deutsche (f). *I[ch] bin DOY-tshər / DOY-tshə.*	I'm German.
Ich bin Österreicher (m) / Österreicherin (f). *I[ch] bin [OE]S-tayr-rei-[ch]ər / [OE]S-tayr-rei-[ch]ə-rin.*	I'm Austrian.
Ich bin Türke (m) / Türkin (f). *I[ch] bin T[UE]r-kə / T[UE]R-kin.*	I'm Turkish.
Ich bin Schweizer (m) / Schweizerin (f). *I[ch] bin SHVEIT-sər / SHVEIT-sə-rin.*	I'm Swiss.
Ich bin Italiener (m) / Italienerin (f). *I[ch] bin ee-tal-YAY-nər / ee-tal-YAY-nə-rin.*	I'm Italian.
Ich bin Franzose (m) / Französin (f). *I[ch] bin fran-TSOH-zə / fran-ts[oe]-zin.*	I'm French.
Ich bin Pole (m) / Polin (f). *I[ch] bin POH-lə / POH-lin.*	I'm Polish.
Ich bin Tscheche (m) / Tschechin (f). *I[ch] bin TSHE-[ch]ə / TSHE-[ch]in.*	I'm Czech.
Ich bin Spanier (m) / Spanierin (f). *I[ch] bin SHPAH-nee-ər / SHPAH-nee-ə-rin.*	I'm Spanish.
Ich bin Portugiese (m) / Portugiesin (f). *I[ch] bin por-too-GEE-zə / por-too-GEE-zin.*	I'm Portuguese.
Ich bin Grieche (m) / Griechin (f). *I[ch] bin GREE-[ch]ə / GREE-[ch]in.*	I'm Greek.
Ich bin Niederländer (m) / Niederländerin (f). *I[ch] bin NEE-dayr-len-dər / NEE-dayr-len-dər-in.*	I'm Dutch.
Ich bin Belgier (m) / Belgierin (f). *I[ch] bin BEL-gee-ər / BEL-gee-ayr-in.*	I'm Belgian.
Ich bin Däne (m) / Dänin (f). *I[ch] bin DE-nə / DE-nin.*	I'm Danish.
Ich bin Vietnamese (m) / Vietnamesin (f). *I[ch] bin vee-et-nah-MAY-zə / vee-et-nah-MAY-zin.*	I'm Vietnamese.

Ich bin Nordafrikaner (m) / Nordafrikanerin (f).	I'm North African.
I[ch] bin nord-af-ree-KAH-nər / nord-af-ree-KAH-nə-rin.	
Ich bin Iraner (m) / Ich bin Iranerin (f).	I'm Iranian.
I[ch] bin ee-RAH-nər / ee-RAH-nə-rin.	
Ich bin Japaner (m) / Japanerin (f).	I'm Japanese.
I[ch] bin yah-PAH-nər / yah-PAH-nə-rin.	
Ich bin Schwede (m) / Schwedin (f).	I'm Swedish.
I[ch] bin SHVAY-də / SHVAY-din.	
Ich bin Norweger (m) / Norwegerin (f).	I'm Norwegian.
I[ch] bin NOR-vay-gər / NOR-vay-gə-rin.	
Ich bin Amerikaner (m) / Amerikanerin (f).	I'm American.
I[ch] bin ah-may-ree-KAH-nər / ah-may-ree-KAH-nə-rin.	
Ich bin Russe (m) / Russin (f).	I'm Russian.
I[ch] bin RUS-sə / RUS-sin.	

For full coverage of nationalities, see English / German dictionary.

depressed	**niedergeschlagen**
	NEE-dər-gə-shlah-gen
anxious	**besorgt**
	bə-ZORKT
stressed	**gestresst**
	gə-SHTREST
confused	**verwirrt**
	fer-VIRT
enthusiastic	**begeistert**
	be-GEIS-tert

PROFESSIONS

What do you do for a living?	**Was machen Sie beruflich?**
	Vas ma-[kh]en zee bə-ROOF-li[ch]?
Here is my business card.	**Hier ist meine Karte.**
	Heer ist meî-nə KAR-tə.

SOCIALIZING

I am _____.	**Ich bin _____.**
	I[ch] bin _____.
a doctor	**Arzt / Ärztin**
	artst / AYRTS-tin
an engineer	**Ingenieur / Ingenieurin**
	in-shen-Y[OE]R / in-shen-Y[OE]R-in
a lawyer	**Anwalt / Anwältin**
	AN-valt / AN-vel-tin
a salesperson	**Verkäufer / Verkäuferin**
	fer-KOY-fər / fer-KOY-fə-rin
a writer	**Autor / Autorin**
	OW-tohr / ow-TOH-rin
an editor	**Redakteur / Redakteurin**
	ray-dak-T[OE]R / ray-dak-T[OE]-rin
a designer	**Designer / Designerin**
	dee-ZEI-nər / dee-ZEI-nə-rin
an educator	**Erzieher / Erzieherin**
	ayr-TSEE-ər / ayr-TSEE-ə-rin
an artist	**Künstler / Künstlerin**
	K[UE]NST-lər / K[UE]NST-lə-rin
a craftsperson	**Handwerker / Handwerkerin**
	HANT-ver-kər / HANT-ver-kə-rin
a homemaker	**Hausfrau / Hausmann**
	HOWS-frow / HOWS-man
an accountant	**Buchhalter / Buchhalterin**
	BOO[CH]-hal-tər / BOO[CH]-hal-tə-rin
a nurse	**Krankenpfleger / Krankenpflegerin**
	KRANG-ken-pflay-gər / KRANG-ken-pflay-gə-rin

a musician	**Musiker / Musikerin**
	MOO-zik-kər / MOO-zik-kə-rin
a military professional	**beim Militär**
	beim mil-lee-TAYR
a government employee	**Regierungsangestellter**
	ray-GEE-rungs-an-gə-shtel-tər
a web designer	**Webdesigner**
	WEB-dee-SEI-nər
a computer programmer	**Programmierer**
	proh-grah-MEER-ər

TOPICS OF CONVERSATION

As in the United States, the weather and current affairs are common conversation topics.

THE WEATHER

It's so ____.	**Es ist so ____.**
	Es ist zoh ____.
Is it always so ____?	**Ist es immer so ____?**
	Ist es IM-mər zoh ____?
sunny	**sonnig**
	ZON-ni[ch]
rainy	**regnerisch**
	RAYG-ne-rish
cloudy	**bewölkt**
	bə-V[OE]LKT
humid	**feucht**
	foy[ch]t
warm	**warm**
	vahrm
cool	**kalt**
	kalt
windy	**windig**
	VIN-di[ch]

Do you know the weather forecast for tomorrow?	**Wissen Sie, wie morgen das Wetter wird?** *Vis-sen zee, vee MOR-gen das VET-tər virt?*

THE ISSUES

What do you think about ____?	**Was denken Sie über ____?** *Vas deng-ken zee [ue]-bər ____?*
the government	**die Regierung** *dee ray-GEE-rung*
democracy	**Demokratie** *day-moh-krah-TEE*
socialism	**Sozialismus** *zoh-tsee-ah-LIS-mus*
American Democrats	**die Demokraten in Amerika** *dee day-moh-KRAH-ten in ah-MAY-ree-kah*
American Republicans	**die Republikaner in Amerika** *dee ray-poo-blee-KAH-nər in ah-MAY-ree-kah*
the environment	**die Umwelt** *dee UM-velt*
climate change	**den Klimawandel** *dayn KLEE-mah-van-del*
the economy	**die Wirtschaft** *dee VIRT-shaft*
the economic situation in ____	**die Wirtschaftslage in ____** *dee VIRT-shafts-lah-gə in ____*
the political situation in ____	**die politische Lage in ____** *dee poh-LEE-ti-shə lah-gə in ____*
the upcoming election in ____	**die bevorstehende Wahl in ____** *die bə-FOHR-shtay-en-də vahl in ____*

the war in ____

den Krieg in ____
dayn kreek in ____

What political party do
you belong to?

Welcher Partei gehören Sie an?
*Vel-[ch]ər par-TEI gə-h[oe]-ren
zee an?*

RELIGION

Do you go to church /
temple / mosque?

**Gehen Sie in die Kirche / den
Tempel / die Moschee?**
*Gay-en zee in dee KIR-[ch]ə / dayn
TEM-pel / dee moh-SHAY?*

Are you religious?

Sind Sie religiös?
Zint zee rel-li-gee-[oe]s?

I'm ____ / I was
raised ____.

**Ich bin ____ / Ich wurde ____
erzogen.**
*I[ch] bin ____ / I[ch] vur-də ____
ayr-TSOH-gen.*

Protestant

protestantisch
proh-tes-TAN-tish

Catholic

katholisch
kah-TOH-lish

Jewish

jüdisch
Y[UE]H-dish

Muslim

muslimisch
moos-LEE-mish

Buddhist

buddhistisch
boo-DIS-tish

Greek Orthodox

griechisch-orthodox
GREE-[ch]ish-or-toh-doks

Hindu

hinduistisch
hin-doo-IS-tish

agnostic

agnostisch
ahg-NOS-tish

atheist

atheistisch
ah-tay-IS-tish

I'm spiritual but I don't attend services.
Ich bin gläubig, gehe aber nicht zu Gottesdiensten.
I[ch] bin GLOY-bi[ch[, gay-ə ah-bər ni[ch]t tsoo GOT-tes-deens-ten.

I don't believe in that.
Ich bin nicht gläubig.
I[ch] bin ni[ch]t GLOY-bi[ch].

That's against my beliefs.
Das ist gegen meinen Glauben.
Das ist GAY-gen mei-nen GLOW-ben.

I'd rather not talk about it.
Darüber möchte ich eigentlich nicht sprechen.
DAH-r[ue]-bər m[oe][ch]-tə i[ch] ei-gent-li[ch] ni[ch]t shpre-[ch]en.

MUSICAL TASTES

What kind of music do you like?
Welche Art von Musik mögen Sie?
Vel-[ch]ə ahrt fon moo-ZEEK m[oe]-gen zee?

I like _____.
Ich mag _____.
I[ch] mahk _____.

rock music
Rockmusik
ROCK-moo-zeek

classic rock
Classic Rock
KLAS-sic rock

hip-hop
Hiphop
HIP-hop

techno
Techno
TEK-noh

classical
Klassik
KLAS-sik

jazz
Jazz
Zhays

country music
Country-Musik
KAN-tree-moo-seek

reggae
Reggae
RAY-gay

opera	**Opern**
	OH-payrn
show-tunes / musicals	**Shows / Musicals**
	Shows / MYOO-zi-kəls
pop	**Pop**
	Pop

HOBBIES

What do you like to do in your spare time?	**Was machen Sie in Ihrer Freizeit?**
	Vas ma-[kh]en zee in ee-rər FREI-tseit?
I like ____.	**Ich ____.**
	I[ch] ____.
playing the guitar	**spiele gern Gitarre**
	shpee-lə gern gee-TAR-rə
playing the piano	**spiele gern Klavier**
	shpee-lə gern klah-VEER

For other instruments, see the English / German dictionary.

painting	**male gern**
	MAH-lə gern
drawing	**zeichne gern**
	TSEI[CH]-nə gern
dancing	**tanze gern**
	TANT-sə gern
reading	**lese gern**
	LAY-zə gern
watching TV	**sehe gern fern**
	zay-ə gern FAYRN
blogging	**Bloggen**
	BLOG-gə gern
shopping	**gehe gern einkaufen**
	gay-ə gern EIN-kow-fen
going to the movies	**gehe gern ins Kino**
	gay-ə gern ins KEE-noh
hiking	**gehe gern wandern**
	gay-ə gern VAN-dern

camping	**gehe gern campen**
	gay-ə gern KEM-pen
traveling	**reise gern**
	REI-zə gern
eating out	**esse gern auswärts**
	ES-sə gern OWS-vayrts
cooking	**koche gern**
	KO-[kh]ə gern
sewing	**nähe gern**
	NAY-ə gern
sports	**treibe Sport**
	TREI-be sport

What kind of books do you like to read?

Welche Art von Büchern lesen Sie gern?
Vel-[ch]ə ahrt fon B[UE]-[ch]ern lay-zen zee gern?

I like _____.

Ich mag _____.
I[ch] mahk _____.

novels	**Romane**
	roh-MAH-nə
mysteries	**Mystery-Romane**
	MIS-te-ree-roh-mah-nə
classics	**Klassiker**
	KLAS-sik-kər
biographies	**Biografien**
	bee-oh-gra-FEE-en
autobiographies	**Autobiografien**
	ow-toh-bee-oh-gra-FEE-en
romance novels	**Liebesromane**
	LEE-bes-roh-mah-nə
historical novels	**historische Romane**
	his-TOH-ri-shə roh-mah-nə
memoirs	**Memoiren**
	Mem-MWAH-ren

non-fiction	**Sachliteratur**
	ZA[KH]-lee-te-rah-toor
What kind of movies do you like?	**Welche Art von Filmen mögen Sie?**
	Vel-[ch]ə ahrt fon FIL-men m[oe]-gen zee?
I like ____.	**Ich mag ____.**
	I[ch] mahk ____.
action films	**Actionfilme**
	EKT-shen-fil-mə
thrillers	**Thriller**
	thril-ler
drama	**Dramas**
	DRAH-mas
comedy	**Komödien**
	Koh-M[OE]-dee-en
old movies	**alte Filme**
	AL-tə fil-mə
documentary films	**Dokumentarfilme**
	Doh-koo-men-TAHR-fil-mə
Do you like to dance?	**Tanzen Sie gerne?**
	TANT-sən zee gerne?
Would you like to go out?	**Würden Sie gern ausgehen?**
	V[ue]r-den zee gern OWS-gay-en?
May I buy you dinner sometime?	**Darf ich Sie vielleicht mal zum Essen einladen?**
	Darf i[ch] zee fee-lei[ch]t mahl tsum ES-sen ein-lah-den?
What kind of food do you like?	**Welche Art von Essen mögen Sie?**
	Vel-[ch]ə ahrt fon es-sen M[OE]-gen zee?

For a full list of food types, see Dining in Chapter 4.

Would you like to ____?	**Würden Sie gern ____?**
	V[ue]r-den zee gern ____?
go to a movie	**ins Kino gehen**
	ins KEE-noh gay-en

go to a concert	**zu einem Konzert gehen**
	tsoo ei-nem kon-TSERT gay-en
go to the zoo	**in den Zoo gehen**
	in dayn TSOH gay-en
go to the beach	**an den Strand gehen**
	an dayn SHTRANT gay-en
go to a museum	**ein Museum besuchen**
	ein moo-ZAY-oom bə-ZOO-[ch]en
go for a walk in the park	**im Park spazieren gehen**
	im PAHRK shpah-TSEE-ren gay-en
go out dancing	**tanzen gehen**
	TANT-sen gay-en
Would you like to get ____?	**Hätten Sie Lust auf ____?**
	Het-ten zee LUST owf ____?
lunch	**ein Mittagessen**
	ein MIT-tah-ges-sen
coffee	**einen Kaffee**
	ei-nen kaf-FAY
dinner	**ein Abendessen**
	ein AH-bent-es-sen

For dating terms, see Nightlife in Chapter 10.

PARTING WAYS

Keep in touch.	**Lassen Sie uns in Verbindung bleiben.**
	Las-sen zee uns in fer-BIN-dung blei-ben.
Please write or email.	**Schicken Sie mir einen Brief oder eine E-Mail.**
	Shik-ken zee meer ei-nen BREEF oh-dər ei-nə EE-mayl.

Here's my phone number / email.

Hier ist meine Telefonnummer / E-Mail-Adresse.
Heer ist mei-nə te-le-FOHN-num-mər / EE-mayl-ah-dres-sə.

Call me.

Rufen Sie mich an.
Roo-fen zee mi[ch] AN.

May I have your phone number / email please?

Könnten Sie mir bitte Ihre Telefonnummer / E-Mail-Adresse geben?
K[oe]n-ten zee meer bit-ə ee-rə te-le-FOHN-num-mər / EE-mayl-ah-dres-sə gay-ben?

May I have your card?

Geben Sie mir Ihre Visitenkarte?
Gay-ben zee meer ee-rə vee-ZEE-ten-kar-tə?

Are you on Facebook / Twitter?

Sind Sie bei Facebook / Twitter?
Zint zee bei FAYS-book / tvit-tər?

Find me on Facebook / Twitter.

Sie finden mich bei Facebook / Twitter.
Zee FIN-den mi[ch] bei FAYS-book / tvit-tər.

CHAPTER SIX

MONEY & COMMUNICATIONS

This chapter covers money, the mail, phone, Internet service, and other tools you need to connect with the outside world.

MONEY

I need to exchange money.
Ich muss Geld umtauschen.
I[ch] mus GELT um-tow-shen.

Do you accept ___?
Akzeptieren Sie ___?
Ak-tsep-TEE-ren zee ___?

credit cards
Kreditkarten
Kray-DEET-kar-ten

bills
Scheine
SHEI-nə

coins
Münzen
M[UE]NT-sen

checks
Schecks
Shecks

money transfers
Überweisungen
[Ue]-bər-VEI-zung-en

May I wire transfer funds here?
Kann ich hier Überweisungen vornehmen?
Kan i[ch] heer [ue]-bər-VEI-zung-en FOHR-nay-men?

Would you please tell me where to find ___?
Wo finde ich hier ___?
Voh fin-də i[ch] heer ___?

a bank
eine Bank
ei-nə BANK

a credit bureau
ein Kreditinstitut
ein kray-DEET-ins-tee-toot

an ATM
einen Geldautomaten
ei-nen GELT-ow-toh-mah-ten

a currency exchange
eine Geldwechselstube
ei-nə GELT-vek-sel-shtoo-bə

A receipt, please.	**Geben Sie mir bitte eine Quittung.** *Gay-ben zee meer bit-ə ei-nə KVIT-tung.*
Would you tell me ____?	**Sagen Sie mir bitte ____?** *Zah-gen zee meer bit-ə ____?*
the exchange rate for dollars to Euros	**den Wechselkurs von Dollar in Euro** *dayn VEK-sel-kurs fon dol-lahr in OY-roh*
the exchange rate for pounds to Euros	**den Wechselkurs von Pfund in Euro** *dayn VEK-sel-kurs fon pfunt in OY-roh*
Is there a service charge?	**Gibt es eine Servicegebühr?** *Geept es ei-nə ZER-vis-gə-b[ue]r?*

ATM Machine

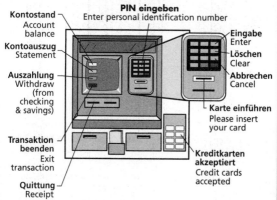

Kontostand — Account balance

Kontoauszug — Statement

Auszahlung — Withdraw (from checking & savings)

Transaktion beenden — Exit transaction

Quittung — Receipt

PIN eingeben — Enter personal identification number

Eingabe — Enter

Löschen — Clear

Abbrechen — Cancel

Karte einführen — Please insert your card

Kreditkarten akzeptiert — Credit cards accepted

Außer Betrieb

Before you stick your coins or bills in a vending machine, watch out for the little sign that says *Außer Betrieb* ("Out of Order").

Listen Up: Bank Lingo

Unterschreiben Sie bitte hier. *Un-tər-shrei-ben zee bit-ə HEER.*	Please sign here.
Hier ist Ihre Quittung. *Heer ist ee-rə KVIT-tung.*	Here is your receipt.
Zeigen Sie mir bitte Ihren Ausweis. *Tsei-gen zee meer bit-ə ee-ren OWS-veis.*	May I see your ID, please?
Nur gegen bar. *Noor gay-gen BAHR.*	Cash only.

May I have a cash advance on my credit card?	**Könnte ich bitte eine Barauszahlung über meine Kreditkarte bekommen?** *K[oe]n-tə i[ch] bit-ə ei-nə BAHR-ows-tsah-lung [ue]-bər mei-nə kray-DEET-kar-tə bə-kom-men?*
Will you accept a credit card?	**Akzeptieren Sie eine Kreditkarte?** *Ak-tsep-TEE-ren zee ei-nə kray-DEET-kar-tə?*
May I have smaller bills, please?	**Könnte ich bitte kleinere Scheine bekommen?** *K[oe]n-tə i[ch] bit-ə klei-ne-rə SHEI-nə bə-kom-men?*

Can you make change?	**Können Sie wechseln?**
	K[oe]n-nen zee VEK-seln?
I only have bills.	**Ich habe nur Scheine.**
	I[ch] hah-bə noor SHEI-nə.
Some coins, please.	**Geben Sie mir bitte ein paar Münzen.**
	Gay-ben zee meer bit-ə ein pahr M[UE]NT-sen.

PHONE SERVICE

Where can I buy a SIM card?	**Wo kann ich eine SIM-Karte kaufen?**
	Voh kan i[ch] ei-nə SIM-kar-tə KOW-fen?
Where can I buy or rent a cell phone?	**Wo kann ich ein Mobiltelefon kaufen oder mieten?**
	Voh kan i[ch] ein moh-BEEL-te-le-fohn KOW-fen oh-dər MEE-ten?
What rate plans do you have?	**Welche Tarife bieten Sie an?**
	Vel-[ch]ə tah-REE-fə bee-ten zee an?
Is this good throughout the country?	**Funktioniert das im ganzen Land?**
	Funk-tsee-oh-NEERT das im GANT-sen lant?
Is data included in the rate?	**Sind im Tarif Datenverbindungen enthalten?**
	Zint im tah-REEF dah-ten-fer-bin-dung-en ent-HAL-ten?
I'd like a pay-as-you-go SIM card.	**Ich hätte gern eine Prepaid-SIM-Karte.**
	I[ch] HET-tə gern ei-nə PREE-payt-SIM-kar-tə.
May I have a prepaid calling card?	**Könnte ich bitte eine Prepaid-Telefonkarte haben?**
	K[oe]n-tə i[ch] bit-ə ei-nə PREE-payt-te-le-fohn-kar-tə hah-ben?

MONEY & COMMUNICATIONS

Where can I buy a phone card?	**Wo kann ich eine Telefonkarte kaufen?** *Voh kan i[ch] ei-nə te-le-fohn-kar-tə KOW-fen?*
May I add more minutes to my phone card?	**Kann ich meine Telefonkarte aufladen?** *Kan i[ch] mei-nə te-le-fohn-kar-tə OWF-lah-den?*

MAKING A CALL

May I dial direct?	**Kann ich direkt wählen?** *Kan i[ch] dee-REKT vay-len?*
Operator please.	**Die Vermittlung, bitte.** *Dee fer-MIT-lung, bit-ə.*
I'd like to make an international call.	**Ich möchte ein Auslandsgespräch führen.** *I[ch] m[oe][ch]-tə ein OWS-lants-gə-shpre[kh] f[ue]-ren.*
I'd like to make a collect call.	**Ich möchte ein R-Gespräch führen.** *I[ch] m[oe][ch]-tə ein ER-gə-shpre[kh] f[ue]-ren.*
I'd like to use a calling card.	**Ich möchte eine Telefonkarte verwenden.** *I[ch] m[oe][ch]-tə ei-nə te-le-FOHN-kar-tə vayr-ven-den.*
Bill my credit card.	**Belasten Sie meine Kreditkarte.** *Bə-LAS-ten zee mei-nə kray-DEET-kar-tə.*
May I bill the charges to my room?	**Kann ich die Kosten über mein Zimmer abrechnen?** *Kan i[ch] dee kos-ten [ue]-bər mein TSIM-mər ap-ray[ch]-nen?*
May I bill the charges to my home phone?	**Kann ich die Kosten über meine Telefonrechnung abrechnen?** *Kan i[ch] dee kos-ten [ue]-bər mei-nə te-le-FOHN-ray[ch]-nung ap-ray[ch]-nen?*

Listen Up: Telephone Lingo

Hallo?
HAH-loh?

Hello?

Welche Nummer?
Vel-[ch]ə NUM-mər?

What number?

Es tut mir leit, die Leitung ist besetzt.
Es toot meer leid, dee lei-tung ist bə-ZETST.

I'm sorry, the line is busy.

Legen Sie bitte auf, und wählen Sie erneut.
Lay-gen zee bit-ə OWF, unt vay-len zee ayr-NOYT.

Please hang up and redial.

Leider nimmt niemand ab.
Lei-dər nimt nee-mant AP.

I'm sorry, nobody is answering.

Auf Ihrer Karte sind noch zehn Minuten übrig.
Owf ee-rər kar-tə zint no[kh] TSAYN mee-noo-ten [ue]p-ri[ch].

Your card has ten minutes left.

Information, please.

Die Auskunft, bitte.
Dee OWS-kunft, bit-ə.

I'd like the number for ___.

Ich hätte gern die Nummer von ___.
I[ch] HET-tə gern dee num-mər fon ___.

I just got disconnected.	**Die Verbindung wurde gerade unterbrochen.**
	Dee fer-BIN-dung vur-də gə-rah-də un-tər-BRO-[kh]en.
The line is busy.	**Die Leitung ist belegt.**
	Dee lei-tung ist bə-LAYKT.

INTERNET ACCESS

Would you tell me where to find an Internet café?	**Wo finde ich ein Internetcafé?**
	Voh fin-də i[h] ein IN-ter-net-kaf-fay?
Is there Wi-Fi?	**Gibt es dort WLAN-Zugang?**
	Geept es dort VAY-lahn-tsoo-gang?
How much do you charge per minute / hour?	**Wie viel kostet das pro Minute / Stunde?**
	Vee feel kos-tet das proh mee-NOO-tə / SHTUN-də?
Can I print here?	**Kann ich hier etwas ausdrucken?**
	Kan i[ch] heer et-vas OWS-druk-ken?
Can I burn a CD?	**Kann ich eine CD brennen?**
	Kan i[ch] ei-nə tsay-DAY bren-nen?
Would you please help me change the language preference to English?	**Könnten Sie mir bitte die Sprache auf Englisch umstellen?**
	K[oe]n-ten zee meer bit-ə dee shprah-[kh]ə owf ENG-lish um-shtel-len?
May I scan something?	**Kann ich etwas einscannen?**
	Kan i[ch] et-vas EIN-sken-nen?
Can I upload photos from my digital camera?	**Kann ich Bilder von meiner Digitalkamera hochladen?**
	Kan i[ch] BIL-dər fon mei-nər dee-gee-TAHL-kam-me-rah hoh[ch]-lah-den?

Do you have a computer with a USB port?
Haben Sie einen Computer mit USB-Anschluss?
Hah-ben zee ei-nen kom-pyoo-tər mit oo-es-BAY-an-shlus?

Do you have a Mac?
Haben Sie einen Mac?
Hah-ben zee ei-nen MEK?

Do you have a PC?
Haben Sie einen PC?
Hah-ben zee ei-nen pay-TSAY?

Do you have a newer version of this software?
Haben Sie eine neuere Version dieser Software?
Hah-ben zee ei-nə noy-ay-rə ver-zee-OHN dee-zər soft-wayr?

MAIL

Where is the post office?
Wo finde ich das Postamt?
Voh fin-də i[ch] das POST-amt?

May I send an international package?
Kann ich ein Paket ins Ausland versenden?
Kan i[ch] ein pah-KAYT ins OWS-lant fer-zen-den?

Do I need a customs form?
Benötige ich ein Zollformular?
Bə-n[oe]-ti-gə i[ch] ein TSOL-for-moo-lahr?

Do you sell insurance for packages?	**Bieten Sie Paketversicherungen an?** *Bee-ten zee pah-KAYT-fer-zi-[ch]e-rung-en an?*
Please mark it fragile.	**Kennzeichnen Sie das Paket bitte als zerbrechlich.** *Ken-tsei[ch]-nen zee das pah-kayt bit-ə als tsayr-BRAY[CH]-li[ch].*
Please handle with care.	**Behandeln Sie es bitte vorsichtig.** *Bə-han-deln zee es bit-ə FOHR-zi[ch]-ti[ch].*
Do you have twine?	**Haben Sie Paketschnur?** *Hah-ben zee pah-KAYT-shnoor?*
Where is a DHL office?	**Wo finde ich eine DHL-Niederlassung?** *Voh fin-də i[ch] ei-nə day-hah-EL-nee-dər-las-sung?*
Do you sell stamps?	**Verkaufen Sie Briefmarken?** *Fer-kow-fen zee BREEF-mar-ken?*
Do you sell postcards?	**Verkaufen Sie Postkarten?** *Fer-kow-fen zee POST-kar-ten?*
How much to send that express / air mail?	**Wie viel kostet der Expressversand / Luftpostversand?** *Vee feel kos-tet dayr eks-PRES-fer-zant / LUFT-post-fer-zant?*
Do you offer overnight delivery?	**Bieten Sie einen Übernachtversand an?** *Bee-ten zee ei-nen [ue]-bər-NA[KH]T-fer-zant an?*
How long will it take to reach the United States?	**Wie lange dauert der Versand in die USA?** *Vee lang-ə dow-ert dayr fer-zant in dee oo-es-AH?*
I'd like to buy an envelope.	**Ich möchte ein Kuvert kaufen.** *I[ch] m[oe][ch]-tə ein koo-VAYR kow-fen.*

May I send it airmail?	**Kann ich das per Luftpost senden?** *Kan i[ch] das payr LUFT-post zen-den?*
I'd like to send it certified / registered mail.	**Ich möchte das als Einschreiben senden.** *I[ch] m[oe][ch]-tə das als EIN-shrei-ben zen-den.*

Listen Up: Postal Lingo

Der Nächste, bitte! *Dayr NAYKS-tə, bit-ə!*	Next!
Stellen Sie das bitte hier ab. *Shtel-len zee das bit-ə HEER ap.*	Please, set it here.
Welchen Service möchten Sie? *Vel-[ch]en ZER-vis m[oe][ch]-ten zee?*	What kind of service would you like?
Was kann ich für Sie tun? *Vas kan i[ch] f[ue]r zee TOON?*	How can I help you?
Abgabeschalter *AP-gah-bə-shal-tər*	dropoff window
Abholschalter *AP-hohl-shal-tər*	pickup window

CHAPTER SEVEN

CULTURE

CINEMA

Is there a movie theater nearby?	**Gibt es hier in der Nähe ein Kino?** *Geept es heer in dayr nay-ə ein KEE-noh?*
What's playing tonight?	**Was läuft heute Abend?** *Vas LOYFT hoy-tə ah-bent?*
Is that in English or German?	**Ist das auf Englisch oder auf Deutsch?** *Ist das owf ENG-lish oh-dər owf doytsh?*
Are there English subtitles?	**Gibt es englische Untertitel?** *Geept es eng-li-shə UN-tər-tee-tel?*
Is the theater air conditioned?	**Ist das Kino klimatisiert?** *Ist das kee-noh klee-mah-tee-ZEERT?*
How much is a ticket?	**Wie viel kostet eine Karte?** *Vee feel kos-tet ei-nə KAR-tə?*
Do you have a discount for ___?	**Gibt es einen Rabatt für ___?** *Geept es ei-nen rah-BAT f[ue]r ___?*
seniors	**Senioren** *zayn-YOH-ren*
students	**Studenten** *shtoo-DEN-ten*
children	**Kinder** *KIN-dər*
What time is the movie showing?	**Wann läuft der Film?** *Van LOYFT dayr film?*
How long is the movie?	**Wie lang dauert der Film?** *Vee lang DOW-ert dayr film?*

May I buy tickets in advance?	**Kann ich schon vorher Karten kaufen?** *Kan i[ch] shohn FOHR-her kar-ten kow-fen?*
Is it sold out?	**Ist die Vorstellung ausverkauft?** *Ist dee fohr-shtel-lung OWS-fer-kowft?*
When does it begin?	**Wann beginnt die Vorstellung?** *Van bə-GINT dee fohr-shtel-lung?*

PERFORMANCES

Are there any plays showing right now?	**Finden derzeit irgendwelche Aufführungen statt?** *Fin-den dayr-tseit ir-gent-vel-[ch]ə OWF-f[ue]-rung-en shtat?*
Is there a dinner theater?	**Gibt es hier ein Theater mit angeschlossener Gastronomie?** *Geept es heer ein tay-AH-tər mit an-gə-shlos-sen-ər gas-troh-noh-MEE?*
Where can I buy tickets?	**Wo kann ich Karten kaufen?** *Voh kan i[ch] KAR-ten kow-fen?*
Are there student discounts?	**Gibt es einen Studentenrabatt?** *Geept es ei-nen shtoo-DEN-ten-rah-bat?*
I need ___ seats.	**Ich benötige ___ Plätze.** *I[ch] bə-n[oe]-ti-gə ___ PLET-sə.*

For a full list of numbers, see p8.

An aisle seat.	**Einen Gangplatz, bitte.** *Ei-nen GANG-plats, bit-ə.*
An orchestra seat, please.	**Einen Orchesterplatz, bitte.** *Ei-nen or-KES-tər-plats, bit-ə.*

CULTURE

Listen Up: Box Office Lingo

Was möchten Sie gern sehen?
Vas m[oe][ch]-ten zee gern ZAY-en?

What would you like to see?

Wie viele?
Vee FEE-lə?

How many?

Für zwei Erwachsene?
F[ue]r tsvei ayr-VAK-se-nə?

For two adults?

Popcorn?
POP-corn?

Popcorn?

Mit Butter? Gesalzen?
Mit BUT-tər? Gə-ZALT-sen?

With butter? Salt?

Darf's sonst noch was sein?
Darfs ZONST no[kh] vas zein?

Would you like anything else?

What time does the play start?

Wann beginnt die Vorstellung?
Van bə-GINT dee fohr-shtel-lung?

Is there an intermission?

Gibt es eine Pause?
Geept es ei-nə POW-zə?

Is there an opera house nearby?

Gibt es hier in der Nähe eine Oper?
Geept es heer in dayr nay-ə ei-nə OH-pər?

Is there a local symphony?	**Gibt es hier ein örtliches Symphonieorchester?**
	Geept es heer ein [oe]rt-li-[ch]es zim-foh-NEE-or-kes-tər?
May I purchase tickets over the phone?	**Kann ich die Karten telefonisch bestellen?**
	Kan i[ch] dee kar-ten te-le-FOH-nish bə-shtel-len?
What time is the box office open?	**Welche Öffnungszeiten hat der Kartenschalter?**
	Vel-[ch]ə [OE]F-nungs-tsei-ten hat dayr kar-ten-shal-tər?
I need space for a wheelchair, please.	**Ich benötige einen Platz für einen Rollstuhl.**
	I[ch] bə-n[oe]-ti-gə ei-nen plats f[ue]r ei-nen ROL-shtool.
Do you have private boxes available?	**Verfügen Sie über Privatlogen?**
	Fer-f[ue]-gen zee [ue]-bər pree-VAHT-loh-zhen?
Is there a church that gives concerts?	**Gibt es hier eine Kirche, in der Konzerte gegeben werden?**
	Geept es heer ei-nə kir-[ch]ə, in dayr kon-TSAYR-tə gə-gay-ben vayr-den?
A program, please.	**Ein Programm, bitte.**
	Ein proh-GRAM, bit-ə.
Please show us to our seats.	**Zeigen Sie uns bitte unsere Plätze.**
	Tsei-gen zee uns bit-ə un-zay-rə PLET-sə.

MUSEUMS, GALLERIES & ATTRACTIONS

Do you have a museum guide?	**Haben Sie einen Museumsführer?** *Hah-ben zee ei-nen moo-ZAY-ooms-f[ue]-rər?*
Do you have guided tours?	**Bieten Sie Fremdenführungen an?** *Bee-ten zee FREM-den-f[ue]-rung-en an?*
What are the museum hours?	**Wann hat das Museum geöffnet?** *Van hat das moo-zay-oom gə-[OE]F-net?*
Do I need an appointment?	**Benötige ich einen Termin?** *Bə-n[oe]-ti-gə i[ch] ei-nen tayr-MEEN?*
What is the admission fee?	**Wie hoch ist der Eintrittspreis?** *Vee hoh[ch] ist dayr EIN-trits-preis?*
Do you have ____?	**Haben Sie ____?** *Hah-ben zee ____?*
student discounts	**Studentenrabatte** *shtoo-DEN-ten-rah-bat-tə*
senior discounts	**Seniorenrabatte** *zayn-YOH-ren-rah-bat-ə*
Do you have services for the hearing impaired?	**Haben Sie Angebote für Hörgeschädigte?** *Hah-ben zee AN-gə-boh-tə f[ue]r H[OE]R-gə-shay-dik-tə?*
Do you have audio tours in English?	**Werden Audioführungen in englischer Sprache angeboten?** *Vayr-den OW-dee-oh-f[ue]-rung-en in eng-li-shə SHPRAH-[ch]ə an-gə-boh-ten?*

CHAPTER EIGHT

SHOPPING

This chapter covers the phrases you'll need to shop in a variety of settings, from the mall to the town square artisan market. We also threw in the terminology you'll need to visit the barber or hairdresser.

For coverage of food and grocery shopping, see p90.

GENERAL SHOPPING TERMS

Could you please tell me ___?	**Könnten Sie mir bitte sagen, ___?** *K[oe]n-ten zee meer bit-ə zah-gen ___?*
how to get to a mall	**wie ich zu einem Einkaufszentrum komme** *vee i[ch] tsoo ei-nem EIN-kowfs-tsen-trum kom-mə*
the best place for shopping	**wo man hier am besten shoppen kann** *voh man heer am bes-ten SHOP-pen kan*
how to get downtown	**wie ich in die Stadt komme** *vee i[ch] in dee SHTAT kom-mə*
Where can I find a ___?	**Wo finde ich ___?** *Voh fin-də i[ch] ___?*
shoe store	**ein Schuhgeschäft** *ein SHOO-gə-sheft*
men's / women's / children's clothing store	**ein Bekleidungsgeschäft für Herren / Damen / Kinder** *ein bə-KLEI-dungs-gə-sheft f[ue]r HER-ren / DAH-men / KIN-dər*

designer fashion shop	**ein Geschäft mit Designermode**
	ein gə-SHEFT mit dee-ZEI-nər-moh-də
vintage clothing store	**ein Second-Hand-Geschäft**
	ein sek-kend-HENT-gə-sheft
jewelry store	**einen Juwelier**
	ei-nen yoo-vay-LEER
bookstore	**eine Buchhandlung**
	ei-nə BOO[CH]-hant-lung
toy store	**ein Spielwarengeschäft**
	ein SHPEEL-vah-ren-gə-sheft
stationery store	**eine Schreibwarenhandlung**
	ei-nə SHREIB-vah-ren-hant-lung
antique shop	**einen Antiquitätenhändler**
	ei-nen an-tee-kvee-TAY-ten-hent-lər
cigar shop	**einen Tabakladen**
	ei-nen TAH-bak-lah-den
souvenir shop	**ein Souvenirgeschäft**
	ein zoo-vay-NEER-gə-sheft
flea market	**einen Flohmarkt**
	ei-nen FLOH-markt

CLOTHES SHOPPING

I'd like to buy ____.	**Ich möchte ____ kaufen.**
	I[ch] m[oe][ch]-tə ____ kow-fen.
men's shirts	**Herrenhemden**
	HER-ren-hem-den
women's shoes	**Damenschuhe**
	DAH-men-shoo-ə
children's clothes	**Kinderbekleidung**
	KIN-dər-bə-klei-dung
toys	**Spielwaren**
	SHPEEL-vah-ren

For a full list of numbers, see p8.

I'm looking for a size ____.	**Ich suche etwas in Größe ____.**
	I[ch] zoo-[ch]ə et-vas in gr[oe]-sə ____.
small	**S**
	es
medium	**M**
	em
large	**L**
	el
extra-large	**XL**
	IKS-el
I'm looking for ____.	**Ich suche ____.**
	I[ch] ZOO-[ch]ə ____.
a silk blouse	**eine Seidenbluse**
	ei-nə ZEI-den-bloo-zə
cotton pants	**eine Baumwollhose**
	ei-nə BOWM-vol-hoh-zə
a hat	**einen Hut**
	ei-nen HOOT
sunglasses	**eine Sonnenbrille**
	ei-nə ZON-nen-bril-lə
underwear	**Unterwäsche**
	UN-tər-ve-shə
cashmere	**nach etwas aus Kaschmir**
	nah[kh] et-vas ows KASH-meer
socks	**nach Socken**
	nah[kh] ZOK-ken
sweaters	**nach Pullovern**
	nah[kh] pul-LOH-vern
a coat	**eine Jacke**
	ei-nə YA-kə
a swimsuit	**einen Badeanzug**
	ei-nen BAH-də-an-tsook
May I try it on?	**Kann ich das anprobieren?**
	Kan i[ch] das AN-proh-bee-ren?

Ohrringe
OHR-ring-ə

Halskette
HALS-ket-tə

Armbanduhr
ARM-bant-oor

Kleid
Kleit

Hemd
Hemt

Krawatte
Krah-VAT-tə

Jackett
Shah-KET

Gürtel
G[UE]r-tel

Hose
HOH-zə

Schuhe
SHOO-ə

Do you have fitting rooms?	**Haben Sie Umkleidekabinen?** *Hah-ben zee UM-klei-də-kah-bee-nen?*
Thanks, I'll take it.	**Danke, das nehme ich.** *Dank-ə, das NAY-mə i[ch].*
Do you have that in ___?	**Haben Sie das ___?** *Hah-ben zee das ___?*
a smaller / larger size	**kleiner / größer** *KLEI-nər / GR[OE]-sər*
a different color	**in einer anderen Farbe** *in ei-nər an-de-ren FAR-bə*
How much is it?	**Wie viel kostet das?** *Vee feel KOS-tet das?*

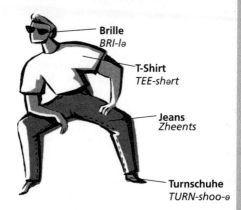

Brille
BRI-lə

T-Shirt
TEE-shərt

Jeans
Zheents

Turnschuhe
TURN-shoo-ə

ARTISAN MARKET SHOPPING

Is there a craft / an artisan market?

Gibt es hier einen Handwerksmarkt / Künstlermarkt?
Geept es heer ei-nen HANT-verks-markt / K[UE]NST-lər-markt?

That's beautiful. May I look at it?

Das ist wunderschön. Darf ich mir das näher ansehen?
Das ist vun-dər-SH[OE]N. Darf i[ch] meer das NAY-ər an-zay-en?

When is the farmers' market open?

Wann hat der Bauernmarkt geöffnet?
Van hat dayr BOW-ern-markt gə-[oe]f-net?

Is that open every day of the week?

Ist das die ganze Woche über geöffnet?
Ist das dee GANT-sə vo-[kh]ə [ue]-bər gə-[oe]f-net?

How much does that cost?

Wie viel kostet das?
Vee feel KOS-tet das?

How much for two?	**Wie viel für zwei Stück?**
	Vee feel f[ue]r TSVEI sht[ue]k?
Do I get a discount if I pay in cash?	**Bekomme ich einen Nachlass bei Barzahlung?**
	Bə-kom-mə i[ch] ei-nen na[kh]-las bei BAHR-tsah-lung?
No thanks, maybe I'll come back.	**Nein, danke. Vielleicht komme ich später nochmal vorbei.**
	Nein, dank-ə. Fee-lei[ch]t kom-mə i[ch] SHPAY-tər no[kh]-mahl fohr-bei.
Would you take € ___?	**Sagen wir ___ Euro?**
	Zah-gen veer ___ OY-roh?
For a full list of numbers, see p8.	
That's a deal!	**Abgemacht!**
	AP-gə-ma[kh]t!
Do you have a less expensive one?	**Haben Sie eine günstigere Ausführung?**
	Hah-ben zee ein-ə G[UE]NS-tee-ge-rə ows-f[ue]-rung?
Is there tax?	**Fällt Steuer an?**
	Felt SHTOY-ər an?
May I have the VAT forms?	**Könnte ich bitte die Formulare für die Mehrwertsteuer haben?**
	K[oe]n-tə i[ch] bit-ə dee fohr-moo-lah-rə f[ue]r dee MAYR-vayrt-shtoy-ər hah-ben?

BOOKSTORE / NEWSSTAND SHOPPING

Is there ___ nearby?	**Gibt es in der Nähe ___?**
	Geept es in dayr nay-ə ___?
a bookstore	**eine Buchhandlung**
	ei-nə BOO[CH]-hant-lung
a newsstand	**einen Zeitungsstand**
	ei-nen TSEI-tungs-shtant

Do you have ____ in English?	**Haben Sie ____ in englischer Sprache?**
	Hah-ben zee ____ in eng-li-shər SHPRAH-[kh]ə?
books	**Bücher**
	B[ue]-[ch]ər
newspapers	**Zeitungen**
	Tsei-tung-en
magazines	**Zeitschriften**
	Tseit-shrif-ten
books about local history	**Bücher zur örtlichen Geschichte**
	B[ue]-[ch]ər tsoor [oe]rt-li-[ch]en gə-SHI[CH]-tə
picture books	**Bilderbücher**
	BIL-dər b[ue]-[ch]ər

SHOPPING FOR ELECTRONICS

With some exceptions, shopping for electronic goods in Germany, Switzerland or Austria is generally not recommended for North American travelers. Many DVDs, CDs, and other products contain different signal coding from that used in the United States or Canada to help deter piracy. In addition, electronic goods are generally more expensive than in the United States or Canada. They can be even more epensive if the exchange rate is high.

Can I play this in the United States / United Kingdom?	**Lässt sich das in den USA / im Vereinigten Königreich abspielen?**
	Lest zi[ch] das in dayn oo-es-AH / im fer-ei-nik-ten K[OE]-nig-rei[ch] ap-shpee-len?

Will this game work on my game console in the United States / United Kingdom?	**Funktioniert dieses Spiel auf meiner Spielekonsole in den USA / im Vereinigten Königreich?** *Funk-tsee-oh-neert dee-zes shpeel owf mei-nə SHPEE-lər-kon-zoh-lə in dayn oo-es-AH / im fer-ei-nik-ten K[OE]-nig-rei[ch]?*
Do you have this in a U.S. / U.K. market format?	**Haben Sie das in einem US / UK-kompatiblen Format?** *Hah-ben zee das in ei-nem oo-ES / oo-KAH-kom-pah-tee-blen fohr-MAHT?*
Can you convert this to a U.S. / U.K. market format?	**Können Sie das in ein US / UK-kompatibles Format umwandeln?** *K[oe]n-nen zee das in ein oo-ES / oo-KAH-kom-pah-tee-bles fohr-maht UM-van-deln?*
Is this DVD region encoded?	**Hat diese DVD einen Regionalcode?** *Hat dee-zə DAY-fow-day ei-nen ray-gee-oh-NAHL-koht?*
Will this work with a 110 VAC adapter?	**Funktioniert das mit einem 110-Volt-Adapter?** *Funk-tsee-oh-NEERT das mit ei-nem hun-dert-tsayn-volt-ah-DAP-tər?*
Do you have an adapter plug for 110 to 220?	**Haben Sie einen Adapterstecker von 110 auf 220 Volt?** *Hah-ben zee ei-nen ah-DAP-tər-shtek-kər fon hun-dert-TSAYN owf tsvei-hun-dert-TSVAN-tsi[ch] volt?*
Do you sell electronics adapters here?	**Gibt es hier Elektronikadapter?** *Geept es heer ay-lek-TROH-nik-ah-DAP-tər?*

Is it safe to use my laptop with this adapter?	**Kann ich mein Notebook mit diesem Adapter betreiben?**
	Kan i[ch] mein NOHT-book mit dee-zem ah-dap-tər bə-TREI-ben?
If it doesn't work, may I return it?	**Kann ich den Artikel zurückgeben, wenn er nicht funktioniert?**
	Kan i[ch] dayn ar-tee-kel tsoo-R[UE]K-gay-ben, ven ayr ni[ch]t funk-tsee-oh-NEERT?
May I try it here in the store?	**Kann ich den Artikel hier im Laden ausprobieren?**
	Kan i[ch] dayn ar-tee-kel heer im lah-den OWS-proh-bee-ren?

AT THE BARBER / HAIRDRESSER

May I make an appointment?	**Ich hätte gern einen Termin.**
	I[ch] HET-tə gern ei-nen tayr-MEEN.
Do I need an appointment?	**Benötige ich einen Termin?**
	Bə-n[oe]-ti-gə i[ch] ei-nen tayr-MEEN?
A trim, please.	**Schneiden, bitte.**
	SHNEI-den, bit-ə.
Would you make the color ___?	**Könnten Sie die Farbe bitte ___?**
	K[oe]n-ten zee dee far-bə bit-ə ___?
darker	**dunkler machen**
	DUNG-klər ma-[kh]en
lighter	**heller machen**
	HEL-lər ma-[kh]en
I'd like it curled.	**Ich hätte mein Haar gern gelockt.**
	I[ch] het-tə mein hahr gern gə-LOKT.

Do you do perms?	**Kann ich bei Ihnen eine Dauerwelle bekommen?** *Kan i[ch] bei ee-nen ei-nə DOW-ər-vel-lə bə-kom-men?*
Please use low heat.	**Bitte nicht zu heiß.** *Bit-ə ni[ch]t tsoo HEIS.*
Please don't blow dry it.	**Bitte nicht trockenföhnen.** *Bit-ə ni[ch]t TROK-ken-f[oe]-nen.*
Please dry it curly / straight.	**Föhnen Sie die Haare bitte lockig / glatt.** *F[oe]-nen zee dee hah-rə bit-ə LOK-ki[ch] / GLAT.*
Could you fix my highlights?	**Könnten Sie sich bitte um meine Strähnen kümmern?** *K[oe]n-ten zee zi[ch] bit-ə um mei-nə SHTRAY-nen k[ue]m-mern?*
Could you trim my bangs?	**Könnten Sie bitte meinen Pony schneiden?** *K[OE]N-ten zee bit-ə mei-nen PON-nee shnei-den?*
Do you offer waxes?	**Bieten Sie Wachsenthaarung an?** *Bee-ten zee vaks-ent-HAH-rung an?*
I'd like a Brazilian wax.	**Ich hätte gern ein Brazilian Waxing.** *I[ch] HET-tə gern ein bra-zil-yen VAK-sing.*
Please wax my ____.	**Bitte enthaaren Sie meine ____.** *Bit-ə ent-hah-ren zee mei-nə ____.*
legs	**Beine** *BEI-nə*
bikini line	**Bikinilinie** *bee-KEE-nee-lee-nee-ə*
eyebrows	**Augenbrauen** *OW-gen-brow-en*

under my nose	**Oberlippe**
	OH-bər-lip-pə
Please trim my beard.	**Bitte trimmen Sie meinen Bart.**
	Bit-ə trim-men zee mei-nen BAHRT.
A shave, please.	**Rasieren, bitte.**
	Rah-ZEE-ren, bit-ə.
Use a fresh blade please.	**Verwenden Sie bitte eine neue Klinge.**
	Fer-ven-den zee bit-ə ei-nə noy-ə KLING-ə.

CHAPTER NINE

SPORTS & FITNESS

GETTING FIT

Is there a gym nearby?	**Gibt es ein Fitnessstudio in der Nähe?**
	Geept es ein FIT-nes-shtoo-dee-oh in dayr nay-ə?
Does the hotel have a gym?	**Gibt es im Hotel einen Fitnessraum?**
	Geept es im hoh-TEL ei-nen FIT-nes-rowm?
Do you have free weights?	**Haben Sie Hanteln und Gewichte?**
	Hah-ben zee HAN-teln unt gə-WI[CH]-tə?
Is there a pool?	**Gibt es ein Schwimmbad?**
	Geept es ein SHVIM-baht?
Do I have to be a member?	**Muss ich Mitglied sein?**
	Mus i[ch] MIT-gleet zein?
I need to get a locker please.	**Ich hätte gern einen Spind.**
	I[ch] HET-ə gern ei-nen SHPINT.

Do you have a lock?	**Haben Sie ein Schloss?**
	Hah-ben zee ein SHLOS?
Do you have a treadmill?	**Haben Sie ein Laufband?**
	Hah-ben zee ein LOWF-bant?
Do you have a stationary bike?	**Haben Sie ein Trainingsrad?**
	Hah-ben zee ein TRAY-nings-raht?
May I have clean towels?	**Könnte ich bitte saubere Handtücher bekommen?**
	K[oe]n-tə i[ch] bit-ə zow-be-rə HANT-t[ue]-[ch]ər bə-kom-men?
Where are the showers / locker-rooms?	**Wo finde ich die Duschen / Umkleiden?**
	Voh fin-də i[ch] dee DOO-shen / UM-klei-den?
Do you have aerobics classes?	**Bieten Sie Aerobic-Kurse an?**
	Bee-ten zee ay-RO-bik-kur-zə an?
Are there yoga / pilates classes?	**Gibt es Yogakurse / Pilateskurse?**
	Geept es YOH-gah-koor-zə / Pee-LAH-tes-koor-zə?

CATCHING A GAME

Where is the stadium?	**Wo finde ich das Stadion?**
	Voh fin-də i[ch] das SHTAH-dee-on?
Who is playing?	**Wer spielt?**
	Vayr shpeelt?
Who is the best goalie?	**Wer ist der beste Torwart?**
	Vayr ist dayr bes-tə TOHR-vart?
Where can I watch a soccer game?	**Wo kann ich ein Fußballspiel sehen?**
	Voh kan i[ch] ein FOOS-bal-shpeel zay-en?
Where can I see a volleyball game?	**Wo kann ich ein Volleyballspiel sehen?**
	Voh kan i[ch] ein VOL-lee-bal-shpeel zay-en?

Are there any women's teams?	**Gibt es Frauenteams?** *Geept es FROW-en teems?*
Which is the best team?	**Welches Team ist das beste?** *Vel-[ch]es teem ist das BES-tə?*
Will the game be on television?	**Wird das Spiel im Fernsehen übertragen?** *Virt das shpeel im FAYRN-zayn [ue]-bər-trah-gen?*
Where can I buy tickets?	**Wo kann ich Karten kaufen?** *Voh kan i[ch] KAR-ten kow-fen?*
The best seats, please.	**Die besten Plätze, bitte.** *Dee bes-ten PLET-sə, bit-ə.*
The cheapest seats, please.	**Die billigsten Plätze, bitte.** *Dee bil-liks-ten PLET-sə, bit-ə.*
How close are these seats?	**Wie nah sind diese Plätze?** *Vee NAH zint dee-zə plet-sə?*
May I have box seats?	**Könnte ich bitte Logenplätze haben?** *K[oe]n-tə i[ch] bit-ə LOH-zhen-plet-sə hah-ben?*
Wow! What a game!	**Wow! Was für ein Spiel!** *Wow! Vas f[ue]r ein shpeel!*
Go go go!	**Los, los, los!** *LOHS, LOHS, LOHS!*

Goal!	**Tor!**
	TOHR!
What's the score?	**Wie lautet der Spielstand?**
	Vee low-tet dayr SHPEEL-shtant?
Who's winning?	**Wer gewinnt?**
	Vayr gə-VINT?

HIKING

Where can I find a guide to hiking trails?	**Wo finde ich einen Führer für Wandertouren?**
	Voh fin-də i[ch] ei-nen f[ue]-rər f[ue]r VAN-dər-too-ren?
Do we need to hire a guide?	**Benötigen wir einen Führer?**
	Bə-n[oe]-ti-gen veer ei-nen F[UE]-rər?
Where can I rent equipment?	**Wo kann ich Ausrüstung mieten?**
	Voh kan i[ch] OWS-r[ue]s-tung mee-ten?
Where can we go mountain climbing?	**Wo können wir hier bergsteigen?**
	Voh K[OE]-nen veer heer BAYRK-shtei-gen?
Are the routes ____?	**Sind die Routen ____?**
	Zint dee roo-ten ____?
well marked	**gut gekennzeichnet**
	goot gə-KEN-tsei[ch]-net

in good condition	**in gutem Zustand**
	in goo-tem TSOO-shtant
What is the altitude there?	**Wie hoch ist es dort?**
	Vee HOH[CH] ist es dort?
How long will it take?	**Wie lange dauert die Tour?**
	Vee lang-ə dow-ert dee toor?
Is it very difficult?	**Ist die Tour sehr schwierig?**
	Ist dee toor zayr SHVEE-ri[ch]?
Are the campsites marked?	**Sind die Zeltplätze gekennzeichnet?**
	Zint dee tselt-plet-sə gə-KEN-tsei[ch]-net?
Can we camp off the trail?	**Können wir abseits der Strecke campieren?**
	K[oe]n-nen veer AP-seits dayr shtrek-kə kam-pee-ren?
Is it okay to build fires here?	**Ist hier Feuermachen erlaubt?**
	Ist heer foy-ər-ma-[kh]en ayr-LOWPT?
Do we need permits?	**Benötigen wir eine Genehmigung?**
	Bə-n[oe]-ti-gen veer ei-nə gə-NAY-mi-gung?

For more camping terms, see p72.

BOATING & FISHING

I'd like to go fishing.	**Ich würde gern angeln gehen.**
	I[ch] v[ue]r-də gern ANG-eln gayn.
Can I rent a boat?	**Kann ich ein Boot leihen?**
	Kan i[ch] ein BOHT lei-en?
When do we sail?	**Wann legen wir ab?**
	Van lay-gen veer AP?
How long is the trip?	**Wie lange dauert die Reise?**
	Vee LANG-ə dow-ert dee rei-zə?

Where are the life preservers?	**Wo befinden sich die Schwimmwesten?** *Voh bə-fin-den zi[ch] dee SHVIM-ves-ten?*
Can I purchase bait?	**Kann ich Köder kaufen?** *Kan i[ch] K[OE]-dər kow-fen?*
Can I rent a pole?	**Kann ich eine Angel leihen?** *Kan i[ch] ei-nə ANG-el lei-en?*
Are we going up river or down?	**Fahren wir flussauf- oder flussabwärts?** *Fah-ren veer flus-OWF oh-dər flus-AP-vayrts?*
How far are we going?	**Wie weit fahren wir?** *Vee VEIT fah-ren veer?*
How fast are we going?	**Wie schnell fahren wir?** *Vee SHNEL fah-ren veer?*
How deep is the water here?	**Wie tief ist das Wasser hier?** *Vee teef ist das VAS-sər heer?*
I got one!	**Ich hab einen!** *I[ch] HAHP ei-nen!*
I can't swim.	**Ich kann nicht schwimmen.** *I[ch] kan ni[ch]t SHVIM-men.*
Help! Lifeguard!	**Hilfe! Rettungsschwimmer!** *HIL-fə! RET-tungs-shvim-mər!*
Can we go ashore?	**Können wir an Land gehen?** *K[oe]n-nen veer an LANT gay-en?*

GOLFING

I'd like to reserve a tee-time, please.	**Ich möchte eine Tee-Time reservieren.** *I[ch] m[oe][ch]-tə ei-nə TEE-teim re-zer-VEE-ren.*
Do we need to be members to play?	**Müssen wir Mitglied sein, um spielen zu dürfen?** *M[ue]s-sen veer MIT-gleet zein, um shpee-len tsoo d[ue]r-fen?*
How many holes is your course?	**Wie viele Löcher hat Ihr Platz?** *Vee fee-lə l[oe]-[ch]ər hat eer PLATS?*
What is par for the course?	**Wie hoch ist das Par auf diesem Platz?** *Vee hoh[kh] ist das PAHR owf dee-zem plats?*
What is the dress code for players?	**Wie ist die Kleiderordnung für Spieler?** *Vee ist dee KLEI-dər-ord-nung f[ue]r SHPEE-lə?*
I need to rent clubs.	**Ich möchte Schläger mieten.** *I[ch] m[oe][ch]-tə SHLAY-gər mee-ten.*
I need to purchase a sleeve of balls.	**Ich möchte Golfbälle kaufen.** *I[ch] m[oe][ch]-tə GOLF-bel-lə kow-fen.*
I need a glove.	**Ich benötige einen Handschuh.** *I[ch] bə-n[oe]-ti-gə ei-nen HANT-shoo.*
I need a new hat.	**Ich brauche einen neuen Hut.** *I[ch] brow-[kh]ə ei-nen noy-en HOOT.*

Do you require soft spikes? **Muss ich weiche Spikes tragen?**
Mus i[ch] WEI-[ch]ə shpeiks trah-gen?

Do you have carts? **Haben Sie Golfwagen?**
Hah-ben zee GOLF-vah-gen?

I'd like to hire a caddy. **Ich würde gern einen Caddy mieten.**
I[ch] v[ue]r-də gern ei-nen KED-dee mee-ten.

Do you have a driving range? **Haben Sie eine Driving Range?**
Hah-ben zee ei-nə DREI-ving raynzh?

How much are the greens fees? **Wie hoch ist die Green Fee?**
Vee hoh[ch] ist dee GREEN fee?

Is it very hilly? **Ist der Platz sehr hügelig?**
Ist dayr plats zayr H[UE]-ge-li[ch]?

CHAPTER TEN

NIGHTLIFE

For coverage of movies and cultural events, see p130, Chapter Seven, "Culture."

CLUB HOPPING

Where can I find ____?	**Wo finde ich ____?** *Voh fin-də i[ch] ____?*
a good nightclub	**einen guten Nachtclub** *ei-nen goo-ten NA[KH]T-klup*
a club with a live band	**einen Club mit Liveband** *ei-nen klup mit LEIF-bent*
a techno club	**einen Technoclub** *ei-nen TEK-noh-klup*
a jazz club	**einen Jazzclub** *ei-nen TCHES-klup*
a gay / lesbian club	**einen Schwulen- /** **Lesbenclub** *ei-nen SHVOO-len / LES-ben-* *klup*
a club where I can dance	**einen Tanzclub** *ei-nen TANTS-klup*
a club with salsa music	**einen Club mit Salsa-Musik** *ei-nen KLUP mit SAL-sah-* *moo-zeek*
the most popular club in town	**den beliebtesten Club der** **Stadt** *dayn bə-LEEP-tes-ten klup* *dayr shtat*
a singles bar	**eine Singlebar** *ei-nə SINGL-bahr*
What's the cover charge?	**Wie viel kostet der Eintritt?** *Vee feel kos-tet dayr EIN-trit?*

Do they have a dress code?	**Ist eine bestimmte Kleidung vorgeschrieben?**
	Ist ei-nə bə-shtim-tə KLEI-dung fohr-gə-shree-ben?
Is it expensive?	**Ist es dort teuer?**
	Is es dort TOY-ər?
What's the best time to go?	**Wann geht man dort am besten hin?**
	Van gayt man dort am bes-ten HIN?
What kind of music do they play there?	**Welche Art von Musik wird dort gespielt?**
	Vel-[ch]ə ahrt von moo-ZEEK virt dort gə-shpeelt?
Is there a smoking area?	**Gibt es einen Raucherbereich?**
	Geept es ei-nen ROW-[kh]ər-bə-rei[ch]?
I'm looking for ____.	**Ich suche ____.**
	I[ch] ZOO-[ch]ə ____.
a good cigar shop	**ein gutes Zigarrengeschäft**
	ein goo-tes tsee-GAR-ren-gə-sheft
a pack of cigarettes	**eine Packung Zigaretten**
	ei-nə pak-kung tsee-gah-RET-ten
I'd like ____.	**Ich hätte gern ____.**
	I[ch] HET-tə gern ____.
a drink, please	**etwas zu trinken**
	et-vas tsoo TRING-ken
a bottle of beer, please	**ein Bier aus der Flasche**
	ein beer ows dayr FLASH-ə
a beer on tap, please	**ein Bier vom Fass**
	ein beer fom FAS
a shot of ____, please	**einen ____**
	ei-nen ____

For a full list of drinks, see p82.

NIGHTLIFE

Make it a double, please!	**Einen Doppelten, bitte!**
	Ei-nen DOP-pel-ten, bit-ə!
With ice, please.	**Mit Eis, bitte.**
	Mit EIS, bit-ə.
How much for a bottle / glass of beer?	**Wie viel kostet eine Flasche / ein Glas Bier?**
	Vee feel kos-tet ei-nə FLASH-ə / ein GLAHS beer?
I'd like to buy a drink for that woman / man over there.	**Ich würde der Dame / dem Herrn da drüben gern einen Drink spendieren.**
	I[ch] v[ue]r-də dayr DAH-mə / daym HER-ren dah dr[ue]-ben gern ei-nen DRINK shpen-dee-ren.
A pack of cigarettes, please.	**Eine Packung Zigaretten, bitte.**
	Ei-nə pa-kung tsee-gah-RET-ten, bit-ə.

Do You Mind if I Smoke?

Darf ich hier rauchen? *Darf i[ch] heer row-[ch]en?*	May I smoke here?
Haben Sie eine Zigarette? *Hah-ben zee ei-nə tsee-gah-RET-tə?*	Do you have a cigarette?
Haben Sie Feuer? *Hah-ben zee FOY-ər?*	Do you have a light?
Darf ich Ihnen Feuer geben? *Darf i[ch] ee-nen FOY-ər gay-ben?*	May I offer you a light?
Rauchen verboten. *Row-[kh]en fer-BOH-ten.*	Smoking not permitted.

Do you have a lighter or matches?	**Hast du Feuer?**
	Hast doo FOY-ər?
Do you smoke?	**Rauchst du?**
	ROW[KH]ST doo?
Would you like a cigarette?	**Darf ich dir eine Zigarette anbieten?**
	Darf i[ch] deer ei-nə tsee-gah-RET-tə an-bee-ten?
May I run a tab?	**Kann ich die Getränke bezahlen, wenn ich gehe?**
	Kan i[ch] dee gə-trenk-ə bə-tsah-len, venn i[ch] GAY-ə?
What's the cover?	**Was kostet der Eintritt?**
	Vas kos-tet dayr EIN-trit?

ACROSS A CROWDED ROOM

Excuse me, may I buy you a drink?	**Verzeihung. Darf ich dich auf einen Drink einladen?**
	Fer-TSEI-ung. Darf i[ch] di[ch] owf ei-nen DRINK ein-lah-den?
I wanted to meet you.	**Ich wollte dich treffen.**
	I[ch] VOL-tə di[ch] TREF-fen.
Are you single?	**Bist du Single?**
	Bist doo SING-el?
You look amazing.	**Du siehst umwerfend aus.**
	Doo zeest UM-vayr-fent ows.
You look like the most interesting person in the room.	**Du bist mit Abstand die interessanteste Person im Raum.**
	Doo bist mit ap-shtant dee in-tay-res-AN-tes-tə payr-zohn im rowm.
Would you like to dance?	**Möchtest du gern tanzen?**
	M[oe][ch]-test doo gern TANT-sen?
Do you like to dance fast or slow?	**Tanzt du lieber schnell oder langsam?**
	Tantst doo lee-bər SHNEL oh-dər lang-zahm?

Give me your hand.	**Gib mir deine Hand.** *Geep meer dei-nə HANT.*
What would you like to drink?	**Was möchtest du trinken?** *Vas m[oe][ch]-test doo TRING-ken?*
You're a great dancer.	**Du tanzt großartig.** *Doo tantst GROHS-ar-ti[ch].*
Do you like this song?	**Magst du dieses Lied?** *MAHKST doo dee-zes leet?*
You have nice eyes!	**Du hast wunderschöne Augen!** *Doo hast VUN-dər-sh[oe]-nə ow-gen!*

For a full list of features, see p169.

For a full list of features, see p169.

May I have your phone number / email address?	**Gibst du mir deine Telefonnummer / E-Mail-Adresse?** *Geepst doo meer dei-nə te-le-FOHN-num-mər / EE-mayl-ah-dres-sə?*

GETTING CLOSER

You're very attractive.

Du siehst unglaublich gut aus.
Doo zeest un-glowp-li[ch] GOOT ows.

I like being with you.

Ich bin gern mit dir zusammen.
I[ch] bin GERN mit deer tsoo-zam-men.

I like you.

Ich mag dich.
I[ch] MAHK di[ch].

I want to hold you.

Ich möchte dich in den Arm nehmen.
I[ch] m[oe][ch]-tə di[ch] in dayn ARM nay-men.

Kiss me.

Küss mich.
K[UE]SS mi[ch].

May I give you ____?

Darf ich dich ____?
Darf i[ch] di[ch] ____?

a hug

umarmen
um-ar-men

a kiss

küssen
K[UE]S-sen

Would you like ____?

Möchtest du gern ____?
M[oe]ch-test doo gern ____?

a back rub

eine Rückenmassage
ei-nə R[UE]K-ken-mah-sah-shə

a massage

eine Massage
ei-nə mah-SAH-shə

GETTING INTIMATE

Would you like to come inside?	**Möchtest du mit reinkommen?** *M[oe][ch]-test doo mit REIN-kom-men?*
May I come inside?	**Darf ich noch mit reinkommen?** *Darf i[ch] no[kh] mit REIN-kom-men?*
Let me help you out of that.	**Lass mich dir damit helfen.** *Las mi[ch] deer dah-mit HEL-fen.*
Would you help me out of this?	**Könntest du mir damit bitte behilflich sein?** *K[oe]n-test doo meer dah-mit bit-ə bə-HILF-li[ch] zein?*
You smell so good.	**Du riechst so gut.** *Doo REE[CH]ST zoh goot.*
You're beautiful / handsome.	**Du bist wunderschön / sehr gut aussehend.** *Doo bist vun-dər-SH[OE]n / zayr GOOT-ows-zay-ent.*
May I?	**Darf ich?** *DARF i[ch]?*
OK?	**OK?** *o-KAY?*
Like this?	**So?** *Zoh?*
How?	**Wie?** *Vee?*

HOLD ON A SECOND

Please don't do that.	**Das möchte ich nicht.**
	Das M[OE][CH]-tə i[ch] ni[ch]t.
Stop, please.	**Hör bitte auf.**
	H[oe]r bit-ə OWF.
Do you want me to stop?	**Soll ich aufhören?**
	Zol i[ch] OWF-h[oe]-ren?
Let's just be friends.	**Lass uns einfach Freunde sein.**
	Las uns ein-fa[kh] FROYN-də zein.
Do you have a condom?	**Hast du ein Kondom?**
	Hast doo ein kon-DOHM?
Are you on birth control?	**Nimmst du die Pille?**
	Nimst doo dee PIL-lə?
I have a condom.	**Ich habe ein Kondom.**
	I[ch] hah-bə ein kon-DOHM.
Do you have anything you should tell me first?	**Sollte ich vorher noch etwas wissen?**
	Zol-tə i[ch] fohr-her no[kh] et-vas VIS-sen?

BACK TO IT

That's it.	**Genau so.**
	Gə-now ZOH.
That's not it.	**Nicht so.**
	Ni[ch]t ZOH.
Here.	**Hier.**
	Heer.
There.	**Da.**
	Dah.

For a full list of features, see p169.
For a full list of body parts, see p169.

More.	**Weiter.**
	VEI-tər.
Harder.	**Härter.**
	HAYR-tər.

NIGHTLIFE

Faster.	**Schneller.**
	SHNEL-lər.
Deeper.	**Tiefer.**
	TEE-fər.
Slower.	**Langsamer.**
	LANG-zah-mər.
Easier.	**Sanfter.**
	SANF-tər.

COOLDOWN

You're great.	**Du bist fantastisch.**
	Doo bist fan-tas-tish.
That was great.	**Das war fantastisch.**
	Das vahr fan-tas-tish.
Would you like ____?	**Möchtest du gern ____?**
	M[oe][ch]-test doo gern ____?
a drink	**etwas zu trinken**
	et-vas tsoo TRING-ken
a snack	**einen Imbiss**
	ei-nen IM-bis
a shower	**duschen**
	DOO-shen
May I stay here?	**Kann ich hierbleiben?**
	Kan i[ch] HEER-blei-ben?
Would you like to stay here?	**Möchtest du bleiben?**
	M[oe][ch]-test doo BLEI-ben?
I'm sorry. I have to go now.	**Es tut mir leid. Ich muss jetzt gehen.**
	Es toot meer LEIT. I[ch] mus yetst gay-en.
Where are you going?	**Wohin gehst du?**
	Voh-hin GAYST doo?
I have to work early.	**Ich muss früh arbeiten.**
	I[ch] mus fr[ue] AR-bei-ten.

I'm flying home in the morning.	**Ich fliege morgen früh nach Hause.**
	I[ch] flee-gə mor-gen fr[ue] nah[kh] HOW-zə.
I have an early flight.	**Mein Flug geht frühmorgens.**
	Mein flook gayt fr[ue]-MOR-gens.
I think this was a mistake.	**Ich glaube, das war ein Fehler.**
	I[ch] GLOW-bə, das vahr ein FAY-lər.
Will you make me breakfast too?	**Bekomme ich auch ein Frühstück?**
	Bə-kom-mə i[ch] ow[kh] ein FR[UE]-sht[ue]k?
Stay. I'll make you breakfast.	**Geh nicht. Ich mach dir Frühstück.**
	GAY ni[ch]t. I[ch] ma[kh] deer FR[UE]-sht[ue]k.

IN THE CASINO

How much is this table?	**Wie hoch ist der Einsatz an diesem Tisch?**
	Vee hoh[kh] ist dayr EIN-zats an dee-zem tish?
Deal me in.	**Ich bin dabei.**
	I[ch] bin dah-BEI.
Put it on red!	**Setzen Sie das auf Rot!**
	Zet-sen zee das owf ROHT!
Put it on black!	**Setzen Sie das auf Schwarz!**
	Zet-sen zee das owf SHVARTS!
Let it ride!	**Los geht's!**
	LOHS gayts!
Snake-eyes!	**Schlangenaugen!**
	SHLANG-en-ow-gen!
Seven.	**Sieben.**
	ZEE-ben.

For a full list of numbers, see p8.

NIGHTLIFE

I'll pass.	**Ich passe.** *I[ch] PAS-sə.*
Hit me!	**Karte!** *KAR-tə!*
Split.	**Split.** *Split.*
Are the drinks complimentary?	**Sind die Getränke gratis?** *Zint dee gə-trenk-ə GRAH-tis?*
May I bill it to my room?	**Kann ich die Kosten über mein Zimmer abrechnen?** *Kan i[ch] dee kos-ten [ue]-bər mein TSIM-mər ap-ray[ch]-nen?*
I'd like to cash out.	**Ich möchte meinen Gewinn auszahlen lassen.** *I[ch] m[oe][ch]-tə mei-nen gə-VIN ows-tsah-len las-sen.*
I'll hold.	**Ich schiebe.** *I[ch] SHEE-bə.*
I'll see your bet.	**Ich gehe mit.** *I[ch] gay-ə MIT.*
I call.	**Ich will sehen.** *I[ch] vil ZAY-en.*
Full house!	**Full House!** *Ful HOWS!*
Royal flush.	**Royal Flush.** *Roy-əl FLASH.*
Straight.	**Straße.** *SHTRAH-sə.*

CHAPTER ELEVEN

HEALTH & SAFETY

This chapter covers the terms you'll need to maintain your health and safety—including the most useful phrases for the pharmacy, the doctor's office, and the police station.

AT THE PHARMACY

Please fill this prescription.
Ich möchte das Rezept hier einlösen.
I[ch] m[oe][ch]-tə das ray-tsept heer EIN-l[oe]-sen.

Do you have something for ____?
Haben Sie etwas gegen ____?
Hah-ben zee et-vas gay-gen ____?

a cold
eine Erkältung
ei-nə ayr-KEL-tung

a cough
Husten
HOOS-ten

I need something ____.
Ich brauche etwas ____.
I[ch] brow-[kh]ə et-vas ____.

to help me sleep
zum Einschlafen
tsum EIN-shlah-fen

to help me relax
zum Entspannen
tsum ent-SHPAN-nen

I want to buy ____.
Ich hätte gern ____.
I[ch] HET-tə gern ____.

condoms
Kondome
kon-DOH-mə

an antihistamine
ein Antihistamin
ein an-tee-his-tah-MEEN

antibiotic cream
eine antibiotische Salbe
ei-nə an-tee-bee-OH-ti-shə ZAL-bə

aspirin	**Aspirin** *as-pee-REEN*
non-aspirin pain reliever	**ein aspirinfreies Schmerzmittel** *ein as-pee-REEN-frei-es SHMAYRTS-mit-tel*
medicine with codeine	**ein Medikament mit Kodein** *ein may-dee-kah-ment mit koh-day-EEN*
insect repellant	**ein Insektenschutzmittel** *ein in-SEK-ten-shuts-mit-tel*
I need something for ___.	**Ich brauche etwas gegen ___.** *I[ch] brow-[kh]ə et-vas gay-gen ___.*
corns	**Hühneraugen** *H[UE]-nər-ow-gen*
congestion	**Verstopfung** *fer-SHTOP-fung*
warts	**Warzen** *VAHRT-sen*
constipation	**Darmträgheit** *DARM-trayk-heit*
diarrhea	**Durchfall** *DUR[CH]-fal*
indigestion	**Verdauungsstörungen** *fer-DOW-ungs-sht[oe]-run-gen*
nausea	**Übelkeit** *[UE]-bel-keit*
motion sickness	**Reisekrankheit** *REI-zə-krank-heit*
seasickness	**Seekrankheit** *ZAY-krank-heit*
acne	**Akne** *AHK-nə*

AT THE DOCTOR'S OFFICE

I would like to see ___.	**Ich brauche einen Termin bei einem ___.**
	I[ch] brow-[kh]ə ei-nen tayr-MEEN bei ei-nem ___.
a doctor	**Arzt**
	artst
a chiropractor	**Chiropraktiker**
	kee-roh-PRAK-tee-kər
a gynecologist	**Frauenarzt**
	FROW-en-artst
an eye specialist	**Augenspezialisten**
	OW-gen-shpay-tsee-yah-lis-ten
an ears / nose / throat specialist	**Ohrenspezialisten / Nasenspezialisten / Halsspezialisten**
	OH-ren-shpay-tsee-yah-lis-ten / NAH-zen-shpay-tsee-yah-lis-ten / HALS-shpay-tsee-yah-lis-ten
a dentist	**Zahnarzt**
	TSAAHN-artst
an optometrist	**Optiker**
	OP-tee-kər
a dermatologist	**Hautarzt**
	HOWT-artst
Do I need an appointment?	**Benötige ich einen Termin?**
	Bə-n[oe]-tig-gə i[ch] ei-nen tayr-MEEN?
Do I have to pay up front?	**Muss ich im Voraus bezahlen?**
	Mus i[ch] im FOHR-rows bə-tsah-len?
It's an emergency.	**Das ist ein Notfall.**
	Das ist ein NOHT-fal.

HEALTH & SAFETY

I need an emergency prescription refill.	**Ich benötige dringend eine erneute Rezepteinlösung.** *I[ch] bə-n[oe]ti-gə dring-gent ei-nə ayr-noy-tə ray-TSEPT-ein-l[oe]-sung.*
Please call a doctor.	**Rufen Sie bitte einen Arzt.** *Roo-fen zee bit-ə ei-nen ARTST.*
I need an ambulance.	**Ich brauche einen Krankenwagen.** *I[ch] brow-[kh]ə ei-nen KRANK-en-vah-gen.*

SYMPTOMS

For a full list of body parts, see p169.

My ____ hurts.	**Mein ____ schmerzt. (sing.) / Meine ____ schmerzen. (pl.)** *Mein ____ shmayrtst. / Mei-nə ____ shmayrt-sen.*
My ____ is stiff.	**Mein ____ ist steif. (sing.) / Meine ____ sind steif. (pl.)** *Mein ____ ist shteif. / Mei-nə ____ zint shteif.*
I think I'm having a heart attack.	**Ich glaube, ich habe einen Herzinfarkt.** *I[ch] glow-bə, i[ch] hah-bə ei-nen HAYRTS-in-farkt.*
I think I'm having an allergic reaction.	**Ich glaube, ich habe eine allergische Reaktion.** *I[ch] glow-bə, i[ch] hah-bə ei-nə al-LAYR-gi-shə ray-AK-tsee-ohn.*
I can't move.	**Ich kann mich nicht bewegen.** *I[ch] kan mi[ch] ni[ch]t bə-VAY-gen.*
I fell.	**Ich bin gestürzt.** *I[ch] bin gə-SHT[UE]RTST.*

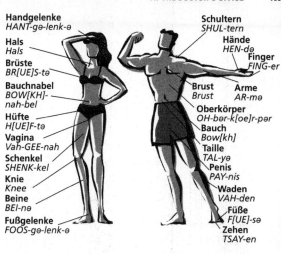

Handgelenke
HANT-gə-lenk-ə

Hals
Hals

Brüste
BR[UE]S-tə

Bauchnabel
BOW[KH]-nah-bel

Hüfte
H[UE]F-tə

Vagina
Vah-GEE-nah

Schenkel
SHENK-kel

Knie
Knee

Beine
BEI-nə

Fußgelenke
FOOS-gə-lenk-ə

Schultern
SHUL-tern

Hände
HEN-də

Finger
FING-er

Brust
Brust

Arme
AR-mə

Oberkörper
OH-bər-k[oe]r-pər

Bauch
Bow[kh]

Taille
TAL-yə

Penis
PAY-nis

Waden
VAH-den

Füße
F[UE]-sə

Zehen
TSAY-en

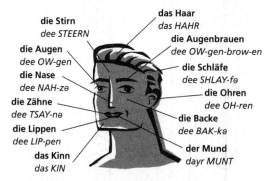

die Stirn
dee STEERN

das Haar
das HAHR

die Augenbrauen
dee OW-gen-brow-en

die Augen
dee OW-gen

die Schläfe
dee SHLAY-fə

die Nase
dee NAH-zə

die Ohren
dee OH-ren

die Zähne
dee TSAY-nə

die Backe
dee BAK-kə

die Lippen
dee LIP-pen

das Kinn
das KIN

der Mund
dayr MUNT

I fainted.	**Ich habe das Bewusstsein verloren.** *I[ch] hah-bə das bə-VUST-zein fer-loh-ren.*
I have a cut on my ___.	**Ich habe eine Schnittwunde in meiner / meinem ___.** *I[ch] hah-bə ei-nə SHNIT-vun-də in mei-nər / mei-nem ___.*
I have a headache.	**Ich habe Kopfschmerzen.** *I[ch] hah-bə KOPF-shmayrt-sen.*
My vision is blurry.	**Ich sehe verschwommen.** *I[ch] zay-ə fer-SHVOM-men.*
I feel dizzy.	**Ich fühle mich benommen.** *I[ch] f[ue]-lə mi[ch] bə-NOM-men.*
I think I'm pregnant.	**Ich glaube, ich bin schwanger.** *I[ch] glow-bə, i[ch] bin SHVANG-ər.*
I don't think I'm pregnant.	**Ich glaube nicht, dass ich schwanger bin.** *I[ch] glow-bə ni[cht]t, das i[ch] SHVANG-ər bin.*
I think I have an infection.	**Ich glaube, ich habe eine Infektion.** *I[ch] glow-bə i[ch] hah-bə ei-nə in-fek-tsee-ohn.*
I'm having trouble walking.	**Ich habe Probleme beim Gehen.** *I[ch] hah-bə proh-blay-mə beim GAY-en.*
I can't get up.	**Ich kann nicht aufstehen.** *I[ch] kan ni[ch]t owf-shtay-en.*
I was mugged.	**Ich wurde überfallen.** *I[ch] vur-də [ue]-bər-FAL-len.*
I was raped.	**Ich wurde vergewaltigt.** *I[ch] vur-də fer-gə-val-tikt.*

A dog attacked me.	**Ich wurde von einem Hund angegriffen.** *I[ch] vur-də fon ei-nem HUNT an-gə-grif-fen.*
A snake bit me.	**Ich wurde von einer Schlange gebissen.** *I[ch] vur-də fon ei-nər SHLANG-ə gə-bis-sen.*
I can't move my ____ without pain.	**Ich kann mein / meinen / meine ____ nicht schmerzfrei bewegen.** *I[ch] kan mein / mei-nen / mei-nə ____ ni[ch]t schmerts-frei bə-VAY-gen.*
I think I sprained my ankle	**Ich glaube, ich habe mir den Fuß verstaucht.** *I[ch] glow-bə, i[ch] hah-bə meer dayn FOOS fer-shtow[kh]t.*

MEDICATIONS

Please fill this prescription.	**Ich möchte das hier abholen.** *I[ch] m[oe][ch]-tə das heer AP-hoh-len.*
I need a prescription for ____.	**Ich brauche ein Rezept für ____.** *I[ch] brow-[kh]ə ein ray-TSEPT f[ue]r ____.*
I need morning-after pills.	**Ich brauche Pillen für den Morgen danach.** *I[ch] brow-[kh]ə PIL-len f[ue]r dayn mor-gen da-NAH[KH].*
I need birth control pills.	**Ich brauche Antibabypillen.** *I[ch] brow-[kh]ə an-tee-BAY-bee-pil-len.*

I lost my eyeglasses and need new ones.	**Ich habe meine Brille verloren und benötige eine neue.** *I[ch] hah-bə mei-nə BRIL-lə fer-loh-ren unt bə-n[oe]-ti-gə ei-nə NOY-ə.*
I need new contact lenses.	**Ich benötige neue Kontaktlinsen.** *I[ch] bə-n[oe]-ti-gə noy-ə kon-TAKT-lin-zen.*
I need erectile dysfunction pills.	**Ich benötige Pillen gegen Erektionsstörungen.** *I[ch] bə-n[oe]-ti-gə pil-len gay-gen ay-rek-tsee-OHNS-sht[oe]-rung-en.*
I am allergic to ___.	**Ich bin allergisch gegen ___.** *I[ch] bin al-LAYR-gish gay-gen ___.*
penicillin	**Penizillin** *pen-nee-tsee-LEEN*
antibiotics	**Antibiotika** *an-tee-bee-YOH-tee-kah*
sulfa drugs	**schwefelhaltige Medikamente** *SHVAY-fel-hal-tig-gə may-dee-kah-men-tə*
steroids	**Steroide** *shtay-roh-EE-də*
I have asthma.	**Ich habe Asthma.** *I[ch] hah-bə AST-mah.*

DENTAL PROBLEMS

I have a toothache.	**Ich habe Zahnschmerzen.** *I[ch] hah-bə TSAHN-shmayrt-sen.*
I chipped a tooth.	**Ich habe einen abgebrochenen Zahn.** *I[ch] hah-bə ei-nen ap-gə-bro-[ch]e-nen TSAHN.*
My bridge came loose.	**Meine Brücke hat sich gelöst.** *Mei-nə BR[UE]-kə hat zi[ch] gə-l[oe]st.*
I lost a crown.	**Ich habe eine Krone verloren.** *I[ch] hah-bə ei-nə KROH-nə fer-loh-ren.*
I lost a denture plate.	**Ich habe eine Zahnprotese verloren.** *I[ch] hah-bə ei-nə TSAHN-proh-tay-zə fer-loh-ren.*

AT THE POLICE STATION

I'm sorry, did I do something wrong?	**Verzeihung, habe ich etwas falsch gemacht?** *Fer-TSEI-ung, hah-bə i[ch] et-vas FALSH gə-ma[kh]t?*
I am ___.	**Ich bin ___.** *I[ch] bin ___.*
American	**Amerikaner (m.) / Amerikanerin (f.)** *ah-may-ree-KAH-nər / ah-may-ree-KAH-nə-rin*
British	**Brite (m.) / Britin (f.)** *BREE-tə / BREE-tin*
Canadian	**Kanadier (m.) / Kanadierin (f.)** *kah-NAH-dee-ər / kah-NAH-dee-ə-rin*

For full coverage of nationalities, see p108.

For full coverage of nationalities, see p108.

HEALTH & SAFETY

Listen Up: Police Lingo

Führerschein, Fahrzeug- und Versicherungspapiere, bitte. *F[ue]-rər-shein, fahr-tsoyg-unt fer-ZI-[CH]E-rungs-pah-pee-rə, bit-ə.*	Your license, registration and insurance, please.
Die Strafe beträgt 10 €. Sie können direkt bezahlen. *Dee shtrah-fə bay-traykt tsayn OY-roh. Zee k[oe]n-nen dee-REKT bay-tsah-len.*	The fine is €10. You can pay me directly.
Ihren Ausweis, bitte? *EE-ren OWS-veis, bit-ə?*	Your passport please?
Wohin sind Sie unterwegs? *Voh-hin zint zee un-tər-VAYKS?*	Where are you going?
Warum haben Sie es denn so eilig? *Vah-rum hah-ben zee es den zoh EI-li[ch]?*	Why are you in such a hurry?

The car is a rental.	**Das Auto ist ein Mietwagen.** *Das ow-toh ist ein MEET-vah-gen.*
Do I pay the fine to you?	**Zahle ich die Strafe direkt an Sie?** *Tsah-lə i[ch] dee shtrah-fə dee-rekt an ZEE?*
Do I have to go to court?	**Komme ich vor Gericht?** *Kom-mə i[ch] fohr gə-RI[CH]T?*
I'm sorry, my German isn't very good.	**Verzeihung, mein Deutsch ist nicht besonders gut.** *Fer-TSEI-ung, mein doytsh ist ni[ch]t bə-zon-ders GOOT.*
I need an interpreter.	**Ich benötige einen Dolmetscher.** *I[ch] bə-n[oe]ti-gə ei-nen DOL-met-shər.*
I'm sorry, I don't understand the ticket.	**Verzeihung, ich verstehe den Strafzettel nicht.** *Fer-TSEI-ung, i[ch] fer-shtay-ə dayn SHTRAHF-tset-tel ni[ch]t.*
May I call my embassy?	**Darf ich meine Botschaft anrufen?** *Darf i[ch] mei-nə BOHT-shaft an-roo-fen?*
I was robbed.	**Ich wurde ausgeraubt.** *I[ch] vur-də ows-gə-rowpt.*
I was mugged.	**Ich wurde überfallen.** *I[ch] vur-də [ue]-bər-FAL-len.*
I was raped.	**Ich wurde vergewaltigt.** *I[ch] vur-də fer-gə-VAL-tikt.*
Do I need to make a report?	**Muss ich eine Aussage machen?** *Mus i[ch] ei-nə OWS-zah-gə ma-[kh]en?*
Somebody broke into my room.	**In mein Zimmer wurde eingebrochen.** *In mein tsim-mər vur-də EIN-gə-bro-[kh]en.*

Someone stole ____.	**Mir wurde ____ gestohlen.**
	Meer vur-də ____ gə-shtoh-len.
my purse	**meine Handtasche**
	mei-nə HANT-tash-ə
my wallet	**meine Geldbörse**
	mei-nə GELT-b[oe]r-zə
my cell phone	**mein Mobiltelefon**
	mein moh-BEEL-te-le-fohn
my passport	**mein Ausweis**
	mein OWS-veis
my laptop	**mein Laptop**
	mein LEP-top
my backpack	**mein Rucksack**
	mein RUK-zak
my camera	**meine Kamera**
	mei-nə KAM-mə-rah

DICTIONARY KEY

n	noun	m	masculine
v	verb	f	feminine
adj	adjective	gn	gender neutral
prep	preposition	s	singular
adv	adverb	pl	plural
pron	pronoun		

All verbs are listed in infinitive (to + verb) form, cross-referenced to the appropriate conjugations page. Adjectives are listed first in masculine singular form, followed by the feminine ending.

For food terms, see the Menu Reader (p85) and Grocery section (p90) in Chapter 4, Dining.

A

able, to be able to (can) *v*
  können p26
above *adj über* p6
accept *v* p21 *akzeptieren*
  Do you accept credit cards?
  *Akzeptieren Sie
  Kreditkarten?* p32
accident *n der Unfall m* p51
  I've had an accident. *Ich
  hatte einen Unfall.*
account *n das Konto gn*
  **I'd like to transfer to / from
  my checking / savings
  account.** *Ich möchte etwas
  auf mein / von meinem
  Girokonto / Sparkonto
  überweisen.*
acne *n die Akne f* p166
across *prep über* p5
  across the street *auf der
  anderen Straßenseite*
actual *adj tatsächlich,
  eigentlich, wirklich* p15
adapter *n der Adapter m*

adapter plug *n der
  Adapterstecker m*
address *n die Adresse f*
  What's the address?
  Wie lautet die Adresse?
admission fee *n der
  Eintrittspreis f* p134
in advance *im Voraus*
African-American *adj
  afroamerikanisch*
afternoon *n der Nachmittag
  m* p13
  in the afternoon
  nachmittags
age *n das Alter gn*
  What's your age? *Wie alt
  sind Sie? (formal) / Wie alt
  bist du? (informal)*
agency *n die Agentur / das
  Büro f/gn*
  car rental agency *die
  Autovermietung f*
agnostic *adj agnostisch*
air conditioning *n die
  Klimaanlage f* p61

Would you lower / raise the air conditioning? *Könnten Sie die Klimaanlage bitte auf eine niedrigere / höhere Temperatur einstellen?*

airport *n der Flughafen m*

I need a ride to the airport. *Ich muss zum Flughafen.*
How far is it from the airport? *Wie weit ist das vom Flughafen entfernt?*

airsickness bag *n die Spucktüte f* p42

aisle (in store) *n der Gang m*

Which aisle is it in? *In welchem Gang finde ich das?*

alarm clock *n der Wecker m* p68

alcohol *n der Alkohol m*

Do you serve alcohol? *Haben Sie alkoholische Getränke?*
I'd like nonalcoholic beer. *Ich hätte gerne ein alkoholfreies Bier.*

all *n Alles* p11

all *adj ganz; alle*

all of the time *die ganze Zeit*
That's all, thank you. *Danke, das ist alles.*

allergic *adj allergisch* p68

I'm allergic to ___. *Ich bin allergisch gegen ___.* See p79 and 172 for common allergens.

I think I'm having an allergic reaction. *Ich glaube, ich habe eine allergische Reaktion.* p168

also *auch adv* p15

altitude *n die Höhe f* p150

aluminum *n das Aluminium gn*

ambulance *n der Krankenwagen m*

Call an ambulance. *Rufen Sie einen Krankenwagen.* p7

American *n der Amerikaner m, die Amerikanerin f* p110

amount *n die Menge (things) / der Betrag (money) f/m*

angry *adj wütend*

animal *n das Tier gn*

another *adj noch ein / eine / einen* p81

answer *n die Antwort f*

answer, to answer (phone call, question) *v* p21 *beantworten (question) / entgegennehmen (phone call)*

Answer me, please. *Antworten Sie mir bitte.*

antibiotic *n das Antibiotikum gn*

I need an antibiotic. *Ich brauche ein Antibiotikum.*

antihistamine *n das Antihistamin gn* p165

anxious *adj besorgt* p109

any *adj beliebig*

anything n alles / irgend etwas
anywhere adv überall / irgendwo
April n der April m p14
appointment n der Termin m p134
 Do I need an appointment? Benötige ich einen Termin?
are v See be, to be p23
arrive v ankommen
arrival(s) n die Ankunft f
art n die Kunst f
art exhibit die Kunstausstellung
art adj Kunst-
art museum das Kunstmuseum
artist n der Künstler m, die Künstlerin f
Asian adj asiatisch p73
ask for (request) v bitten um p24
ask a question v fragen p21
aspirin n das Aspirin gn p166
assist v helfen p24
assistance n die Hilfe f
asthma n das Asthma gn p172
 I have asthma. Ich habe Asthma.
atheist adj atheistisch p113
ATM n der Geldautomat m
 I'm looking for an ATM. Ich suche einen Geldautomaten.
attend v teilnehmen (meeting) / behandeln (doctor) p21, 24

audio adj Audio- p58
August n der August m p14
aunt n die Tante f p105
Australian n der Australier m, die Australierin f
Austrian n der Österreicher m, die Österreicherin p108
autumn n der Herbst m p14
available adj verfügbar p133

B
baby n das Baby gn p107
baby adj Baby- / für Babys p91
 Do you sell baby food? Verkaufen Sie Babynahrung?
babysitter n der Babysitter m
 Do you have babysitters who speak English? Haben Sie englischsprachige Babysitter?
back n der Rücken m
 My back hurts. Mein Rücken schmerzt.
backpack n der Rucksack m
back rub n die Rückenmassage f p159
backed up (toilet) adj verstopft
 The toilet is backed up. Die Toilette ist verstopft.
bad schlecht adj p15
bag n die Tasche f, die Tüte f
 airsickness bag die Spucktüte p42
 My bag was stolen. Meine Tasche wurde gestohlen.

I lost my bag. *Ich habe meine Tasche verloren.*

bag *v einpacken* p21

baggage *n das Gepäck gn* p33

baggage *adj Gepäck-* p42

baggage claim *Gepäckausgabe*

bait *n der Köder m*

balance (on bank account) *n der Kontostand m*

balance *v balancieren* p21 *(something shaky) / begleichen (invoice)* p24

balcony *n der Balkon m* p62

bald *adj kahl* p15

ball (sport) *n der Ball m*

ballroom dancing *n der Gesellschaftstanz m*

band (musical ensemble) *n die Band f* p154

band-aid *n das Pflaster gn*

bank *n die Bank f* p122

Can you help me find a bank? *Könnten Sie mir bitte helfen, eine Bank zu finden?*

bar *n die Bar f*

barber *n der (Herren-) Frisör m*

bass (instrument) *n der Bass m*

bath (spa) *n das Bad gn*

bathroom (restroom) *n die Toilette / das WC f/gn* p64

Where is the nearest public bathroom? *Wo finde ich das nächste öffentliche WC?*

bathtub *n die Badewanne f* p64

bathe, to bathe oneself *v baden / ein Bad nehmen* p21, 24

battery (for flashlight) *n die Batterie f*

battery (for car) *n die Batterie f*

bee *n die Biene f*

I was stung by a bee. *Ich wurde von einer Biene gestochen.*

be *v sein* p23

beach *n der Strand m* p118

beach *v stranden*

beard *n der Bart m*

beautiful *adj schön* p107

bed *n das Bett gn* p60

beer *n das Bier gn* p82

beer on tap *das Bier vom Fass*

begin *v beginnen / anfangen* p24

behave *v sich benehmen* p24

well behaved *brav* p15

behind *adv hinter* p5

Belgian *n der Belgier m, die Belgierin f* p108

below *adv unter* p6

belt *n der Gürtel m* p138

conveyor belt *das Transportband*

berth *n die Koje f*

best *am besten*

bet *v wetten* p21

better *besser*

big *adj groß* p12

bilingual *adj zweisprachig*

ENGLISH—GERMAN

bill (currency) n der (Geld-)Schein m

bill v berechnen p21

billion n die Milliarde f p15

biography n die Biografie f

bird n der Vogel m

birth control n die Pille f p161

birth control adj Antibaby- p171

I'm out of birth control pills. Ich habe keine Antibabypillen mehr.

I need more birth control pills. Ich brauche mehr Antibabypillen.

bit (small amount) n ein bisschen gn

black adj schwarz p163

blanket n die (Bett-)Decke f p41

bleach n das Bleichmittel gn

blend v mischen p15

blind adj blind

block v blockieren p21

blogging v Bloggen p21

blond(e) adj blond

blouse n die Bluse f p137

blue adj blau

blurry adj verschwommen p170

board n die Tafel f

on board an Bord

board v einsteigen / an Bord gehen p24

boarding pass n die Bordkarte f p39

boat n das Boot gn

bomb n die Bombe f

book n das Buch gn p141

bookstore n die Buchhandlung f p140

bordello n der Puff m p15

boss n der Chef m, die Chefin f

bottle n die Flasche f p82

May I heat this (baby) bottle someplace? Kann ich dieses (Baby-)Fläschchen irgendwo aufwärmen?

bottle opener n der Flaschenöffner f p68

box (seat) n die Loge f p148

box office n der Kartenverkauf m

boy n der Junge m

boyfriend n der Freund m p104

braid n der Zopf m

braille, American n die englische Blindenschrift f

brake n die Bremse f p48

emergency brake die Notbremse

brake v bremsen p21

brandy n der Brandy m p83

brave adj tapfer p15

Brazilian n das Brasilianer m

Brazilian wax n das Brazilian Waxing m p144

bread n das Brot p86

break v (zer-)brechen p24

breakfast n das Frühstück gn

What time is breakfast?
Um wie viel Uhr gibt es Frühstück?
bridge (across a river, dental) *n die Brücke f* p173
briefcase *n der Aktenkoffer m* p43
bright *adj hell*
broadband *n Breitband-*
bronze *adj bronzefarben*
brother *n der Bruder m* p104
brown *adj braun*
brunette *n die Brünette f*
Buddhist *n der Buddhist m, die Buddhistin f* p113
budget *n das Budget gn*
buffet *n das Buffet gn*
bug *n der Käfer m, das Insekt gn*
bulkhead seat *n der Sitz hinter der Trennwand m* p35
burn *v brennen* p24

Can I burn a CD here? *Kann ich hier eine CD brennen?* p126
bus *n der Bus m* p54

Where is the bus stop?
Wo ist die nächste Bushaltestelle?
Which bus goes to ____?
Welcher Bus fährt nach ____?
business *n das Unternehmen gn*
business *adj Geschäfts-* p66

business center *das Geschäftszentrum*

busy *adj gut besucht* (restaurant), *besetzt* (phone)
butter *n die Butter f* p87
buy *v kaufen* p21

C
café *n das Café gn* p31

Internet café *das Internetcafé*
call *v rufen* (shout) *anrufen* (phone) p24
camera *n die Kamera f* p176
camp *v zelten* p21
camper *n das Wohnmobil* (van) / *der Wohnwagen* (trailer) gn/m
camping *adj Camping-*

Do we need a camping permit? *Benötigen wir eine Campingerlaubnis?*
campsite *n der Campingplatz m*
can *n die Dose f*
can (able to) *v können* p26
Canada *n Kanada*
Canadian *adj kanadisch*
cancel *v stornieren* p21

My flight was canceled.
Mein Flug wurde storniert.
canvas *n die Leinwand f* (for painting), *der Stoff m* p43 (material)
cappuccino *n der Cappuccino m*
car *n das Auto gn*

car rental agency *die Autovermietung*

I need a rental car. *Ich benötige einen Mietwagen.*

card *n die Karte f*

Do you accept credit cards? *Akzeptieren Sie Kreditkarten?*

May I have your business card? *Könnte ich bitte Ihre Visitenkarte haben?*

car seat (child's safety seat) *n der Kindersitz m*

Do you rent car seats for children? *Vermieten Sie Kindersitze?*

carsickness *n die Autokrankheit f*

cash *n das Bargeld gn* p50

cash only *Nur Bargeld* p50

cash *v einlösen (check)* p21

to cash out (gambling) *auszahlen lassen* p164

cashmere *n der Kaschmir m*

casino *n das Kasino gn* p59

cat *n die Katze f*

cathedral *n der Dom m* p15

Catholic *adj katholisch* p113

cavity (tooth cavity) *n das Loch gn*

I think I have a cavity. *Ich glaube, ich habe ein Loch im Zahn.*

CD *n die CD f* p45

CD player *n der CD-Player m* p45

celebrate *v feiern* p21

cell phone *n das Mobiltelefon / das Handy gn* p176

centimeter *n der Zentimeter m*

chamber music *n die Kammermusik f*

change (money) *n das Wechselgeld gn*

I'd like change, please. *Geben Sie mir bitte Wechselgeld.*

This isn't the correct change. *Das Wechselgeld stimmt leider nicht.*

change, to change (money, clothes) *v wechseln* p21

changing room *n die Umkleidekabine f*

charge, to charge (money) *v abbuchen* p21

charge, to charge (a battery) *v aufladen* p24

charmed *adj entzückt*

charred (meat) *adj verschmort* p78

charter *v chartern* p21

cheap *adj billig*

check *n der Scheck m* p120

Could I have the check, please? *Könnte ich bitte die Rechnung haben?*

check *v überprüfen / sich vergewissern* p21

checked (pattern) *adj kariert*

check-in *n der Check-In / das Einchecken m/gn* p30

Is online check-in available?
Gibt es einen Online-Check-in?

What time is check-in?
Um wie viel Uhr wird eingecheckt?

check-out *n* der Check-Out / das Auschecken *m/gn*

check-out time *Uhrzeit für das Auschecken*

What time is check-out?
Um wie viel Uhr wird ausgecheckt?

check out *v* auschecken **p21**

cheese *n* der Käse *m* **p89**

chicken *n* das Hähnchen *gn* **p88**

child *n* das Kind *gn*

My child is missing. *Mein Kind ist ist weg.*

children *n* Kinder *gn* **p106**

Are children allowed? *Sind Kinder erlaubt?*

Do you have children's programs? *Haben Sie ein Programm für Kinder?*

Do you have a children's menu? *Haben Sie ein Kindermenü?*

chiropractor *n* der Chiropraktiker *m* **p167**

church *n* die Kirche *f* **p113**

cigar *n* die Zigarre *f* **p38**

cigarette *n* die Zigarette *f*

a pack of cigarettes *eine Schachtel Zigaretten*

cinema *n* das Kino *gn*

city *n* die Stadt *f* **p61**

claim *n* die Reklamation *f*

I'd like to file a claim. *Ich möchte etwas reklamieren.*

clarinet *n* die Klarinette *f*

class *n* die Klasse *f* **p34**

business class *die Business-Klasse*

economy class *die Economy-Klasse*

first class *die Erste Klasse*

classical (music) *adj* klassisch

clean *adj* sauber

clean *v* reinigen **p21**

Please clean the room today. *Reinigen Sie bitte heute das Zimmer.*

clear *v* räumen **p21**

clear *adj* klar

climbing *n* das Klettern *gn*

climb *v* klettern (mountain) / steigen (stairs) **p21, 24**

to climb a mountain *bergsteigen*

to climb stairs *Treppen steigen*

close *v* schließen **p24**

close (near) *nah* **p5**

closed *adj* gesperrt **p50**

cloudy *adj* bewölkt **p111**

clover *n* der Klee *m*

go clubbing *v* einen Nachtclub besuchen **p21**

cocktail *n* der cocktail *m* **p82**

coat *n* die Jacke *f* **p137**

ENGLISH—GERMAN

coffee n der Kaffee m p84
iced coffee der Eiskaffee
cognac n der Kognak m p83
coin n die Münze f
cold n die Erkältung f p100
I have a cold. Ich habe eine Erkältung.
cold adj kalt p81
I'm cold. Mir ist kalt.
It's cold out. Es ist kalt draußen.
coliseum n das Sportstadion gn
collect adj unfrei
I'd like to place a collect call. Ich möchte ein R-Gespräch führen.
collect v sammeln p21
college n die Hochschule f
color n die Farbe f p138
color v färben p21
computer n der Computer m
computer programmer n der Programmierer m p111
concert n das Konzert gn p118
condition n der Zustand m
in good / bad condition in gutem / schlechtem Zustand
condom n das Kondom gn p161
Do you have a condom? Hast du ein Kondom?
not without a condom nicht ohne Kondom
condor n der Kondor m
confirm v bestätigen p21
I'd like to confirm my reservation. Ich möchte meine Reservierung bestätigen.

confused adj verwirrt
congested adj überfüllt
connection speed n die Verbindungs-geschwindigkeit f
consequently adv folglich p15
consistent adj konsequent p15
constipated adj verstopft
I'm constipated. Ich habe Verstopfung.
contact lens n die Kontaktlinse f
I lost my contact lens. Ich habe meine Kontaktlinse verloren.
continue v fortsetzen p21
convertible n das Cabrio gn
cook v kochen p21
I'd like a room where I can cook. Ich hätte gerne ein Zimmer mit Kochgelegenheit.
cookie n der Keks m p90
copper adj Kupfer-
corner n die Ecke f
on the corner an der Ecke
correct v korrigieren p21
correct adj richtig
Am I on the correct train? Bin ich im richtigen Zug?
cost v kosten p21
How much does it cost? Wie viel kostet das?
Costa Rican adj costa-ricanisch
costume n das Kostüm gn

cotton n die Baumwolle f p137

cough n der Husten m p165

cough v husten **p21**

counter (in bar) n die Theke f p77

country music n die Country-Musik f p114

court (legal) n das Gericht gn p51, 175

court (sport) n der Platz m

courteous adj zuvorkommend p72

cousin n der Cousin m, die Cousine f

cover charge (in bar) n der Eintrittspreis m

cow n die Kuh f

crack (in glass object) n der Sprung m

craftsperson n der Handwerker m, die Handwerkerin f p110

cream n die Sahne f p87

credit card n die Kreditkarte f p120

Do you accept credit cards? Akzeptieren Sie Kreditkarten?

crib n das Kinderbett gn p62

crown (dental) n die Krone f

curb n der Bordstein m

curl n die Locke f

curly adj gelockt

currency exchange n die Geldwechselstube f p31, 120

Where is the nearest currency exchange? Wo finde ich die nächste Geldwechselstube?

current adj aktuell p15

current (water) n die Strömung f

customs n der Zoll m

cut (wound) n der Schnitt m p170

I have a bad cut. Ich habe eine tiefe Schnittwunde.

cut v schneiden **p24**

cybercafé n das Internetcafé gn

Where can I find a cybercafé? Wo finde ich ein Internetcafé?

Czech n der Tscheche m, die Tschechin f p108

D

damaged adj beschädigt p43

Damn! expletive Verdammt!

dance v tanzen **p21**

danger n die Gefahr f p50

Danish n der Däne m, die Dänin f p108

dark n die Dunkelheit f

dark adj dunkel

daughter n die Tochter f p107

day n der Tag m p46

the day before yesterday vorgestern p4

these last few days die letzten paar Tage

dawn n die Morgendämmerung f

at dawn bei Tagesanbruch

dazzle v blenden p15

deaf adj taub

deal (bargain) n das Schnäppchen gn

> **What a great deal!** Was für ein großartiges Schnäppchen!

deal (cards) v geben p24

> **Deal me in.** Ich bin dabei.

December n der Dezember m p14

declare v verzollen (customs) p21

> **I have nothing to declare.** Ich habe nichts zu verzollen.

declined adj abgelehnt

> **Was my credit card declined?** Wurde meine Kreditkarte nicht akzeptiert?

deep adj tief p151

delay n die Verspätung f p34, 37

> **How long is the delay?** Wie viel beträgt die Verspätung?

delighted adj erfreut

democracy n die Demokratie f

dent v verbeulen p21

> **He / She dented the car.** Er / Sie hat das Auto verbeult.

dentist n der Zahnarzt m p167

denture n das Gebiss gn

> **denture plate** die Zahnprothese

departure n die Abreise f

depressed adj niedergeschlagen p109

dermatologist n der Hautarzt m p167

designer n der Designer m, die Designerin f p109

dessert n die Nachspeise f p86

> **dessert menu** die Dessertkarte

destination n das Ziel gn

diabetic adj Diabetiker- p35, 78

dial (a phone) v wählen p21

> **dial direct** durchwählen

diaper n die Windel f

> **Where can I change a diaper?** Wo kann ich hier Windeln wechseln?

diarrhea n der Durchfall m p166

dictionary n das Wörterbuch gn

different (other) adj anders p70, 138

difficult adj schwierig p150

dinner n das Abendessen gn p75, 85, 118

directory assistance (phone) n die Telefonauskunft f

dirty adj schmutzig p70

disability n die Behinderung f

disappear v verschwinden p24

disco n die Disko f

disconnected adj unterbrochen p126

> **Operator, I was disconnected.** Vermittlung, mein Gespräch wurde unterbrochen.

discount n der Preisnachlass m
Do I qualify for a discount? Bekomme ich einen Preisnachlass?
dish n das Gericht g n p79
dive v tauchen p21
scuba dive tauchen (mit Atemgerät)
divorced adj geschieden
dizzy adj benommen p170
do v tun p24
doctor n der Arzt m, die Ärztin f p7, 109, 167
I need a doctor. Ich brauche einen Arzt.
doctor's office n die Arztpraxis f
dog n der Hund m p19, 37
service dog der Blindenhund p37, 58
dollar n der Dollar m
dome n die Kuppel f p15
door n die Tür f
double adj Doppel- p9
double bed das Doppelbett p60
double vision doppelt sehen
down adj abwärts p6
download v herunterladen p24
downtown n das Stadtzentrum g n
dozen n das Dutzend g n p11
drain n der Abfluss m
drama n das Drama g n

drawing (work of art) n die Zeichnung f
dress (garment) n das Kleid g n
dress (general attire) n die Kleidung f p155
What's the dress code? Welche Kleidung ist vorgeschrieben?
dress v anziehen p24, 29
Should I dress up for that affair? Muss ich mich dafür herausputzen?
dressing (salad) n das Dressing g n
dried adj getrocknet / Trocken- p98
drink n das Getränk g n p164
I'd like a drink. Ich hätte gerne etwas zu trinken.
drink v trinken p24
drip v tropfen p21
drive v fahren p24
driver n der Fahrer m p51
driving range n die Driving Range f
drum n die Trommel f
dry adj trocken
This towel isn't dry. Dieses Handtuch ist nicht trocken.
dry v trocknen p21
I need to dry my clothes. Ich muss meine Kleidung trocknen.
dry cleaner n die chemische Reinigung f
dry cleaning n das chemische Reinigen g n

duck n die Ente f

Dutch n der Niederländer m, die Niederländerin f p108

duty-free adj zollfrei

duty-free shop n der Duty-Free-Shop m p32

DVD n die DVD f p45

Do the rooms have DVD players? Gibt es auf den Zimmern einen DVD-Player?

Where can I rent DVDs or videos? Wo kann ich DVDs oder Videos ausleihen?

E

early adj früh p13

It's early. Es ist früh.

eat v essen p24

to eat out auswärts essen

economy n die Wirtschaft f

editor n der Redakteur m, die Redakteurin f p109

educator n der Erzieher m, die Erzieherin f p109

eggs n die Eier f p91

eight adj acht p8

eighteen adj Achtzehn p8

eighth adj achter p10

eighty adj achtzig p8

election n die Wahl f p112

electrical hookup n der Elektroanschluss m p72

elevator n der Aufzug m p58

eleven adj elf p8

email n die E-Mail f p118

May I have your email address? Kann ich Ihre (formal) / deine (informal) E-Mail-Adresse haben?

email message die E-Mail-Nachricht

email v eine E-Mail senden p21

embassy n die Botschaft f

emergency n der Notfall m

emergency brake n die Notbremse f

emergency exit n der Notausgang m p35

employee n der Mitarbeiter m, die Mitarbeiterin f

employer n der Arbeitgeber m

engine n der Motor m p47

engineer n der Ingenieur m, die Ingenieurin f p109

England n England

English n, adj englisch, der Engländer m, die Engländerin f p2

Do you speak English? Sprechen Sie Englisch? p2

enjoy v genießen p24

enter v betreten p24

Do not enter. Kein Eingang.

enthusiastic adj begeistert p109

entrance n der Eingang m p33

envelope n das Kuvert gn p128

environment n die Umwelt f

escalator n die Rolltreppe f

espresso n der Espresso m

exchange rate n der Wechselkurs m p121

What is the exchange rate for US / Canadian dollars? *Welcher Wechselkurs gilt für US-Dollar / kanadische Dollar?*

excuse (pardon) v entschuldigen p21

Excuse me. *Entschuldigung.*

exhausted adj erschöpft

exhibit n die Ausstellung f

exit n der Ausgang m p33

not an exit *kein Ausgang*

exit v verlassen p24

expensive adj teuer p74, 140, 155

explain v erklären p21

express adj Express- p34, 55

express check-in *der Express-Check-In*

extra (additional) adj zusätzlich p67

extra-large adj besonders groß

eye n das Auge gn p167

eyebrow n die Augenbraue f

eyeglasses n die Brille f

eyelash n die Wimper f

F

fabric n der Stoff m

face n das Gesicht gn

faint v ohnmächtig werden p24

fall (season) n der Herbst m

fall v fallen p24

family n die Familie f p104

fan n der Ventilator (blower) / der Fan (sport) m

far weit p5

How far is it to _____? *Wie weit ist es nach / zur / zum _____?*

fare n der Fahrpreis m

fast adj schnell p50, 151

fat adj beleibt

father n der Vater m p104

faucet n der Wasserhahn m

fault n der Fehler m p51

I'm at fault. *Es war mein Fehler.*

It was his fault. *Es war sein Fehler.*

February n der Februar m p14

fee n die Gebühr f

female adj weiblich

fiancé(e) n der Verlobte m, die Verlobte f p105

fifteen adj fünfzehn p8

fifth adj fünfter p10

fifty adj fünfzig m p8

find v finden p24

fine (for traffic violation) n die Strafe f p50, 174

fine gut p1

I'm fine. *Mir geht es gut.*

fire! n Feuer! gn

first adj erste / erster / erstes p10

fishing pole n die Angelrute f

fitness center n das Fitness-Center gn p59

ENGLISH—GERMAN

fit (clothes) v passen
> **Does this look like it fits?**
> Passt mir das?

fitting room n die
Umkleidekabine f

five adj fünf p8

flight n der Flug m p32
> **Where do domestic flights arrive / depart?** Wo finde ich den Ankunftsbereich / Abflugbereich für Inlandsflüge?
> **Where do international flights arrive / depart?** Wo finde ich den Ankunftsbereich / Abflugbereich für Auslandsflüge?
> **What time does this flight leave?** Welche Abflugzeit hat dieser Flug?

flight attendant der
Flugbegleiter m / die
Flugbegleiterin f

floor n die Etage f
> **ground floor** das Erdgeschoß
> **second floor** das erste Stockwerk

Note that in German, the second floor is called the first, the third is the second, etc.

flower n die Blume f

flush (gambling) n der Flush m

flush v spülen p21
> **This toilet won't flush.**
> Die Toilettenspülung funktioniert nicht.

flute n die Flöte f

food n das Essen gn p81

foot (body part, measurement) n (der) Fuß

forehead n die Stirn f

formula n die Formel f
> **Do you sell infants' formula?** Haben Sie Säuglingsanfangsnahrung?

forty adj vierzig p8

forward adj vorwärts p6

four adj vier p8

fourteen adj vierzehn p8

fourth adj vierter p10
> **one-fourth** ein Viertel

fragile adj zerbrechlich p128

freckle n die Sommersprosse f

French n der Franzose m, die
Französin f p108

fresh adj frisch p79,92

Friday n der Freitag m p13

friend n der Freund m, die
Freundin f p104

front adj Vorder- p35
> **front desk** die Rezeption p66
> **front door** die Vordertür

fruit n die Frucht f p93

fruit juice n der Fruchtsaft m

full, to be full (after a meal) adj satt

Full house! n Full House!

fuse n die Sicherung f

G

garlic n der Knoblauch m p97

gas n das Gas (for cooking) n,
das Benzin (for cars) gn

gas gauge *die Tankanzeige*
out of gas *kein Benzin mehr*
gate (at airport) *n das Gate gn* p30
German *n der/die Deutsche m/f* p108
gift *n das Geschenk gn*
gin *n der Gin m* p83
girl *n das Mädchen gn*
girlfriend *n die Freundin f* p104
give *v geben* p24
glass *n das Glas gn* p81
Do you have it by the glass? *Schenken Sie es als offenes Getränk aus?*
I'd like a glass please. *Ich hätte gerne ein Glas.*
glasses (eye) *n die Brille f*
I need new glasses. *Ich brauche eine neue Brille.*
glove *n der Handschuh m* p152
gluten-free *adj glutenfreie* p35
go *v gehen* p24
goal (sport) *n das Tor gn*
goalie *n der Torwart m* p147
gold *adj Gold-*
golf *n das Golf(-spiel) gn*
golf, to go golfing *v Golf spielen* p21
good *adj gut* p59, 73
goodbye *n der Abschied m* p101
government *n die Regierung f* p112
GPS coordinates *n die GPS-Koordinaten f* p49

GPS system *n das GPS-System n* p45
grade (school) *n die Note f*
gram *n das Gramm gn*
grandfather *n der Großvater m*
grandmother *n die Großmutter f*
grandparents *n die Großeltern pl only*
grape *n die Traube f*
gray *adj grau*
great *adj großartig*
Greek *n der Grieche m, die Griechin f* p108
Greek Orthodox *adj griechisch-orthodox* p113
green *adj grün*
groceries *n die Lebensmittel gn*
group *n die Gruppe f*
grow (get larger) *v wachsen* p24
Where did you grow up? *Wo sind Sie (formal) / bist du (informal) aufgewachsen?*
guard *n der Wachmann m*
security guard *der Sicherheitsbeamte* p31
guest *n der Gast m*
guide (of tours) *n der Fremdenführer / die Fremdenführerin m/f*
guide (publication) *n der Reiseführer m*
guide *v führen* p21
guided tour *n die Fremdenführung f*

guitar *n die Gitarre f* p115
gym *n das Fitnessstudio gn* p146
gynecologist *n der Frauenarzt m*

H

hair *n das Haar gn, die Haare pl*
haircut *n der Haarschnitt m*
> **I need a haircut.** *Ich muss mir mir die Haare schneiden lassen.*
> **How much is a haircut?** *Wie viel kostet ein Haarschnitt?*

hairdresser *n der Frisör m, die Frisörin f*
hair dryer *n der Haartrockner m* p69
half *n die Hälfte f*
one-half *halb-* p99
hallway *n der Gang m*
hand *n die Hand f* p158
handicapped-accessible *adj behindertengerecht*
handle *v handhaben* p21
handsome *adj gut aussehend* p107, 160
hangout (hot spot) *n der Treff m*
hang out (to relax) *v entspannen / abhängen (slang)* p21, 24
hang up (to end a phone call) *v auflegen* p21
hanger *n der Kleiderbügel m*
happy *adj fröhlich* p107
hard *adj schwierig* (difficult), *hart* (firm) p43

hat *n der Hut m*
have *v haben* p24
hazel *adj nussbraun*
headache *n die Kopfschmerzen pl* p100, 170
headlight *n der Scheinwerfer m*
headphones *n der Kopfhörer m*
hear *v hören* p21
hearing-impaired *adj hörgeschädigt*
heart *n das Herz gn*
heart attack *n der Herzinfarkt m* p168
hello *n Hallo* p1
Help! *n Hilfe!*
help *v helfen* p24
hen *n die Henne f*
her *adj ihr*
herb *n das Kraut gn*
here *n hier* p5
high *adj hoch*
highlights (hair) *n die Strähnchen pl* p144
highway *n die Autobahn f*
hike *v wandern* p21
him *pron ihm / ihn*
hip-hop *n Hiphop* p114
his *adj sein / seine*
historical *adj historisch*
history *n die Geschichte f* p141
hobby *n das Hobby gn*
hold *v halten* p24
> **to hold hands** *Händchen halten*

Would you hold this for me? *Könnten Sie (formal) / Kannst du (informal) das bitte für mich halten?*

hold (to pause) *v innehalten* p24

Hold on a minute! *Einen Moment bitte!*
I'll hold. *Ich warte.*

hold (gambling) *v schieben* p21

holiday *n der Feiertag m*

home *n das Zuhause gn, das Haus gn*

homemaker *n die Hausfrau f*

horn *n die Hupe f*

horse *n das Pferd gn*

hostel *n die Jugendherberge f* p59

hot *adj heiß* p84

hot chocolate *n die heiße Schokolade f* p84

hotel *n das Hotel gn* p59

Do you have a list of local hotels? *Haben Sie eine Liste der örtlichen Hotels?*

hour *n die Stunde f* p126

hours (at museum) *n die Öffnungszeiten pl*

how *adv wie* p3

humid *adj feucht* p111

hundred *n Hundert*

hurry *v sich beeilen* p21

I'm in a hurry. *Ich bin in Eile.*
Hurry, please! *Beeilung, bitte!*

hurt *v verletzen* p21

Ouch! That hurts! *Autsch! Das tut weh!*

husband *n der Ehemann m* p104

I

I *pron ich* p3

ice *n das Eis gn* p80

identification *n die Papiere pl* p39

indigestion *n die Verdauungsstörung f*

inexpensive *adj günstig*

infant *n das Kleinkind gn*

Are infants allowed? *Sind Kleinkinder erlaubt?*

infection *n die Infektion f* p170

information *n die Information f*

information booth *n der Informationsstand m*

insect repellent *n das Insektenschutzmittel gn* p166

inside *adj drinnen* p77

insult *v beleidigen* p21

insurance *n die Versicherung f* p46

intercourse (sexual) *n der (Geschlechts-)Verkehr m*

interest rate *n der Zinssatz m*

intermission *n die Pause f*

Internet *n das Internet gn* p69

Wi-Fi *WLAN* p69

Do you have Internet access? *Haben Sie einen Internetanschluss?*

Where can I find an Internet café? *Wo finde ich ein Internetcafé?*

interpreter *n der Dolmetscher / die Dolmetscherin m/f* p175

I need an interpreter. *Ich benötige einen Dolmetscher.*

introduce *v vorstellen* p21

I'd like to introduce you to ____. *Ich möchte Sie (formal) / dich (informal) mit ____ bekannt machen.*

Ireland *n Irland*

iPod connection *n der iPod-Anschluss f* p45

Irish *n der Ire m, die Irin f*

is *v See* **be (to be)** p23

Italian *n der Italiener m, die Italienerin f* p108

J

jacket *n die Jacke f* p40

January *n der Januar m* p14

Japanese *adj japanisch* p110

jazz *n der Jazz m* p114

Jewish *adj jüdisch* p113

jog, to run *v joggen* p21

juice *n der Saft m* p91

June *n der Juni m* p14

July *n der Juli m* p14

K

keep *v behalten* p24

kid *n das Kind gn*

Are kids allowed? *Sind Kinder erlaubt?*

Do you have kids' programs? *Haben Sie ein Programm für Kinder?*

Do you have a kids' menu? *Haben Sie ein Kindermenü?*

kilo *n das Kilo gn* p11

kilometer *n der Kilometer m*

kind (type) *n die Art f*

What kind is it? *Um welche Art handelt es sich?*

kiss *n der Kuss m* p159

kitchen *n die Küche f* p66

know (something) *v (etwas) wissen* p24

know (someone) *v (jemanden) kennen* p24

kosher *adj koscher* p78

L

lactose-intolerant *adj mit Laktoseunverträglichkeit* p79

land *v landen* p21

landscape *n die Landschaft f*

language *n die Sprache f*

laptop *n das Notebook gn* p143

large *adj groß*

last *v dauern* p21

last *adv letzter* p10

late *adj spät* p13

Please don't be late. *Bitte pünktlich sein.*

later *adv später*

See you later. *Bis später.*
laundry n die Wäscherei
f p67
lavender adj *Lavendel-*
law n das Gesetz gn
lawyer n der Anwalt / die
Anwältin m/f p109
least n das Mindeste gn
least adj mindestens
leather n das Leder gn p43
leave (depart) v abreisen p21
left adj links p6
on the left *auf der linken
Seite*
leg n das Bein gn
lemonade n die Limonade f
less adj weniger
lesson n die
Unterrichtseinheit f
license n die Lizenz f
driver's license *der
Führerschein*
lifeguard n der
Rettungsschwimmer! m
p151
life preserver n die
Schwimmweste f
light n (lamp) das Licht gn p41
light (for cigarette) n das
Feuer gn p156
May I offer you a light?
*Darf ich Ihnen (formal) /
dir (informal) Feuer
geben?*
lighter (cigarette) n das
Feuerzeug m p157
like, desire v gern haben p24

I would like ____. *Ich hätte
gerne ____.*
like v gefallen p28
I like this place. *Mir gefällt
es hier.*
limo n die Limousine f p51
liquor n das alkoholische
Getränk gn p38
liter n der Liter m p11
little adj klein (size), gering
(amount)
live v leben p21
Where do you live? *Wo
bleiben Sie? (formal) / Wo
bleibst du? (informal)*
living n der Lebensunterhalt
m
What do you do for a
living? *Was machen Sie
(formal) / machst du
(informal) beruflich?*
local adj örtlich p46
lock n das Schloss gn p147
lock v abschließen p24
I can't lock the door.
*Die Tür lässt sich nicht
abschließen.*
I'm locked out. *Ich bin
ausgesperrt.*
locker n der Spind m p146
storage locker *der
Aufbewahrungsschrank*
locker room *die Umkleide*
p147
long adv lang p12
For how long? *Für wie
lange?*

long *adj* lang
look *v* (to observe) *umsehen* p24
  I'm just looking. *Ich sehe mich nur um.*
  Look here! *Schau her!*
look *v* (to appear) *aussehen* p24
  How does this look? *Wie sieht das aus?*
look for (to search) *v suchen* p21
  I'm looking for a porter. *Ich suche einen Träger für mein Gepäck.*
loose *adj locker*
lose *v verlieren* p24
  I lost my passport. *Ich habe meinen Ausweis verloren.*
  I lost my wallet. *Ich habe meine Geldbörse verloren.*
  I lost my key. *Ich habe meinen Schlüssel verloren.*
  I'm lost. *Ich habe mich verirrt.*
lost *See* **lose**
loud *adj laut* p71
loudly *adv laut*
lounge *n das Foyer gn*
lounge *v faulenzen* p21
love *n die Liebe f*
love *v lieben* p21
  to love (family) *lieben*
  to love (a friend) *mögen*
  to love (a lover) *lieben*
  to make love *miteinander schlafen*

low *adj niedrig*
lunch *n das Mittagessen gn* p74
luggage *n das Gepäck gn* p52
  Where do I report lost luggage? *Wo kann ich verloren gegangenes Gepäck melden?*
  Where is the lost luggage claim? *Wo finde ich die Ausgabe für verloren gegangenes Gepäck?*

M

machine *n die Maschine f*
made of *adj aus*
magazine *n die Zeitschrift f*
maid (hotel) *n das Zimmermädchen gn*
maiden *adj Mädchen-*
  That's my maiden name. *Das ist mein Mädchenname.*
mail *n die Post f*
  air mail *die Luftpost*
  registered mail *das Einschreiben*
mail *v versenden* p21
make *v machen* p21
makeup *n das Make-up gn*
make up (apologize) *v wiedergutmachen* p21
make up (apply cosmetics) *v schminken* p21
male *n der Mann m* p39
male *adj männlich*
mall *n das Einkaufszentrum gn*

man n der Mann m
manager n der Manager / die Managerin m/f
manual (instruction booklet) n das Handbuch gn p46
many adj viele p11
map n die Karte f p49
March (month) n der März m p14
market n der Markt m p139
  flea market der Flohmarkt m p136
  open-air market der Freiluftmarkt m
married adj verheiratet p105
marry v heiraten p21
massage v massieren p21
match (sport) n das Spiel gn
match n das Streichholz gn
  book of matches das Streichholzbriefchen
match v passen p21
  Does this match my outfit? Passt das zu meinem Outfit?
May (month) n der Mai m p14
may v aux dürfen p24
  May I? Darf ich?
meal n die Mahlzeit f
meat n das Fleisch gn p82
meatball n die Frikadelle f
medication n das Medikament gn
medium (size) adj mittel
medium rare (meat) adj halb gar p77

medium well (meat) adj halb durch p78
member n das Mitglied gn
menu n die Speisekarte f p75
  May I see a menu? Darf ich die Speisekarte haben?
  children's menu Kindermenü
  diabetic menu Diabetikermenü
  kosher menu koscheres Menü
metal detector n der Metalldetektor m
meter n der Meter m p11
middle adj Mittel-
midnight n Mitternacht f
military n das Militär gn
milk n die Milch f p84
  milk shake der Milchshake
milliliter n der Milliliter m
millimeter n der Millimeter m
minute n die Minute f p126
  in a minute gleich
miss, to miss (a flight) v verpassen p21
missing adj fehlend
mistake n der Fehler m
moderately priced adj der mittleren Preiskategorie p59
mole (facial feature) n das Muttermal gn
Monday n der Montag m p13
money n das Geld gn p120
  money transfer die Überweisung

ENGLISH–GERMAN

month *n* der Monat *m* p4
morning *n* der Morgen *m* p13
  in the morning *morgens*
mosque *n* die Moschee *f*
mother *n* die Mutter *f* p104
mother *v* bemuttern p21
motorcycle *n* das Motorrad *gn*
mountain *n* der Berg *m*
  mountain climbing *das Bergsteigen* p149
mouse *n* die Maus *f*
mouth *n* der Mund *m*
move *v* bewegen p21
movie *n* der Film *m* p130
much *n* viel p11
mug, to mug (someone) *v* überfallen p24
  mugged *adj* überfallen
museum *n* das Museum *gn* p118
music *n* die Musik *f* p114
  live music *die Livemusik*
musician *n* der Musiker *m*, die Musikerin *f* p111
muslim *adj* muslimisch p113
mustache *n* der Schnurrbart *m*
mystery (novel) *n* der Mystery-Roman *m*

N
name *n* der Name *m*
  My name is ___. *Ich heiße ___.* p1
  What's your name? *Wie heißen Sie? (formal) / Wie heißt du? (informal)* p1
napkin *n* die Serviette *f*

narrow *adj* schmal p12
nationality *n* die Nationalität *f*
nausea *n* die Übelkeit *f* p166
near *adj* in der Nähe von p5
nearby *adj* in der Nähe p75
neat (tidy) *adj* ordentlich
need *v* benötigen p21
neighbor *n* der Nachbar *m*, die Nachbarin *f* p104
nephew *n* der Neffe *m* p105
network *n* das Netzwerk *gn*
new *adj* neu p152
newspaper *n* die Zeitung *f*
newsstand *n* der Zeitungsstand *m* p32
New Zealand *n* Neuseeland
New Zealander *adj* der Neuseeländer *m*, die Neuseeländerin *f*
next *prep* neben
  next to *neben*
  the next station *der nächste Halt*
nice *adj* nett
niece *n* die Nichte *f* p105
night *n* die Nacht *f* p13
  at night *nachts*
  per night *pro Übernachtung* p63
nightclub *n* der Nachtclub *m*
nine *adj* neun p8
nineteen *adj* neunzehn p8
ninety *adj* neunzig p8
ninth *adj* neunter p10
no *adv* nein p1
noisy *adj* laut p70
none *n* keiner, keine, kein p11

nonsmoking adj
  Nichtraucher-
  nonsmoking area *der*
    Nichtraucherbereich
  nonsmoking room *das*
    Nichtraucherzimmer
noon n *der Mittag m* p13
Norwegian n *der Norweger*
  m, die Norwegerin f p110
nose n *die Nase f*
novel n *der Roman m*
November n *der November*
  m p14
now adv *jetzt* p4
number n *die Nummer f*
  p125
  Which room number?
    Welche Zimmernummer?
  May I have your phone
    number? *Kann ich bitte*
    Ihre Telefonnummer
    haben?
nurse n *der Krankenpfleger*
  m, die Krankenpflegerin
  f p110
nurse v *stillen* p21
  Do you have a place where
    I can nurse? *Haben Sie*
    einen Raum zum Stillen?
nursery n *die Kinderkrippe f*
  Do you have a nursery?
    Haben Sie eine
    Kinderkrippe?
nut n *die Nuss f*

O
o'clock adv *Uhr* p5
  two o'clock *zwei Uhr*

October n *der Oktober m* p14
offer v *anbieten* p24
officer n *der Polizist m, die*
  Polizistin f
oil n *das Öl gn* p49, 78
okay adv *OK, in Ordnung*
old adj *alt*
olive n *die Olive f*
one adj *ein I eine* p8
one way (traffic sign) adj
  Einbahnstraße
open (business) adj *geöffnet*
  p139
  Are you open? *Haben Sie*
    geöffnet?
opera n *die Oper f* p115
operator (phone) n *die*
  Vermittlung f
optometrist n *der Optiker m,*
  die Optikerin f
orange (color) adj *orange*
orange juice n *der*
  Orangensaft m p40
order, to order (demand) v
  befehlen p24
order, to order (request) v
  bestellen p21
organic adj *Bio-*
Ouch! interj *Au!*
outside n *draußen* p77
overcooked adj *zerkocht*
overheat, to overheat v
  überhitzen p21
  The car overheated. *Das*
    Auto hat sich überhitzt.
overflowing adv *überlaufend*
oxygen tank n *die*
  Sauerstoffflasche f

ENGLISH—GERMAN

P

package n das Paket gn p129
pacifier n der Schnuller m
page, to page (someone) v anpiepen **p21**
paint, to paint v streichen **p24**
painting n das Gemälde gn
pale adj blass p111
paper n das Papier gn
parade n der Umzug m
parent n der Elternteil m
park n der Park m p118
park v parken **p21**

  no parking das Parkverbot
  parking fee die Parkgebühr
  parking garage das Parkhaus

partner n der Partner m, die Partnerin f
party n die Partei f p113

  political party die Partei

party n die Party f
pass v passen **p21**

  I'll pass. Ich passe.

passenger n der Passagier m
passport n der Ausweis m

  I've lost my passport. Ich habe meinen Ausweis verloren.

pay v bezahlen **p21**

  Do I have to pay up front? Muss ich im Voraus bezahlen?

peanut n die Erdnuss f
pedestrian adj Fußgänger-
pediatrician n der Kinderarzt m, die Kinderärztin f

  Can you recommend a pediatrician? Können Sie mir einen Kinderarzt empfehlen?

permit n die Genehmigung f

  Do we need a permit? Benötigen wir eine Genehmigung?

permit v erlauben **p21**
phone n das Telefon gn p123

  May I have your phone number? Kann ich bitte Ihre Telefonnummer haben?
  Where can I find a public phone? Wo finde ich eine Telefonzelle?
  phone operator die Vermittlung
  Do you sell prepaid phones? Verkaufen Sie Prepaid-Telefone?

phone adj Telefon-

  Do you have a phone directory? Haben Sie ein Telefonbuch?

phone call n der Telefonanruf m

  I need to make a collect phone call. Ich möchte ein R-Gespräch führen.
  an international phone call ein Auslandsgespräch

photocopy v (foto-)kopieren **p21**
piano n das Klavier gn p115
pillow n das Kissen gn p41

down pillow *das Daunenkissen*

pink *adj rosa*

pizza *n die Pizza f*

place *v platzieren* **p21**

plastic *n der Kunststoff m*

play *n das Theaterstück gn*

play, to play (a game) *v spielen* **p21**

play, to play (an instrument) *v spielen* **p21**

playground *n der Spielplatz m*

Do you have a playground? *Haben Sie einen Spielplatz?*

please (polite entreaty) *adv bitte*

please, to be pleasing to *v gefallen* **p28**

pleasure *n die Freude f* **p1**

It's a pleasure. *Freut mich.*

plug *n der Stecker m*

plug *v einstecken* **p21**

point *v zeigen, weisen* **p21, 24**

Would you point me in the direction of ___? *Wie komme ich zu / zum / zur ___?*

poison *n das Gift gn* **p15**

police *n die Polizei f* **p7**

Call the police! *Rufen Sie die Polizei!*

police station *n die Polizeiwache f* **p31**

Polish *n der Pole m, die Polin f* **p108**

pool *n der Schwimmbad m* **p146**

pool (the game) *n das Poolbillard gn*

pop music *n die Popmusik f*

popular *adj beliebt* **p154**

port (beverage) *n der Portwein m*

port (for ship) *n der Hafen m*

porter *n der Portier m* **p30**

portion *n die Portion f*

portrait *n das Porträt gn*

Portuguese *n der Portugiese m, die Portugiesin f* **p108**

postcard *n die Postkarte f*

post office *n das Postamt gn*

Where is the post office? *Wo befindet sich das Postamt?*

poultry *n das Geflügel gn*

pound *n das Pfund gn* **p99**

prefer *v bevorzugen* **p21**

pregnant *adj schwanger*

prepared *adj vorbereitet*

prescription *n das Rezept gn* **p39**

price *n der Preis m*

print *v drucken* **p21**

private berth / cabin *n eine eigene Kabine f*

problem *n das Problem gn* **p2**

process *v verarbeiten* **p21**

product *n das Produkt gn*

professional *adj professionell*

program *n das Programm gn*

May I have a program? *Geben Sie mir bitte ein Programm.*

Protestant *n der Protestant m, die Protestantin f*
publisher *n der Verleger m, die Verlegerin f*
puff *n der Hauch / Zug m* p15
pull *v ziehen* p24
purple *adj violett*
purse *n der Geldbeutel m*
push *v drücken* p21
put *v setzen, stellen, legen* p21

Q

quarter *adj Viertel-* p9
  one-quarter *Viertel-*
quiet *adj ruhig*

R

rabbit *n der Hase m*
radio *n das Radio gn*
  satellite radio *das Satellitenradio*
rain *v regnen* p21
  Is it supposed to rain? *Soll es regnen?*
rainy *adj regnerisch* p111
  It's rainy. *Es ist regnerisch.*
ramp (wheelchair) *n die Rampe (Rollstuhl) f*
rare (meat) *adj blutig* p77
rate (for car rental, hotel) *n der Preis m*
  What's the rate per day? *Wie hoch ist der Preis pro Tag?*
  What's the rate per week? *Wie hoch ist der Preis pro Woche?*

rate plan (cell phone) *n die Tariftabelle f*
rather *adv lieber*
read *v lesen* p24
really *adv wirklich*
receipt *n die Quittung f* p121, 122
receive *v erhalten* p21
recommend *v empfehlen* p24
red *adj rot*
redhead *n der Rothaarige m, die Rothaarige f*
reef *n das Riff gn*
refill, to refill (of beverage) *v nachschenken* p21
refill (of prescription) *n die erneute Einlösung f* p168
reggae *adj Reggae-* p114
relative (family) *n der / die Verwandte m/f*
remove *v entfernen* p21
rent *v mieten* p21
  I'd like to rent a car. *Ich möchte ein Auto mieten.*
repeat *v wiederholen* p21
  Would you please repeat that? *Könnten Sie das bitte wiederholen?* p2
reservation *n die Reservierung f*
  I'd like to make a reservation for ___. *Ich möchte eine Reservierung für ___.* p63 See p8 for numbers.
restaurant *n das Restaurant gn*
  Where can I find a good restaurant? *Wo finde ich ein gutes Restaurant?*
restroom *n die Toilette f* p31

Do you have a public restroom? *Gibt es hier eine öffentliche Toilette?*

return, to return (to a place) *v zurückkehren* **p21**

return, to return (something to a store) *v zurückgeben* **p24**

ride *v fahren (vehicle) / reiten (horse)* **p21**

right *adj rechts* **p49**

____ **is on the right.** ____ *befindet sich auf der rechten Seite.*

Turn right at the corner. *Biegen Sie an der Ecke nach rechts ab.*

rights *n die Rechte gn, pl*

civil rights *die Bürgerrechte*

river *n der Fluss m* **p151**

road *n die Straße f* **p50**

Road Closed sign *n das Straßensperrschild gn* **p50**

rob *v ausrauben* **p21**

I've been robbed. *Ich wurde ausgeraubt.*

rock music *n die Rockmusik f*

rock climbing *n das Felsenklettern gn*

rocks (ice) *n die Würfel f, pl*

I'd like it on the rocks. *Ich hätte das gerne auf Eis.*

romance (novel) *n der Liebesroman m*

romantic *adj romantisch*

room (hotel) *n das Zimmer gn*

room for one / two *Einzelzimmer / Doppelzimmer*

room service *der Zimmerservice*

rose *n die Rose f*

royal flush *n der Royal Flush m*

rum *n der Rum m* **p84**

run *v rennen* **p24**

Russian *n der Russe m, die Russin f* **p110**

S

sad *adj traurig* **p107**

safe (for storing valuables) *n der Tresor m* **p69**

Do the rooms have safes? *Verfügen die Zimmer über einen Tresor?*

safe (secure) *adj sicher*

Is this area safe? *Ist dieses Gebiet sicher?*

sail *n das Segel gn*

sail *v ablegen (start) / segeln (on a sailboat)* **p21**

When do we sail? *Wann legen wir ab?* **p150**

salad *n der Salat m* **p98**

salesperson *n der Verkäufer m, die Verkäuferin f* **p109**

salt *n das Salz gn* **p87**

Is that low-salt? *Enthält das wenig Salz?*

satellite *n der Satellit m* **p61**

satellite radio *das Satellitenradio*

satellite tracking *das Navigationssystem*
Saturday *n der Sonntag m* p13
sauce *n die Soße f*
say *v sagen* p21
scan, to scan (document) *v scannen* p21
schedule *n der Fahrplan m*
school *n die Schule f*
scooter *n der Roller m* p44
score *n der Spielstand f* p149
Scottish *adj schottisch*
scratched *adj zerkratzt* p47
scratched surface *die zerkratzte Oberfläche*
sculpture *n die Skulptur f*
seafood *n die Meeresfrüchte f, pl* p79
search *n die Suche f*
hand search *das Abtasten*
search *v suchen* p21
seasick *adj seekrank*
I am seasick. *Ich bin seekrank.*
seasickness pill *n die Tablette gegen Seekrankheit f*
seat *n der Platz m* p35, 131
child seat *der Kindersitz*
second *adj zweiter* p10
security *n der Sicherheitsdienst m* p30
security checkpoint *die Sicherheitsschleuse*
security guard *der Sicherheitsbeamte*

sedan *n die Limousine f*
see *v sehen* p24
May I see it? *Dürfte ich das mal sehen?*
self-serve *adj Selbstbedienungs-*
sell *v verkaufen* p21
seltzer *n das Selters gn* p83
send *v versenden* p21
separated (marital status) *adj getrennt lebend* p105
September *n der September m* p14
serve *v servieren* p21
service *n der Service m* p71
services (religious) *n der Gottesdienst m* p114
service charge *n die Servicegebühr f* p64
seven *adj sieben* p8
seventy *adj siebzig* p8
seventeen *adj siebzehn* p8
seventh *adj siebter* p10
sew *v nähen* p21
sex (gender) *n das Geschlecht gn*
sex, to have (intercourse) *v Sex haben*
shallow *adj seicht*
shampoo *n das Shampoo n*
sheet (bed linen) *n das Bettlaken gn*
shellfish *n das Schalentier gn* p79
ship *n das Schiff gn*
ship *v versenden* p21

How much to ship this to ____? *Wie viel kostet der Versand hiervon nach ____?*

shirt *n das Hemd gn*

shoe *n der Schuh m* p136

shop *n das Geschäft gn*

shop *v einkaufen* p21

I'm shopping for mens' clothes. *Ich bin auf der Suche nach Herrenbekleidung.*

I'm shopping for womens' clothes. *Ich bin auf der Suche nach Damenbekleidung.*

I'm shopping for childrens' clothes. *Ich bin auf der Suche nach Kinderbekleidung.*

short *adj kurz* p12

shorts *n die kurze Hose f* p76

shot (liquor) *n der Kurze m*

shout *v rufen* p24

show (performance) *n die Vorstellung f*

What time is the show? *Wann beginnt die Vorstellung?*

show *v zeigen* p21

Would you show me? *Könnten Sie mir das bitte zeigen?*

shower *n die Dusche f* p61

Does it have a shower? *Gibt es eine Dusche?*

shower *v duschen* p21, 29

shrimp *n die Garnele f* p93

shuttle bus *n der Pendelbus m*

sick *adj krank* p42

I feel sick. *Mir ist schlecht.*

side *n die Beilage f* p79

on the side (e.g., salad dressing) *dazu*

sidewalk *n der Gehweg m*

sightseeing *n das Sightseeing gn*

sightseeing bus *n der Sightseeing-Bus m*

sign *v unterschreiben* p24

Where do I sign? *Wo muss ich unterschreiben?*

silk *n die Seide f* p137

silver *adj Silber-*

SIM card *n die SIM-Karte f* p123

sing *v singen* p24

single (unmarried) *adj ledig* p105

Are you single? *Sind Sie ledig?*

single (one) *adj Einzel-*

single bed *das Einzelbett*

sink *n das Waschbecken gn*

sister *n die Schwester f* p104

sit *v sitzen*

six *adj sechs* p8

sixteen *adj sechzehn* p8

sixty *adj sechzig* p8

size (clothing, shoes) *n die Kleidergröße f* p137

skin *n die Haut f*

sleeping berth *n das Schlafabteil gn*

slow adj langsam
slow v verlangsamen p21
  Slow down! Fahren Sie
  bitte langsamer. p51
slow(ly) adv langsam
  Speak more slowly.
  Sprechen Sie bitte etwas
  langsamer. p102
small adj klein p12
smell v riechen p21
smoke v rauchen p21
smoking n das Rauchen gn
  p31
  smoking area
  Raucherbereich
  No Smoking Rauchen
  verboten p33
snack n der Imbiss m p162
  Snake eyes! n
  Schlangenaugen! p163
snorkel n der Schnorchel m
sock n die Socke f
soda n die Limonade f p41
  diet soda die Diätlimonade
soft adj weich
software n die Software f
sold out adj ausverkauft
some adj etwas
  (uncountable) / einige
  (countable)
someone n jemand p32
something n etwas m p42
son n der Sohn m p104
song n das Lied gn p158
soon adv bald p15
sorry adj leid
  I'm sorry. Tut mir leid.
spa n das Heilbad m p60

Spain n Spanien
Spanish n der Spanier m, die
  Spanierin f p108
spare tire n der Reservereifen
  m
speak v sprechen p24
  Do you speak English?
  Sprechen Sie Englisch?
  Would you speak louder,
  please? Könnten Sie bitte
  etwas lauter sprechen?
  Would you speak slower,
  please? Könnten Sie
  bitte etwas langsamer
  sprechen?
special (featured meal) n die
  Spezialität f
specify v angeben p24
speed limit n die Geschwin-
  digkeitsbegrenzung f p50
  What's the speed limit?
  Welche Geschwindigkeits-
  begrenzung gilt hier?
speedometer n der Tacho m
spell v buchstabieren p21
  How do you spell that? Wie
  schreibt sich das?
spice n das Gewürz gn
spill v verschütten p21
split (gambling) n der Split m
sports n der Sport m p116
spring (season) n der
  Frühling m p14
stadium n das Stadion gn p147
staff (employees) n die
  Mitarbeiter pl p72
stamp (postage) n die
  Briefmarke f

ENGLISH—GERMAN

stair *n* die Stufe *f*
Where are the stairs? *Wo finde ich das Treppenhaus?*
Are there many stairs? *Gibt es viele Stufen?*
stand *v* stehen **p24**
start, to start (commence) *v* beginnen **p21**
start, to start (a car) *v* anlassen **p24**
state *n* der Staat (gov.) / der Status (status) *m*
station *n* der Bahnhof *m* **p51**
Where is the nearest____? *Wo ist die nächste ____?*
gas station *Tankstelle*
bus station *Bushaltestelle*
subway station *U-Bahn-Haltestelle*
Where is the nearest train station? *Wo ist der nächste Bahnhof?*
stay *v* Aufenthalt, bleiben **p24**
We'll be staying for ____ nights. *Wir bleiben ____ Nächte. See numbers, p8.*
steakhouse *n* das Steakhaus *gn* **p73**
steal *v* stehlen **p24**
stolen *adj* gestohlen **p43**
stop *n* die Haltestelle *f* **p54**
Is this my stop? *Ist das hier meine Haltestelle?*
I missed my stop. *Ich habe meine Haltestelle verpasst.*
stop *v* anhalten **p24**

Please stop. *Halten Sie bitte an.*
STOP (traffic sign) *STOP*
Stop, thief! *Haltet den Dieb!*
store *n* das Lager *gn* **p143**
straight *adj* gerade (street) / glatt (hair) **p144**
straight ahead *geradeaus* **p6**
straight (drink) *pur*
Go straight. *Gehen Sie geradeaus* **p49**
straight (gambling) *n* der Straight *m* **p164**
street *n* die Straße *f* **p6**
across the street *gegenüber*
down the street *am Ende der Straße*
Which street? *Welche Straße?*
How many more streets? *Wie viele Straßen noch?*
stressed *adj* gestresst
striped *adj* gestreift
stroller *n* der Kinderwagen *m*
Do you rent baby strollers? *Vermieten Sie Kinderwagen?*
substitution *n* der Ersatz *m*
subway *n* die U-Bahn *f* **p56**
subway line *die U-Bahn-Linie*
subway station *die U-Bahn-Haltestelle*
Which subway do I take for ____? *Mit welcher U-Bahn komme ich zu / zur / zum ____?*
subtitle *n* die Untertitel *m, pl*

suitcase n der Koffer m p43

suite n die Suite f p62

summer n der Sommer m p14

sun n die Sonne f

sunburn n der Sonnenbrand m

  I have a bad sunburn.
  *Ich habe einen starken
  Sonnenbrand.*

Sunday n der Sonntag m p13

sunglasses n die Sonnenbrille f

sunny adj sonnig p111

  It's sunny out. *Draußen
  scheint die Sonne.*

sunroof n das Sonnendach gn

sunscreen n die
  Sonnencreme f

  **Do you have sunscreen
  SPF ____?** *Haben Sie
  Sonnencreme mit
  Lichtschutzfaktor ____?*
  See numbers p8.

supermarket n der
  Supermarkt m

surf v surfen p21

surfboard n das Surfbrett gn

suspiciously adv
  verdächtig p42

swallow v schlucken p21

sweater n der Pullover m p137

Swedish n der Schwede m,
  die Schwedin f p110

swim v schwimmen p24

  Can one swim here? *Kann
  man hier schwimmen?*

swimsuit n der Badeanzug m

swim trunks n die Badehose f

Swiss n der Schweizer m, die
  Schweizerin f p108

symphony n die Symphonie f

T

table n der Tisch m p75

  table for two der Tisch für
  zwei

tailor n der Schneider m, die
  Schneiderin f p67

  **Can you recommend a
  good tailor?** *Können Sie
  mir einen guten Schneider
  empfehlen?*

take v nehmen, bringen p24

  **Take me to the station,
  please.** *Bringen Sie mich
  bitte zum Bahnhof.*

  **How much to take me to
  ____?** *Wieviel kostet die
  Fahrt zu / zur / zum ____?*

takeout menu n das Essen
  zum Mitnehmen gn

talk v sprechen p24

tall adj groß

tanned adj gebräunt

taste (flavor) n der
  Geschmack m

taste n (discernment) der
  Geschmack m

taste v schmecken p21

tax n die Steuer f p140

  value-added tax (VAT)
  Mehrwertsteuer (MwSt.)

taxi n das Taxi gn p51

  Taxi! *Taxi!*

  **Would you call me a taxi,
  please?** *Könnten Sie mir
  bitte ein Taxi rufen?*

tea n der Tee m p84

team n das Team gn p148

Techno n der Techno m p114

television n der Fernseher m

temple n der Tempel m p113

ten adj zehn p8

tennis n das Tennis gn

　tennis court der Tennisplatz

tent n das Zelt gn

tenth adj zehnter p10

terminal n (airport) das
　Terminal gn p33

thank you danke p1

that (near) adj diese / dieser /
　dieses p7

that (far away) adj jene /
　jener / jenes

theater n das Theater gn

them (m/f) sie

there (demonstrative) adv da
　(nearby), dort **(far)**

　**Is / Are there ____ over
　there?** Ist / Sind ____dort
　drüben?

these adj diese p7

thick adj dick

thief adj Dieb! p7

thin adj dünn p92

third adj dritter p10

thirteen adj dreizehn p8

thirty adj dreißig p8

this adj diese / dieser / dieses p7

those jene / jener / jenes
　adj p7

thousand Eintausend p8

three drei p8

Thursday n der Donnerstag
　m p13

thus (therefore) also adv p15

ticket n das Ticket gn p32

　ticket counter der
　　Kartenschalter p30

　one-way ticket das einfache
　　Ticket p53

　round-trip ticket das Hin-
　　und Rückreiseticket p53

tight adj eng

time n die Zeit f p12

　Is it on time? Ist er (train,
　　bus) pünktlich? / Ist es
　　(plane, ship) pünktlich?

　At what time? Um wie
　　viel Uhr?

　What time is it? Wie spät
　　ist es?

timetable n (train) der
　Fahrplan m

tip (gratuity) das Trinkgeld
　gn p85

tire n der Reifen m p47

　I have a flat tire. Ich habe
　　einen platten Reifen.

tired adj müde p107

today n heute

today's special n das Menü
　gn p15

toilet n die Toilette f p69

　The toilet is overflowing.
　　Die Toilette läuft über.

　The toilet is backed up. Die
　　Toilette ist verstopft.

toilet paper n das
　Toilettenpapier gn

　**You're out of toilet
　　paper.** Sie haben kein
　　Toilettenpapier mehr.

toiletries *n die Hygieneartikel m, pl* p91
toll *n die Maut f* p50
tomorrow *n morgen* p4
ton *n die Tonne f*
too (excessively) *adv zu*
too (also) *adv auch* p15
tooth *n der Zahn m* p173
  I lost my tooth. *Ich habe einen Zahn verloren.*
toothache *n die Zahnschmerzen m, pl*
  I have a toothache. *Ich habe Zahnschmerzen.*
toothpaste *n die Zahnpasta f* p67
total *n die Gesamtsumme f*
  What is the total? *Wie hoch ist die Gesamtsumme?*
tour *n der Ausflug m*
  Are guided tours available? *Werden Fremdenführungen angeboten?*
  Are audio tours available? *Werden Audioführungen angeboten?*
towel *n das Handtuch gn*
  May we have more towels? *Könnten wir bitte mehr Handtücher bekommen?*
toy *n das Spielzeug gn*
  toy store *n das Spielwarengeschäft gn*
  Do you have any toys for the children? *Haben Sie Kinderspielzeug?*
traffic *n der Verkehr m*

  How's traffic? *Wie ist der Verkehr?*
traffic laws *die Verkehrsregeln* p46
trail *n der Weg m*
  Are there trails? *Gibt es dort Wege?*
train *n der Zug m* p30, 53
  express train *der Expresszug*
  local train *der Nahverkehrszug*
  Does the train go to ____? *Fährt der Zug nach / zum ____?*
  May I have a train schedule? *Könnte ich bitte einen Zugfahrplan bekommen?*
  Where is the train station? *Wo finde ich den Bahnhof?*
train *v trainieren* p21
transfer *v überweisen* p24
  I need to transfer funds. *Ich möchte eine Überweisung tätigen.*
transmission *n das Getriebe gn*
  automatic transmission *das Automatikgetriebe*
  standard transmission *das Schaltgetriebe*
travel *v reisen* p21
trillion *n die Billion f* p15
trim (hair) *v schneiden* p24
trip *n die Reise f* p100
triple *adj dreifach* p9
trumpet *n die Trompete f*

trunk n der Koffer m (luggage) p43, der Kofferraum m (car)

try, to try (attempt) v versuchen p21, ausprobieren p21

try, to try on (clothing) v anprobieren p21

try, to try (food) v probieren

Tuesday n der Dienstag m p13

Turkish n der Türke m, die Türkin f p108

turn v abbiegen (car) / sich wenden (person) p24
to turn left / right links / rechts abbiegen
to turn off / on ausschalten / einschalten p21

twelve adj zwölf p8

twenty adj zwanzig p8

twine n die Paketschnur f p128

two adj zwei p8

U

umbrella n der Regenschirm m

uncle n der Onkel m p105

undercooked adj noch nicht durch

understand v verstehen p24
I don't understand. Ich verstehe nicht.
Do you understand? Verstanden?

underwear n die Unterwäsche f

university n die Universität f

up adv aufwärts p6

update v aktualisieren p21

upgrade n die höhere Kategorie f p45

upload v hochladen p24, 126

upscale adj gehoben

us pron uns

USB port n der USB-Anschluss m

use v verwenden p21

V

vacation n der Urlaub m p38
on vacation im Urlaub
to go on vacation in Urlaub gehen

vacancy n das freie Zimmer (hotel) gn

van n der Kleinbus m, der Van m

VCR n der Videorekorder m
Do the rooms have VCRs? Gibt es auf den Zimmern einen Videorekorder?

vegan adj vegane p35, 78

vegetable n das Gemüse gn

vegetarian n der Vegetarier m, die Vegetarierin f

vending machine n der Automat m

version n die Version f

very sehr

video n das Video gn
Where can I rent videos or DVDs? Wo kann ich Videos oder DVDs ausleihen?

view n die Aussicht f

ENGLISH–GERMAN

beach view *die Aussicht auf den Strand*
city view *die Aussicht auf die Stadt*
vineyard *n das Weingut gn*
vinyl *n das Vinyl gn* p43
violin *n die Geige f*
visa *n das Visum gn*
Do I need a visa? *Benötige ich ein Visum?*
vision *n die Sicht f*
visit *v besuchen* p21
visually-impaired *adj sehbehindert*
vodka *n der Wodka m* p84
voucher *n der Gutschein m* p38

W

wait *v warten* p21
Please wait. *Warten Sie bitte.*
How long is the wait? *Wie lange muss ich warten? (for me) / Wie lange müssen wir warten? (for us)*
waiter *n der Kellner m, die Kellnerin f*
waiting area *n der Wartebereich m* p31
wake-up call *n der Weckruf m* p68
wallet *n die Geldbörse f* p39
I lost my wallet. *Ich habe meine Geldbörse verloren.*

Someone stole my wallet. *Meine Geldbörse wurde gestohlen.*
walk *v gehen* p24
walker (ambulatory device) *n die Gehhilfe f* p37
walkway *n der Fußgängerweg m*
moving walkway *der Fahrsteig*
want *v wollen* p25
war *n der Krieg m* p113
warm *adj warm* p111
watch *v zusehen* p24
water *n das Wasser gn* p40
Is the water potable? *Ist das Wasser trinkbar?*
Is there running water? *Gibt es fließendes Wasser?* p72
wave *v winken* p21
waxing *n das Enthaaren (mit Wachs) gn*
wear *v tragen* p24
weather forecast *n der Wetterbericht m*
Web designer *n der Webdesigner m* p111
Wednesday *n der Mittwoch m*
week *n die Woche f* p4, 13
this week *diese Woche*
last week *letzte Woche*
next week *nächste Woche*
weigh *v wiegen* p24
I weigh ____. *Ich wiege ____.*

It weighs ____. *Das wiegt ____.* See p8 for numbers.

weights *n die Gewichte gn, pl* p146

welcome *adv willkommen*

You're welcome. *Gern geschehen.*

well *adv gut*

well done (meat) *gut durch* p78

well done (task) *gut gemacht*

I don't feel well. *Ich fühle mich nicht gut.*

western *adj westlich, abendländisch*

whale *n der Wal m*

what *adv was* p3

What sort of ____? *Welche Art von ____?*

What time is ____? *Wann gibt es ____?* p12

wheelchair *n der Rollstuhl m* p37

wheelchair access *der Zugang per Rollstuhl* p64

wheelchair ramp *die Rampe für Rollstuhlfahrer*

power wheelchair *der elektrisch betriebene Rollstuhl*

wheeled (luggage) *adj mit Rollen*

when *adv wann* p3

where *adv wo* p3

Where is ____? *Wo ist ____?*

which *adv welche / welcher / welches* p3

Which one? *Welche / Welcher / Welches?*

white *adj weiß*

who *adv wer* p3

whose *adj wessen / dessen*

wide *adj breit* p12

widow, widower *n die Witwe f, der Witwer m* p105

wife *n die Ehefrau f* p107

wi-fi *n das WLAN gn*

window *n das Fenster gn, der Schalter m* p35, 129

drop-off window *Abgabeschalter*

pickup window *Abholschalter*

windshield *n die Frontscheibe f*

windshield wiper *n der Scheibenwischer m*

windy *adj windig* p111

wine *n der Wein m* p41, 77, 83

winter *n der Winter m* p14

wiper *n der Wischer m*

with *prep mit*

withdraw *v abheben* p24

I need to withdraw money. *Ich möchte Geld abheben.*

without *prep ohne*

woman *n die Frau f*

work *v arbeiten (person), funktionieren (device)* p21

____ doesn't work. *____ funktioniert nicht.*

workout *n das Training m*

worse *schlimmer*

worst *am schlimmsten*

ENGLISH—GERMAN

write *v schreiben* p24
 Would you write that down for me? *Könnten Sie mir das bitte aufschreiben?*
writer *n der Autor m* p109

X
x-ray machine *n das Röntgengerät gn*

Y
yellow *adj gelb*
yes *adv ja*
yesterday *n gestern* p4
 the day before yesterday *vorgestern* p4
yield sign *n das Schild „Vorfahrt gewähren" gn*
you *pron Sie / du / ihr* p3
 you (singular, informal) *du*
 you (singular, formal) *Sie*
 you (plural informal) *ihr*
 you (plural formal) *Sie*
your, yours *adj Ihr / Ihre (formal); dein / deine (informal)*
young *adj jung* p106

Z
zoo *n der Zoo m* p118

A

abbiegen to turn v **p24**
  Biegen Sie links / rechts ab.
  Turn left / right.
abbuchen to charge (money)
  v **p21**
das Abendessen gn dinner n
der Abfluss m drain n
abgelehnt declined adj
  Ihre Kreditkarte wurde
  abgelehnt. Your credit
  card was declined.
abheben to withdraw v **p24**
die Abhebung f withdrawal n
ablegen to sail v **p21**
  Wann legen wir ab? When
  do we sail?
die Abreise f departure
  n **p33**
abreisen to leave (depart)
  v **p21**
abschließen to lock v **p24**
abwärts down adv **p6**
acht eight adj **p8**
achter eighth adj **p9**
  drei Achtel three eighths
achtzehn eighteen adj **p8**
achtzig eighty adj **p8**
der Adapterstecker m
  adapter plug n
der Adler m eagle n
die Adresse f address n
  Wie lautet die Adresse?
  What's the address?
Afro- afro adj

afroamerikanisch African
  American adj
die Agentur / das Büro f/gn
  agency n
der Agnostiker m, **die**
  Agnostikerin f agnostic
  n **p113**
die Akne f acne n **p166**
der Aktenkoffer m briefcase
  n **p43**
aktualisieren to update v **p21**
aktuell current adj **p15**
akzeptieren to accept v **p21**
  Wir akzeptieren
  Kreditkarten. Credit cards
  accepted.
der Alkohol m alcohol n **p82**
die Allergie f allergy n
allergisch allergic adj **p68, 79**
  Ich bin allergisch gegen
  _____. I'm allergic to _____.
  Ich glaube, ich habe eine
  allergische Reaktion.
  *I think I'm having an
  allergic reaction.*
alles / irgend etwas
  anything n
also thus, therefore adv **p15**
alt old adj
das Alter gn age n
  Wie alt sind Sie? (formal) /
  Wie alt bist du? (informal)
  What's your age?
das Aluminium gn
  aluminum n
am besten best. See gut

am schlimmsten *worst. See schlecht*

am wenigsten *least. See wenig*

der Amerikaner *m*, **die Amerikanerin** *f American n* p110

amerikanisch *American adj*

an Bord *on board*

anbieten *to offer v* p24

anders *different (other) adj* p70, 138

angeben *to specify v* p24

die Angelegenheit *f matter, affair*

Kümmern Sie sich um Ihre eigenen Angelegenheiten. *Mind your own business.*

die Angelrute *f fishing pole n*

anhalten *to stop v* p24

Halten Sie bitte an. *Please stop.*

ankommen *to arrive v* p24

die Ankunft *f arrival n*

anlassen *to start (a car) v*

anpiepen *to page (someone) v* p21

anrufen *to call (to phone) v* p24

Antibaby- *birth control adj*

Ich habe keine Antibabypillen mehr. *I'm out of birth control pills.*

das Antibiotikum *gn antibiotic n*

Ich brauche ein Antibiotikum. *I need an antibiotic.*

das Antihistamin *gn antihistamine n* p165

die Antwort *f answer n*

Ich benötige eine Antwort. *I need an answer.*

antworten (auf eine Frage) *to answer (respond to a question) v* p21

Antworten Sie mir bitte. *Answer me, please.*

der Anwalt / die Anwältin *m/f lawyer n* p109

anziehen *to dress v* p24, 29

der April *m April n* p14

arbeiten *to work v* p21

der Arbeitgeber *m employer n*

die Art *f kind (sort, type) n*

Um welche Art handelt es sich? *What kind is it?*

der Arzt *m* / **die Ärztin** *f doctor n* p7, 109, 167

die Arztpraxis *f doctor's office n*

asiatisch *Asian adj* p73

das Aspirin *gn aspirin n* p166

das Asthma *gn asthma n* p172

Ich habe Asthma. *I have asthma.*

atheistisch *atheist adj*

auch *too (also) adv* p15

Audio- *audio adj* p58

das Audio *gn audio n* p134

der Aufenthalt *m wait / stay n* p36

aufladen *to charge (a battery) v* p24

GERMAN—ENGLISH

auflegen hang up (to end a phone call) v **p24**

aufwärts up adv p6

der Aufzug m elevator n p58

das Auge gn eye n p167

die Augenbraue f eyebrow n p144

der August m August n p14

aus made of adj

auschecken to check out (of hotel) v **p21**

der Ausflug m tour n

ausrauben, stehlen to rob v, to steal v **p21**, 24

die Ausrüstung f equipment n p159

ausschalten to turn off (lights) v **p21**

aussehen to look (appear) v **p24**

die Aussicht f view n

  die Aussicht auf den Strand beach view

  die Aussicht auf die Stadt city view

die Ausstellung f exhibit n

Australien Australia n

australisch Australian adj

ausverkauft sold out adj

auswärts essen to eat out

der Ausweis m passport n

auszahlen lassen to cash out (gambling) **p24**, 164

auszahlen to cash v

das Auto gn car n

  die Autovermietung car rental agency

die Autobahn f highway n

die Autokrankheit f carsickness n

der Autor / die Autorin m/f writer n p113

die Autovermietung f car rental agency

Autsch! Ouch! interj

B

das Baby gn baby n p107

Baby-, für Babys for babies adj

  Kinderwagen baby stroller

Babynahrung baby food

der Babysitter m babysitter n

das Bad gn bath, spa n p15

der Badeanzug m swimsuit n

baden to bathe v **p21**

die Badewanne f bathtub n p64

das Badezimmer gn bathroom n, bath n

der Bahnhof m station n p51

  Wo finde ich die nächste Tankstelle? Where is the nearest gas station?

balancieren (something shaky) / begleichen (invoice) to balance v **p21**, 24

bald soon adv p15

der Balkon m balcony n p62

der Ball m ball (sport) n

die Band f band n

Bank- bank adj

  das Bankkonto bank account

die **Bankkarte** bank card

die Bank f bank n p122

die Bar f bar n

die **Pianobar** piano bar

die **Single-Bar** singles bar p166

das **Bargeld** gn cash n p50

Nur Bargeld. Cash only. p50

der **Bass** m bass (instrument) n

die **Batterie** f battery (for flashlight or car) n

die **Baumwolle** f cotton n p137

bearbeiten to process (a transaction) v **p21**

sich **beeilen** to hurry v **p21**

Beeilen Sie sich bitte! Hurry, please!

begeistert enthusiastic adj p109

beginnen to begin v, to start (commence) v **p24**

behalten to keep v **p24**

die **Behinderung** f disability, handicap n

das **Bein** gn leg n

bleibt fat adj

beleidigen to insult v **p21**

der **Belgier** m, die **Belgierin** f Belgian n p108

beliebig any adj

beliebt popular adj p154

bemuttern to mother v **p21**

sich **benehmen** to behave v **p24**

benommen dizzy adj p170

das **Benzin** gn gas n

berechnen to bill v **p21**

der **Berg** m mountain n

das **Bergsteigen** gn mountain climbing n

beschädigt damaged adj p43

besetzt busy adj (phone line), occupied adj p125

besorgt anxious adj p109

besser better. See gut

bestätigen to confirm v **p21**

die **Bestätigung** f confirmation n

bestellen (restaurant) to order v **p21**

besuchen to visit v **p21**

betreten to enter v **p24**

Kein Eingang. Do not enter. **Zutritt verboten.** Entry forbidden.

das **Bett** gn bed n

das **Bettlaken** gn sheet (bed linen) n

die **Beule** f dent n

bevorzugen to prefer v **p21**

bevorzugt preferably adj

bewegen to move v **p21**

bewölkt cloudy adj p111

bezahlen to pay v **p21**

Muss ich im Voraus bezahlen? Do I have to pay up front?

die **Biene** f bee n

das **Bier** gn beer n p82

das **Bier vom Fass** beer on tap, draft beer p155

billig cheap adj

billiger *cheaper*
am billigsten *cheapest*
die Billion *f trillion* n p15
Bio- *organic adj*
Bis später. *See you later.*
bitte *please (polite entreaty)*
  adv p1
blass *pale adj*
blau *blue adj*
bleiben *to stay* v p24
das Bleichmittel *gn bleach* n
blenden *to dazzle, to blind*
  v p15
blind *blind adj*
der Block *m block* n
blockieren *to block* v p21
bloggen *blogging* v p21
der Blonde *m*, **die Blondine** *f*
  blond(e) n
die Blume *f flower* n
die Bluse *f blouse* n p137
blutig *rare (meat) adj* p77
das Boot / Schiff *gn boat* n
  / ship n
die Bordkarte *f boarding*
  pass n p39
der Bordstein *m curb* n
die Botschaft *f embassy* n
der Brandy *m brandy* n p83
brauchen *to need* v p21
braun *brown adj*
brav *well behaved adj* p15
die Brieftasche *f wallet* n
breit *wide adj* p12
Breitband- *broadband* n
die Bremse *f brake* n p48
bremsen *to brake* v p21

das Bremslicht *brake light*
die Motorkontrollleuchte
  check engine light p47
der Scheinwerfer *headlight*
die Ölkontrolllämpchen *oil*
  light p49
brennen *to burn* v p24
die Briefmarke *f stamp*
  (postage) n
die Brieftasche *f wallet* n
die Brille *f eyeglasses* n
bronzefarben *bronze*
  (color) adj
das Brot *gn bread* n p86
die Brücke *f bridge (across*
  a river) n */ bridge (dental*
  structure) n p173
der Bruder *m brother* n p104
der Brünette *m*, **die Brünette**
  f brunette n
buchstabieren *to spell* v p21
Wie schreibt sich das? *How*
  do you spell that?
der Buddhist *m*, **die**
  Buddhistin *f Buddhist* n
  p113
das Budget *gn budget* n
das Buffet *gn buffet* n
der Bus *m bus* n p54
die Bushaltestelle *bus stop*
der Pendelbus *shuttle bus*
der Sightseeing-Bus
  sightseeing bus
die Butter *f butter* n p87
C
das Cabrio *gn convertible* n
das Café *coffee house* n

der Campingplatz m campsite n

der Cappuccino m cappuccino n

die CD f CD n p45

Charter- charter adj

der Charterflug charter flight

chartern to charter (transportation) v p21

der Check-In check-in n p30

der Curbside-Check-In curbside check-in

der Online-Check-In online check-in p34

der Express-Check-In express check-in p34

der Chef m, **die Chefin** f boss n

die chemische Reinigung f dry cleaner n

der Chiropraktiker m chiropractor n p167

der Computer m computer n

die Country-Musik f country music adj

der Cousin m, **die Cousine** f cousin n

die Creme f cream n

cremefarben off-white adj

D

da there (nearby) adv (demonstrative) p161

das Dach gn roof n

das Sonnendach sunroof

die Damentoilette women's restroom

der Däne m, **die Dänin** f Danish n p108

danke thank you

Darf ich Ihnen ___ vorstellen? I'd like to introduce you to ___.

das this n

dauern to last v p21

die Dauerwelle f perm (hair)

die (Bett-)Decke f blanket n p41

dein your, yours adj sing (informal)

die Demokratie f democracy n

der Designer m, **die Designerin** f designer n p109

der Deutsche m, **die Deutsche** f German n p108

der Dezember m December n

Diabetiker- diabetic adj p35, 78

dick thick adj

Dieb! Thief!

der Dienstag m Tuesday n p13

diese these (near) adj pl p7

dieser / diese / dieses this adj p7

der Dollar m dollar n

der Dolmetscher / die Dolmetscherin m/f interpreter n p175

der Dom m cathedral n

der Donnerstag m Thursday n p13

Doppel- double adj p9

dort drüben over there adv

dort there (far) adv (demonstrative) p5

der Download m download n

das Drama gn drama n

draußen outside n p77

drei three adj p8

dreifach triple adj p9

dreißig thirty adj p8

dreizehn thirteen adj p8

das Dressing gn dressing (salad) n

drinnen inside adj p77

dritter third adj p10

die Driving Range f driving range n

drucken to print v p21

drücken to push v p21

du you pron sing (informal)

dunkel dark adj

die Dunkelheit f darkness n

dünn thin (fine, skinny, slender) adj

der Durchfall m diarrhea n p166

durchwählen to dial direct

die Dusche f shower n p64

duschen to shower v p21, 29

das Dutzend gn dozen n p11

die DVD f DVD n p45

E

die Ecke f corner n

an der Ecke on the corner

die Ehefrau f wife n

der Ehemann m husband n

eigentlich / wirklich actual adv p15

ein / eine one adj p8

eine E-Mail senden to send email v p21

einen Nachtclub besuchen to go clubbing v p21

einfach single adj / simple adj

ohne Eis straight up (drink)

das einfache Ticket one-way ticket p32

der Eingang m entrance n p33

einkaufen to shop v p21

das Einkaufszentrum gn mall n

einpacken to bag v p21

einstecken to plug v p21

einsteigen / an Bord gehen to board v p24

die Einwanderungsbehörde f immigration n

das Eis gn ice n p80

die Eismaschine ice machine

der Elefant m elephant n

der Elektroanschluss m electrical hookup n p72

elf eleven adj p8

die E-Mail f email n p118

Kann ich Ihre (formal) / deine (informal) E-Mail-Adresse haben? May I have your email address? p119

die E-Mail-Nachricht *e-mail message*

empfehlen *to recommend* v **p24**

eng *tight adj*

England *England n*

der Engländer *m,* **die Engländerin** *f English n*

englisch *English adj* **p2**

die englische Blindenschrift *f braille (American) n*

die Ente *f duck n*

entfernen *to remove* v **p21**

das Enthaaren (mit Wachs) *gn waxing n*

entschuldigen *to excuse (pardon)* v **p21**

Verzeihung. *Excuse me.*

entspannen / abhängen (slang) *to hang out (relax)* v **p21,** 24

entzückt *charmed adj*

er *he pron* **p3**

erbitten *to request, demand* v **p24**

die Erdnuss *f peanut n*

erfreut *delighted adj*

erhalten *to receive* v **p24**

die Erkältung *f cold (illness) n*

erklären *to explain* v **p21**

erlauben *to permit* v **p21**

die erneute Einlösung *f refill (of prescription) n* **p168**

der Ersatz *m substitution n*

erschöpft *exhausted adj*

erster *first adj* **p10**

der Erzieher *m,* **die Erzieherin** *f educator n* **p109**

der Esel *m donkey n*

das Essen *gn food n* **p81**

essen *to eat* v **p24**

das Essen zum Mitnehmen *takeout food*

die Etage *f floor n*

im Erdgeschoß *ground floor, first floor* **p62**

etwas *bit (small amount) n*

etwas (uncountable) / einige (countable) *some adj*

etwas *gn something n* **p42**

Express- *express adj* **p34,** 55

der Express-Check-In *express check-in* **p34**

F

fahren *to drive, ride* v **p24**

der Fahrer *m driver n* **p51**

der Fahrplan *m schedule n, timetable (train) n* **p53**

der Fahrpreis *m fare n*

fallen *to fall* v **p24**

die Familie *f family n* **p104**

die Farbe *f color n* **p138**

färben *to color* v **p21**

faulenzen *to lounge* v **p21**

der Februar *m February n* **p14**

fehlend *missing adj* **p42**

der Fehler *m fault n* **p51**

Es war mein Fehler. *I'm at fault.* **p51**

Es war sein Fehler. *It was his fault.*

der Fehler *m mistake n* p163

feiern *to celebrate v* **p21**

der Feiertag *m holiday n*

der Fels *m rock n*

auf Eis *on the rocks*

das Fenster *gn window n* p48

der Fernseher *m television n*

das Kabelfernsehen *cable television* p61

das Satellitenfernsehen *satellite television* p61

das Festival *gn festival n*

feucht *humid adj* p111

das Feuer *gn fire n*

das Feuer *gn light (for cigarette) n* p156

Darf ich Ihnen (formal) / dir (informal) Feuer geben? *May I offer you a light?*

das Feuerzeug *gn lighter (cigarette) n*

der Film *m movie n* p130

finden *to find v* **p24**

das Fitness-Center *gn fitness center n* p59

das Fitnessstudio *gn gym n* p146

die Flasche *f bottle n* p82

die Flaschenöffner *f bottle opener n*

das Fleisch *gn meat n* p81

die Flöte *f flute n*

der Flug *m flight n* p32

der Flugbegleiter / die Flugbegleiterin *m / f flight attendant*

der Flughafen *m airport n*

der Fluss *m river n* p151

folglich *consequently adv* p15

das Format *gn format n* p142

die Formel *f formula n*

der Fortschritt *m advance n*

fortsetzen *to continue v* **p21**

(foto-)kopieren *to photocopy v* **p21**

das Foyer *gn lounge n*

fragen *to ask v* **p21**, 24

der Franzose *m,* **die Französin** *f French n* p108

französisch *French adj* p73

die Frau *f woman n*

der Frauenarzt / die Frauenärztin *m/f gynecologist n*

das freie Zimmer (hotel) *gn vacancy n*

der Freitag *m Friday n* p13

der Fremdenführer / die Fremdenführerin *m / f guide (of tours) n*

die Fremdenführung *f guided tour n*

die Freude *f pleasure n*

Freut mich. *It's a pleasure.*

der Freund *m / die Freundin** *f friend n* p104

der Freund *m boyfriend n* p104

die Freundin *f girlfriend n* p104

die Frikadelle *f meatball n*

frisch *fresh adj* p79, 92

der Frisör *m*, **die Frisörin** *f*
hairdresser n

fröhlich *happy adj* p107

die Frontscheibe *f*
windshield n

die Frucht *f fruit n*

der Fruchtsaft *m fruit juice n*

früh *early adj* p13

der Frühling *m spring
(season) n* p14

das Frühstück *gn breakfast n*

führen *to guide v* p21

Full House! *Full house! n*

fünf *five adj* p8

fünfter *m fifth adj*

fünfzehn *m fifteen adj*

fünfzig *fifty adj* p8

(der) Fuß *m foot (body part,
measurement) n*

Fußgänger- *pedestrian adj*

die Fußgängerzone
*pedestrian shopping
district*

der Fußgängerweg *m*
walkway n

der Fahrsteig *moving
walkway*

G

die Gabel *f fork n* p81

der Gang *m aisle (in store)
n I hallway n*

ganz *all adj*

die ganze Zeit *all the time*
Das ist alles. *That's all.*

die Garnele *f shrimp n* p93

das Gas (for cooking) / **das
Benzin** (for cars) *gn gas n*

die Tankanzeige *gas gauge*
kein Benzin mehr *out
of gas*

der Gast *m guest n*

geben *to deal (cards) v* p24

Ich bin dabei. *Deal me in.*
p163

geben *to give v* p24

gebräunt *tanned adj*

die Gebühr *f fee, toll n* p50

der Gedanke *m thought n*

die Gefahr *f danger n* p50

gefallen *to please v to be
pleasing to v* p28

das Geflügel *gn poultry n*

gehen *to go v* p24

die Gehhilfe *f walker
(ambulatory device) n* p37

gehoben *upscale adj*

**Geht es Ihnen (formal) / dir
(informal) gut?** *Are you
okay?*

der Gehweg *m sidewalk n*

die Geige *f violin n*

gelb *yellow adj*

der (Geld-)Schein *m bill
(currency) n*

das Geld *gn money n* p120

die Überweisung *money
transfer* p120

der Geldautomat *m ATM n*

die Geldwechselstube *f
currency exchange n*
p31, 120

gelockt *curly adj*

das Gemälde *gn* painting *n*

das Gemüse *gn* vegetable *n*

die Genehmigung *f* permit *n*

genießen to enjoy *v* **p24**

geöffnet open (business) *adj*

Gepäck- baggage *adj* **p31**

die Gepäckausgabe
baggage claim **p31, 33**

das Gepäck *gn* baggage,
luggage *n* **p52**

**das verloren gegangene
Gepäck** lost baggage

gerade straight *adj*

das Gericht *gn* court (legal)
n **p175**

**das Gericht für
Verkehrsdelikte** traffic
court

das Gericht *gn* dish *n* **p79**

die Gesamtsumme *f* total *n*

**Wie hoch ist die
Gesamtsumme?** What is
the total?

das Geschäft *gn* shop *n*,
store *n*

Geschäfts- business *adj* **p66**

das Geschäftszentrum
business center **p66**

das Geschenk *gn* gift *n*

die Geschichte *f* history *n*
p141

geschieden divorced *adj*

das Geschlecht *gn* sex
(gender) *n*

der (Geschlechts-) Verkehr *m*
intercourse (sexual) *n*

der Geschmack *m* taste
(discernment) *n*

der Geschmack *m* taste,
flavor *n*

der Schokoladengeschmack
chocolate flavor

das Gesicht *gn* face *n*

gesperrt closed *adj* **p50**

gestern yesterday *adv* **p4**

gestohlen stolen *adj* **p43**

gestreift striped *adj*

gestresst stressed *adj*

das Getränk *gn* drink *n* **p164**

das Gratisgetränk
complimentary drink

getrennt lebend separated
(marital status) *adj* **p105**

das Getriebe *gn* transmission *n*

das Automatikgetriebe
automatic transmission
p45

das Schaltgetriebe standard
transmission **p45**

getrocknet / Trocken- dried
adj **p98**

die Gewichte *gn, pl* weights
n **p146**

das Gewürz *gn* spice *n*

Gibt es hier ____? Is / Are
there ____?

**Gibt es hier eine öffentliche
Toilette?** Do you have a
public restroom?

das Gift *gn* poison *n* **p15**

der Gin *m* gin *n* **p83**

die Gitarre *f* guitar *n* **p115**

das Glas *gn* glass (drinking) *n*

Schenken Sie das als offenes Getränk aus? *Do you have it by the glass?* **Ich hätte gerne ein Glas.** *I'd like a glass, please.*

glutenfrei *gluten-free adj*

das Gold *gn* gold *n*

golden *gold (color), golden adj*

Golf spielen *to go golfing v* **p24**

das Golf (-spiel) *gn* golf *n*

der Golfplatz *golf course*

der Gottesdienst *m* service (religious) *n*

das GPS-System *m* GPS system *n* **p45**

das Gramm *gn* gram *n*

grau *gray adj*

der Grieche *m*, **die Griechin** *f* Greek *n* **p108**

griechisch *Greek adj* **p74**

griechisch-orthodox *Greek Orthodox adj* **p113**

groß *big adj*, large *adj* **p12**

größer *bigger, larger* **p70, 138**

am größten *biggest, largest*

Großartig! *Great! interj*

die Großmutter *f grandmother n*

der Großvater *m grandfather n*

grün *green adj*

die Gruppe *f* group *n*

günstig *inexpensive adj*

der Gürtel *m* belt *n* **p138**

das band *conveyor belt* **p40**

gut *fine adj* **p1, 100** *well adv*

gut aussehend *handsome adj* **p107**

gut besucht *busy (restaurant) adj*

Gute Nacht. *Good night.* **p100**

Guten Abend. *Good evening.* **p100**

Guten Morgen. *Good morning.* **p100**

Guten Tag. *Good afternoon.* **p100**

Mir geht es gut. *I'm fine.*

der Gutschein *m* voucher *n*

der Essensgutschein *meal voucher* **p38**

der Zimmergutschein *room voucher* **p38**

H

das Haar *gn* hair *n* **p169**

der Haarschnitt *m* haircut *n*

der Haartrockner *m* hair dryer *n* **p69**

haben *to have v* **p24**

Sex haben *to have sex (intercourse)*

der Hafen *port (for ship mooring) n*

das Hähnchen *gn* chicken *n* **p88**

GERMAN—ENGLISH

halb *half adj*

halb gar *medium rare (meat) adj*

halbes Pfund *half-pound* p99

die Hälfte *f half n*

Hallo *hello n* p1

halten *to hold v* **p24**

> **Händchen halten** *to hold hands*

die Haltestelle *f stop n* p56

> **die Bushaltestelle** *bus stop*

Haltet den Dieb! *Stop, thief!*

die Hand *f hand n* p158

das Handbuch *gn manual (instruction booklet) n* p46

handhaben *to handle v* **p21**

> **Vorsicht!** *Handle with care*

der Handschuh *m glove n* p152

die Handtasche *f purse n* p39

> **Ich habe meine Brieftasche verloren.** *I lost my wallet.*
> **Meine Brieftasche wurde gestohlen.** *Someone stole my wallet.*

das Handtuch *gn towel n*

hart *hard (firm) adj* p43

der Hase *m hare (bunny) n*

der Hauch / Zug *m puff n* p15

die Hausfrau *f homemaker n*

die Haut *f skin n*

der Hautarzt *m dermatologist n*

das Heilbad *gn spa n*

heiraten *to marry v* **p21**

heiß *hot adj, warm adj*

die heiße Schokolade *f hot chocolate n* p84

helfen *to help / to assist v* **p24**

hell *bright adj*

das Hemd *gn shirt n*

der Herbst *m autumn (fall season) n* p14

der (Herren-)Frisör *m barber n*

die Herrentoilette *men's restroom*

herunterladen *to download v* **p24**

das Herz *gn heart n*

der Herzinfarkt *m heart attack n*

heute *today n* p4

hier *here adv* p5

die Hilfe *f assistance n*

die Hilfe *f help n* p50

Hilfe! *Help! n*

das Hin- und Rückreiseticket *round-trip ticket* p53

hinter *behind adj*

der Hiphop *hip-hop n* p114

historisch *historical adj*

das Hobby *gn hobby n*

hoch *high adj* p150

> **höher** *higher*
> **am höchsten** *highest*

hochladen *to upload v* **p24**

die Hochschule *f college n, university n*

die Höhe *f altitude n* p150

die höhere Kategorie *f upgrade n* p45

hören *to hear* v
hören *to listen* v **p21**
hörgeschädigt *hearing-impaired* adj
die Hose f *pair of pants* n
  die Badehose *swim trunks* n
  die kurze Hose *shorts*
das Hotel gn *hotel* n **p59**
der Hund m *dog* n **p19, 37**
  der Blindenhund *service dog* **p37, 58**
hundert *hundred* adj **p8**
die Hupe f *horn* n
der Husten m *cough* n
husten *to cough* v **p21**
der Hut m *hat* n **p137**
die Hygieneartikel m, pl *toiletries* n **p91**

I

Ich hätte gern etwas zu trinken. *I'd like a drink.*
ich *I* pron **p3**
ihr *you* pron pl (informal)
Ihr *you* pron (formal)
ihr / ihre *her / their* adj **p3**
im Voraus *in advance* adv
der Imbiss m *snack* n **p162**
der Impressionismus m *Impressionism* n
in der Nähe *near, nearby* adj
  nah *near* adj
  näher *nearer* (comparative)
  am nächsten *nearest* (superlative)
die Infektion f *infection* n
die Information f *information* n

der Informationsstand m *information booth* n **p31**
der Ingenieur m, **die Ingenieurin** f *engineer* n **p109**
innehalten, warten *to hold (to pause), to wait* v **p21, 24**
das Insektenschutzmittel gn *insect repellent* n
das Internet gn *Internet* n **p126**
  Wo finde ich ein Internetcafé? *Where can I find an Internet café?*
das Internetcafé gn *cybercafé* n
der iPod-Anschluß m *ipod connection* n
der Ire m, **die Irin** f *Irish* n
irisch *Irish* adj
Irland *Ireland* n
italienisch *Italian* adj **p73**
der Italiener m, **die Italienerin** f *Italian* n **p108**

J

ja *yes* adv **p1**
die Jacke f *coat, jacket* n **p40, 137**
das Jahr gn *year* n
  Wie alt sind Sie? (formal) / Wie alt bist du? (informal) *What's your age?*
der Januar m *January* n **p14**
der Jazz m *jazz* n **p114**
jemand *someone* n **p32**

jener / jene / jenes *that (far away)* adj p7

jetzt *now* adv p4

das Joggen *jogging* n

jüdisch *Jewish* adj p113

die Jugendherberge f *hostel* n p59

der Juli m *July* n p14

jung *young* adj p106

der Junge m *boy* n, *kid* n

der Juni m *June* n p14

K

der Käfer m *bug* n p81

der Kaffee (beverage) m *coffee* n

  der Eiskaffee *iced coffee*
  der Espresso m *espresso* n

kahl *bald* adj p15

kalt *cold* adj p81

die Kamera f *camera* n

Kanada m *Canada* n

kanadisch *Canadian* adj

kariert *checked (pattern)* adj

die Karte f *card* n p109

  die Kreditkarte *credit card* p120
  Akzeptieren Sie Kreditkarten? *Do you accept credit cards?*
  die Visitenkarte *business card*

die Karte f *map* n p49

  der Straßenatlas *road map*

der Kartenschalter *ticket counter* p30

der Kartenverkauf m *box office* n

der Kaschmir m *cashmere* n

der Käse m *cheese* n p89

das Kasino gn *casino* n p59

der Katholik m, **die Katholikin** f *Catholic* n p113

die Katze f *cat* n

kein *none, no* adj adv p1

keine freien Zimmer *no vacancy*

der Keks m *cookie* n p90

der Kellner / die Kellnerin m / f *waiter* n

kennen *to know (someone)* v p24

das Kennwort gn *password* n

das Kilo gn *kilo* n p11

das Kind gn, *child* n

  Mein Kind ist weg. *My child is missing.*

die Kinder gn, pl *children* n pl

der Kinderarzt / die Kinderärztin *pediatrician* n

das Kinderbett gn *crib* n p62

die Kinderkrippe f *nursery* n

der Kinderwagen m *stroller* n

das Kino gn *cinema* n

die Kirche f *church* n p113

das Kissen gn *pillow* n p41

  das Daunenkissen *down pillow*

klar *clear* adj

die Klarinette f *clarinet* n

die Klasse f *class* n p34

  die Business-Klasse *business class* p34
  die Economy-Klasse *economy class* p34

die Erste Klasse first class p34
klassisch classical (music) adj
das Klavier gn piano n p115
das Kleid gn dress (garment) n
der Kleiderbügel m hanger n
die Kleidergröße f size (clothing, shoes) n
die Kleidung f dress (general attire) n
klein little adj, small adj p12
kleiner smaller, littler
am kleinsten smallest, littlest
der Kleinbus m van n
das kleine Mädchen gn little girl n
das Kleinkind gn infant n
Kletter- climbing adj
die Kletterausrüstung climbing gear
klettern (mountain) / steigen (stairs) to climb v p21, 24
bergsteigen to climb a mountain
das Klettern gn climbing n
das Felsenklettern rock climbing
die Klimaanlage f air conditioning n p69
der Knoblauch m garlic n p97
kochen to cook v p21
die Kochnische f kitchenette n p61
der Köder m bait n p151
der Koffer m suitcase / trunk (luggage) n p43
der Kofferraum m trunk (of car) n

der Kognak m cognac n p83
die Koje f berth n
das Kondom gn condom n p161
Hast du ein Kondom? Do you have a condom? p161
nicht ohne Kondom not without a condom
können to be able to (can) v, may v aux p26
Kann ich ____? May I ____?
konsequent consistent(ly) adj/adv p15
der Kontakt für den Notfall m emergency contact n
das Konto gn account n p121
der Kontostand m balance (on bank account) n p121
das Konzert gn concert n p118
der Kopfhörer m headphones n
kopieren (fotokopieren) to photocopy v p21
korrekt correct adj
korrigieren to correct v p21
das koschere Essen kosher meal p35, 78
kosten to cost v p21
kosten to taste v, to try (food) v p21
das Kostüm gn costume n
krank sick adj
der Krankenpfleger / die Krankenpflegerin m/f nurse n p110
der Krankenwagen m ambulance n

Rufen Sie einen Krankenwagen. *Call an ambulance.*

kratzen *to scratch* v **p21**

der Kratzer m *scratch* n

das Kraut gn *herb* n

das Kreditinstitut gn *credit bureau* n **p120**

der Krieg m *war* n **p113**

die Krone f *crown (dental)* n

der Kubismus m *Cubism* n

die Küche f *kitchen* n **p66**

die Kuh f *cow* n

Kunst- *art* adj

das Kunstmuseum *art museum*

der Handwerker m, **die Handwerkerin** f *craftsperson / artisan* n

die Kunst f *art* n

die Kunstausstellung *art exhibit*

der Künstler / die Künstlerin m/f *artist* n

der Kunststoff m *plastic* n

kupferfarben *copper* adj

die Kuppel f *dome* n **p15**

kurz *short* adj **p12**

der Kurze m *shot (liquor)* n

der Kuss m *kiss* n **p159**

das Kuvert gn *envelope* n **p128**

L

laktoseintolerant *lactose-intolerant* adj

die Laktoseunverträglichkeit f *lactose intolerance* n **p79**

das Lämpchen *light (on car dashboard)*

landen *to land* v **p21**

langsamer werden *to slow* v **p24**

das Laufband gn *treadmill* n

laufen *to walk* v **p24**

laut *loud, noisy* adj **p70, 71**

das Leben gn *life* n

Was machen Sie (formal / machst du (informal) beruflich? *What do you do for a living?* **p109**

leben *to live* v **p21**

Wo bleiben Sie? (formal) / Wo bleibst du? (informal) *Where do you live?*

die Lebensmittel gn, pl *groceries* n

das Leder gn *leather* n **p43**

ledig *single (unmarried)* adj **p105**

Sind Sie ledig? *Are you single?* **p105**

leid *sorry* adj

Tut mir leid. *I'm sorry.*

letzter / letzte / letztes *last* adv **p10**

das Licht gn *light (lamp)* n **p41, 64**

die Liebe f *love* n

lieben *to love* v **p21**

das Lied gn *song* n **p158**

die Limonade f *soda* n **p41**

die Diätlimonade *diet soda* **p41**

links *left* adj **p6**

das Loch gn *cavity (tooth cavity)* n

die Locke f *curl* n

locker *loose* adj

der **Löffel** m spoon n p81

die **Loge** f box (seat) n p148

die **Luftpost** air mail

der **Expressversand** express mail

der **Versand erster Klasse** first class mail

das **Einschreiben** registered mail

Wo befindet sich das Postamt? Where is the post office?

M

machen to do v, to make v p21

das **Mädchen** gn girl n

die **Mahlzeit** f meal

das **Essen für Diabetiker** diabetic meal

der **Mai** m May (month) n

das **Make-up** gn makeup n

die **Mama** f mom n, mommy n

der **Manager** / die **Managerin** m / f manager n

der **Mann** m man n

männlich male adj

der **Markt** m market n

der **Flohmarkt** flea market p136

der **Freiluftmarkt** open-air market

der **März** m March (month) n

die **Maschine** f machine n

das **Röntgengerät** x-ray machine

der **Automat** vending machine

massieren to massage v p21

die **Maus** f mouse n

medium medium well (meat) adj p78

die **Medizin** f medicine n, medication n

die **Meeresfrüchte** f, pl seafood n p79

die **Menge (things)** / der **Betrag (money)** f / m amount n

das **Menü** gn today's special n p15

messen to measure v p24

der **Metalldetektor** m metal detector n

der **Meter** m meter n

mieten to rent v

das **Militär** gn military n

die **Milliarde** f billion n p15

der **Milliliter** m milliliter n

der **Millimeter** m millimeter n

mindestens at least n

die **Minibar** f minibar n

die **Minute** f minute n p4

sofort in a minute

mischen to blend v p15

mit with prep p80

mit Buffet buffet-style adj

mit Rollen wheeled (luggage) adj

mit wenig Salz low-salt

der **Mitarbeiter** m, die **Mitarbeiterin** f employee n

das **Mitglied** gn member n

die **Mitgliedschaft** f membership n

der **Mittag** noon n p13

das Mittagessen *gn lunch n* p74

mittel *medium adj (size)* p12

Mittel- *middle adj*

Mitternacht *midnight adv* p12

der Mittwoch *m Wednesday n*

das Mobiltelefon / Handy *cell phone* p176

Geben Sie mir bitte Ihre Telefonnummer? *May I have your phone number?* p119

die Telefonvermittlung *f phone operator*

das Prepaid-Telefon *prepaid phones*

der Monat *m month n* p4

der Montag *m Monday n* p13

der Morgen *m morning n* p13

morgens *in the morning* p67

morgen *gn tomorrow adv*

die Morgendämmerung *f dawn n*

bei Tagesanbruch *at dawn* p13

die Moschee *f mosque n* p113

der Motor *m engine n* p47

das Motorrad *gn motorcycle n*

müde *tired adj* p107

der Mund *m mouth n*

die Münze *f coin n*

das Museum *gn museum n* p118

das Musical *gn musical (music genre) n*

die Musik *f music n* p114

die Popmusik *pop music*

musikalisch *musical adj*

der Musiker / die Musikerin *m / f musician n* p111

der Muslim *m, die Muslimin* *f Muslim n* p113

die Mutter *f mother n* p104

das Muttermal *gn mole (facial feature) n*

N

der Nachbar *m, die Nachbarin f neighbor n* p104

der Nachmittag *m afternoon n* p13

nachmittags *in the afternoon*

der Nachname *m last name*

Ich habe meinen Mädchennamen behalten. *I kept my maiden name.*

Nachschenken *v refill (of beverage) v*

die Nachspeise *f dessert n* p86

die Dessertkarte *dessert menu* p86

die Nacht *f night n* p13

nachts *at night* p13, 55

pro Nacht *per night*

der Nachtclub *m nightclub n*

nah, in der Nähe *close, near adj* p5

näher *closer* p5

am nächsten *closest* p5

nähen *to sew* v p21

der Name *m* *name* n

der Vorname *first name*

der Nachname *last name*

die Nase *f* *nose* n p169

die Nationalität *f* *nationality* n

neben *next to* prep p5

der nächste Halt *the next station*

der Neffe *m* *nephew* n p105

nehmen *to take* v **p24**

Wie lange wird das dauern? *How long will this take?*

nett *nice (kind)* adj

das Netzwerk *gn* *network* n

neu *new* adj p152

neun *nine* adj p8

neunter *ninth* adj p10

neunzehn *nineteen* adj p8

neunzig *ninety* n adj p8

Neuseeland *New Zealand* n

der Neuseeländer *m*, die Neuseeländerin *f* *New Zealander* n

die Nichte *f* *niece* n p105

Nichtraucher- *nonsmoking* adj

der Nichtraucherbereich *nonsmoking area*

das Nichtraucherauto *nonsmoking car*

das Nichtraucherzimmer *nonsmoking room*

nichts / keine *none* n p11

der Niederländer *m*, die Niederländerin *f* *Dutch* n p108

niedergeschlagen *depressed* adj p109

niedrig *low* adj

niedriger *lower*

am niedrigsten *lowest*

noch einen / eine / ein *another* adj p5

der Norweger *m*, die Norwegerin *f* *Norwegian* n p110

die Note *f* *grade (school)* n

das Notebook *gn* *laptop* n p143

der Notfall *m* *emergency* n

der November *m* *November* n

die Nummer *f* *number* n p125

die Nuss *f* *nut* n

O

die Öffnungszeiten *f, pl* *hours (at museum)* n

ohne *without* prep p80

ohnmächtig werden *to faint* v **p24**

OK / in Ordnung *Okay* adj adv p14

der Oktober *m* *October* n p14

das Öl *gn* *oil* n p49, 78, 80

die Olive *f* *olive* n

der Onkel *m* *uncle* n p105

die Oper *f* *opera* n p115

das Opernhaus *gn* *opera house* n

der Optiker / die Optikerin *m /*
f optometrist n

orange *orange (color) adj*

der Orangensaft *m orange*
juice n

die Orgel *f organ n*

örtlich *local adj* p46

der Österreicher *m,* **die**
Österreicherin *f Austrian*
n p108

P

das Paket *gn package n* p127

das Papier *paper n*

  der Papierteller *paper plate*
  p91

  die Papierserviette *paper*
  napkin p91

die Papiere *gn, pl*
identification n p39

der Park *m park n* p118

Park- *parking adj*

parken *to park v* **p21**

Parkverbot *no parking*

die Partei *f political party*
n p113

der Partner *m,* **die Partnerin**
f partner n

der Passagier *m passenger*
n p42

passen *to fit (clothes) v* **p21**

passen *to match v* **p21**

passen *to pass (gambling)*
v **p21**

die Pause *f intermission n*

das Penthaus *gn penthouse n*

die Person *f person n*

Person mit Sehbehinderung
visually-impaired person

das Personal *gn staff*
(employees) n p72

das Pferd *gn horse n*

die Pille *f birth control n*
p161

Ich nehme die Pille. *I'm on*
birth control.

die Pizza *f pizza n*

der Platz *m court (sport) n*

der Platz *m seat n* p35

  der Orchesterplatz
  orchestra seat

platzieren *to place v* **p21**

der Pole *m,* **die Polin** *f Polish*
n p108

die Polizei *f police n* p31

Rufen Sei die Polizei! *Call*
the police!

die Polizeiwache *f police*
station n

der Polizist / die Polizistin
m / f officer n

das Poolbillard *gn pool (the*
game) n

der Portier *m porter n*

die Portion *f portion (of*
food) n

das Porträt *gn portrait n*

der Portugiese *m,* **die**
Portugiesin *f Portuguese*
n p108

der Portwein *m port*
(beverage) n

die Post *f mail n/post office*
n p127

die Postkarte *f postcard n*
der Preis *m price n*
  der Eintrittspreis *admission fee, cover charge (in bar) n* p134
  in der mittleren Preiskategorie *moderately priced* p59
der Preisnachlass *m discount n*
  der Kinderrabatt *children's discount*
  der Seniorenrabatt *senior discount*
  der Studentenrabatt *student discount*
Privat- *home adj*
  die Privatadresse *home address*
  die private Telefonnummer *home telephone number*
das Problem *gn problem n* p2
das Produkt *gn product n*
professionell *professional adj*
das Programm *gn program n*
protestantisch *Protestant adj*
der Puff *m bordello n* p15
der Pullover *m sweater n* p40
die Pumpe *f pump n*

Q
das Querformat *gn landscape (painting) n*
die Quittung *f receipt n* p121

R
das Radio *gn radio n*
  das Satellitenradio *satellite radio*

die Rampe für Rollstuhlfahrer *f wheelchair ramp n*
das Rauchen *gn smoking n*
  der Raucherbereich *smoking area* p31
  Rauchen verboten *no smoking* p33
rauchen *to smoke v* p21
räumen *to clear v* p21
die Rechnung *f bill n*
die Rechte *gn, pl rights n pl*
  die Bürgerrechte *civil rights*
rechts *right adj* p49
  ____ befindet sich auf der rechten Seite. *____ is on the right.* p49
  Biegen Sie an der Ecke nach rechts ab. *Turn right at the corner.*
der Redakteur *m*, die Redakteurin *f editor n* p109
der Regenschirm *m umbrella n*
der Reggae *m reggae n* p114
die Regierung *f government n*
regnen *to rain v* p21
regnerisch *rainy adj* p111
der Reifen *m tire n* p48
  der Reservereifen *spare tire n*
die Reise *f trip n* p100
der Reiseführer *m guide (publication) n*
reisen *to travel v* p21
der Reisescheck *m travelers' check n*

GERMAN—ENGLISH

die Reklamation *f claim n*
rennen *to run v* **p24**
die Reservierung *f*
  reservation n
das Restaurant *gn*
  restaurant n

das Steakhaus *steakhouse*

der Rettungsschwimmer *m*
  lifeguard n **p151**
das Rezept *gn prescription*
  n **p39**
die Rezeption *f front desk n*
die Richtung *f direction*

Einbahnstraße *one way*
  (traffic sign)

riechen *to smell v* **p24**
die Rockmusik *m rock n* **p114**
der Roller *m scooter n* **p44**
der Rollstuhl *m wheelchair*
  n **p37**

der Zugang per Rollstuhl
  wheelchair access
die Rampe für
  Rollstuhlfahrer *wheelchair*
  ramp
der elektrisch betriebene
  Rollstuhl *power*
  wheelchair

die Rolltreppe *f escalator n*
der Roman *m novel n*

der Mystery-Roman
  mystery novel
der Liebesroman *romance*
  novel

romantisch *romantic adj*
rosa *pink adj*
die Rose *f rose n*

rot *red adj* **p163**
rothaarig *redhead adj*
der Royal Flush *royal flush*
der Rücken *m back n*
die Rückenmassage *f back*
  rub n **p159**
der Rucksack *m backpack*
  n **p176**
rufen *to call (shout), to shout*
  v **p24**
ruhig *quiet adj*
der Rum *m rum n* **p84**
der Russe *m,* **die Russin** *f*
  Russian n **p110**

S
der Saft *m juice n* **p91**
sagen *to say v* **p21**
der Salat *m salad n* **p98**
das Salz *gn salt n* **p97**
sammeln *to collect v* **p21**
der Samstag *m Saturday n*
  p13
der Satellit *m satellite n*
das Satellitenradio *satellite*
  radio

die Satellitenverfolgung
  satellite tracking

die Sauerstoffflasche *f*
  oxygen tank n
scannen *to scan (document)*
  v **p21**
das Schalentier *gn shellfish*
  n **p79**
der Schalter *m window n*

der Abgabeschalter *drop-*
  off window **p129**

der Abholschalter *pickup window* p129

Schau her! *Look here!*

der Scheck *m check n* p120

der Scheinwerfer *m headlight n*

schieben *to hold (gambling)* v p24

das Schild „Vorfahrt gewähren" *gn yield sign n*

der Schlafwagen *m sleeping car n*

Schlangenaugen! *Snake eyes! n*

schlecht *adj bad adj*

schließen *to close* v p24

schlimmer *worse See schlecht*

das Schloss *gn castle, lock n* p147

schlucken *to swallow* v p21

schmal *narrow adj* p12

schmerzen *to hurt (to feel painful)* v p21

Autsch! Das tut weh! *Ouch! That hurts!*

die Kopfschmerzen *m, pl headache n* p100

die Zahnschmerzen *m, pl toothache n*

Ich habe Zahnschmerzen. *I have a toothache.*

schminken *to make up (apply cosmetics)* v p21

schmutzig *dirty adj* p70

das Schnäppchen *gn deal (bargain) n*

schneiden *to cut* v p24

der Schneider / die Schneiderin *m / f tailor n* p67

schnell *fast adj* p50, 151

der Schnitt *m cut (wound) n*

der Schnorchel *m snorkel (breathing tube) n*

der Schnuller *m pacifier n*

schön *beautiful adj*

schottisch *Scottish adj*

schreiben *to write* v p24

Könnten Sie mir das bitte aufschreiben? *Would you please write that down for me?*

der Schuh *m shoe n*

die Schule *f school n*

die Mittelstufe *junior high / middle school*

die juristische Fakultät *law school*

die medizinische Fakultät *medical school*

die Grundschule *primary school*

die weiterführende Schule *high school*

der Schwan *m swan n*

schwanger *pregnant adj*

schwarz *black adj* p163

der Schwede *m, die Schwedin f Swedish n* p110

das Schwein *gn pig n*

der Schweizer *m, die Schweizerin f Swiss n* p108*

die Schwester f sister n

schwierig difficult adj p150

schwimmen to swim v **p24**

> **Schwimmen verboten.**
> Swimming prohibited.

die Schwimmweste f life
preserver n

sechs six adj p8

sechzehn sixteen adj p8

sechzig sixty adj p8

das Segel gn sail n

das Segeltuch gn canvas
(fabric) n

sehen to see v **p24**

> **Dürfte ich das mal sehen?**
> May I see it?

sehr very p72

seicht shallow adj

die Seide f silk n p137

das Seil gn rope n

sein to be v **p23**

sein / seine his adj

Selbstbedienungs- self-
serve adj

das Selters gn seltzer n p82

senden to send v **p21**

der September m September n

der Service m service n p37

> **außer Betrieb** out of service

die Servicegebühr f service
charge n p64

servieren to serve v **p21**

die Serviette f napkin n

setzen to put (gambling)
v **p21**

> **Setzen Sie das auf Rot /
> Schwarz!** Put it on red /
> black! p163

das Shampoo gn shampoo n

sicher safe (secure) adj

der Sicherheitsdienst m
security n p30

> **die Sicherheitsschleuse**
> security checkpoint
> **der Sicherheitsbeamte**
> security guard p31

die Sicherung f fuse n

sie f she / they

sie them pron pl p4

Sie you pron sing/pl (formal)

sieben seven adj p8

siebter seventh adj p10

siebzehn seventeen adj p8

siebzig seventy adj p8

das Sightseeing gn
sightseeing n

das Silber gn silver n

Silber- silver adj

silbern silver (color) adj

die SIM-Karte f SIM card n

singen to sing v **p24**

**Der Sitz hinter der
Trennwand** m bulkhead
seat n p35

sitzen to sit v **p24**

die Skulptur f sculpture n

die Socke f sock n

die Software f software n

der Sohn m son n p104

der Sommer m summer
n p14

die Sommersprosse f
freckle n

die Sonne f sun n

der Sonnenbrand m
sunburn n

die Sonnenbrille *f sunglasses n* p137

die Sonnencreme *f sunscreen n*

sonnig *sunny adj* p115

der Sonntag *m Sunday n* p13

die Soße *f sauce n*

der Sozialismus *m socialism n*

der Spanier *m,* die Spanierin *f Spanish n* p108

spanisch *Spanish adj* p73

spät *late adj* p12

Bitte pünktlich sein. *Please don't be late.*

später *later adv*

der Spaziergang *m walk n*

der Specht *m woodpecker n*

die Speisekarte *f menu n* p15, 75

das Kindermenü *children's menu*

das Diabetikermenü *diabetic menu*

die Spezialität *f special (featured meal) n*

das Spiel *gn match (sport) n*

die Spielekonsole *f game console n* p142

spielen *to play (a game) v* p21

spielen *to play (an instrument) v* p21

der Spielplatz *m playground n*

der Spielstand *m score n*

das Spielwarengeschäft *gn toy store n*

das Spielzeug *gn toy n*

der Spind *m locker n* p146

der Umkleidesschrank *gym locker*

der Aufbewahrungsschrank *storage locker*

der Split *m split (gambling) n*

der Sport *m sports n*

das Sportstadion *gn coliseum n*

sprechen *to speak v, to talk v* p24

Wir sprechen Englisch. *English spoken here.*

der Sprung *m crack (in glass object) n*

spülen *to flush v* p21

der Staat (gov.) / der Status (status) *m state n*

das Stadion *gn stadium n* p147

die Stadt *f city n* p61

das Stadtzentrum *gn city center n* p30

der Stecker *m plug n*

stehen *to stand v* p24

die Steuer *f tax n* p140

die Mehrwertsteuer (MwSt.) *value-added tax (VAT)*

stillen *to nurse v* p21

die Stirn *f forehead n*

der Stoff *m fabric n*

STOP *STOP (traffic sign)*

stornieren *to cancel v* p21

die Strafe *f fine (for traffic violation) n* p50, 174

die Strähnchen *gn, pl highlights (hair) n* p144

der Strand m beach n p118
stranden to beach v
die Straße f road, street n p6, 50
  am Ende der Straße down the street
  gegenüber across the street
streichen to paint v p24
das Streichholz gn match (fire) n
die Streitkräfte f pl armed forces n pl
die Strömung f current (water) n
die Stufe f stair n
die Suche f search n
  das Abtasten hand search
suchen to look for (to search) v p21
die Suite f suite n p59
der Supermarkt m supermarket n
surfen to surf v p21
  das Surfbrett surfboard n
der (Swimming-) Pool m pool (swimming) n
die Symphonie f symphony n

T
die Tablette f pill n
  die Tablette gegen Seekrankheit f seasickness pill
der Tacho m speedometer n
die Tafel f board n
der Tag m day n p46
  vorgestern the day before yesterday p4

übermorgen the day after tomorrow p4
die Tante f aunt n p105
tapfer brave adj p15
die Tariftabelle f rate plan (cell phone) n
  Haben Sie eine Tariftabelle? Do you have a rate plan?
die Tasche f / **die Tüte** f bag n
tatsächlich actual adj
taub deaf adj
tauchen to dive v p21
tauchen (mit Atemgerät) to scuba dive v
  Ich tauche mit Atemgerät. I scuba dive.
  schnorcheln to snorkel v
tausend thousand adj p8
das Taxi gn taxi n p51
  Taxi! Taxi!
  der Taxistand taxi stand
der Techno m techno n (music)
der Tee m tea n p85
  Tee mit Milch und Zucker tea with milk and sugar
  Tee mit Zitrone tea with lemon
  Kräutertee herbal tea
das Telefon gn phone n
Telefon- phone adj p124
  Geben Sie mir bitte Ihre Telefonnummer? May I have your phone number? p158
  die Telefonvermittlung f phone operator

das Prepaid-Telefon *prepaid phones*

der Telefonanruf *m phone call n*

das R-Gespräch *collect phone call*

das Auslandsgespräch *international phone call*

das Ferngespräch *long-distance phone call*

die Telefonauskunft *phone directory*

die Telefonauskunft *f directory assistance*

der Teller *m plate n p81*

der Tempel *m temple n p113*

das Tennis *gn tennis n p60*

der Termin *m appointment n p134*

das Terminal *gn terminal (airport) n p33*

teuer *expensive adj p74, 140, 155*

das Theater *gn theater n p131*

das Theaterstück *gn play n*

die Theke *f counter (in bar) n p77*

Ticket *gn ticket n p30*

tief *deep adj p151*

das Tier *gn animal n*

der Tisch *m table n p75, 77*

die Tochter *f daughter n p107*

die Toilette *f toilet n p64*

das Toilettenpapier *gn toilet paper n*

die Tonne *f ton n*

das Tor *gn goal (sport) n*

trainieren *to train v p21*

das Training *gn workout n*

die Transaktion *f transaction n*

der Transfer *m transfer n*

die Überweisung *money transfer*

transferieren / überweisen *to transfer v p21, 24*

die Traube *f grape n*

traurig *sad adj p107*

der Treff *m hangout (hot spot) n*

Treppen steigen *to climb stairs*

der Tresor *safe (for storing valuables) n p69*

trimmen *to trim (hair) v p21*

trinken *to drink v p24*

das Trinkgeld *gn tip (gratuity) p85*

inklusive Trinkgeld *tip included p85*

trocken *dry adj*

trocknen *to dry v p21*

die Trommel *f drum n*

die Trompete *f trumpet n*

tropfen *to drip v p21*

der Truthahn *m turkey n*

der Tscheche *m, die Tschechin f Czech n p108*

die Tür *f door n*

das Gate *gate (at airport) p31*

der Türke *m, die Türkin f Turkish n p108*

U

die **U-Bahn** *f subway n*

die **U-Bahn-Linie** *subway line*

die **U-Bahn-Haltestelle** *subway station*

Mit welcher U-Bahn komme ich zu / zur / zum ____? *Which subway do I take for ____?*

die **Übelkeit** *f nausea n* p166

über *above adj* p6, 71

überall / irgendwo *anywhere adv*

überfallen *to mug (assault) v* p24

überfallen werden *to get mugged*

überhitzen *to overheat v* p21

die **Übernachtung mit Frühstück** *f bed-and-breakfast (B & B) n*

überprüfen / sich vergewissern *to check v* p21

die **Uhr** *m clock n, watch n*

Uhr *o'clock adv* p5

zwei Uhr *two o'clock*

die **Uhrzeit** *f time n*

die **Uhrzeit für das Auschecken** *check-out time*

kein Ausgang *not an exit*

der **Notausgang** *emergency exit* p35

die **Umkleide** *f locker room n*

die **Umkleidekabine** *f changing room, fitting room n*

umsehen *to look (observe) v* p24

die **Umwelt** *f environment n*

der **Umzug** *m parade n*

der **Unfall** *m accident n*

unfrei *collect adj*

die **Universität** *f university n*

unter *below adj* p6, 71

unterbrechen *to disconnect v* p24

das **Unternehmen** *gn business n*

unterschreiben *to sign v* p24

Unterschreiben Sie bitte hier. *Sign here.*

die **Untertitel** *m, pl subtitle n*

die **Unterwäsche** *f underwear n*

die **Unze** *f ounce n*

der **Urlaub** *m vacation n* p38

im Urlaub *on vacation*

in Urlaub gehen *to go on vacation*

der **USB-Anschluss** *m USB port n*

V

der **Van** *m van n* p44

der **Vater** *m father n*

der **Vegetarier** *m,* die **Vegetarierin** *f vegetarian n*

das **vegetarische Essen** *vegetarian meal* p35

der **Ventilator** *m fan n*

die Verbindungs-
geschwindigkeit f
connection speed n
verdächtig *suspiciously adv*
p42
verärgert *angry adj* p107
Verdammt! *Damn! expletive*
die Verdauungsstörung f
indigestion n
verfügbar *available adj* p133
verheiratet *married adj* p105
verkaufen *to sell v* p21
der Verkäufer m, die
Verkäuferin f *salesperson
n* p109
der Straßenhändler m, die
Straßenhändlerin f *street
vendor*
der Verkehr m *traffic n* p46
Wie ist der Verkehr? *How's
traffic?*
Es ist viel Verkehr. *Traffic is
terrible.*
der Verkehrsstau m
congestion (traffic) n
der Verkostungsraum m
tasting room n
verlangsamen *to slow v* p21
Fahren Sie bitte langsamer.
Slow down! p51
verlieren *to lose v* p24
der Verlobte m, die Verlobte
f *fiancé(e) n*
die Vermittlung f *operator
(phone) n* p65
verschmort *charred (meat)
adj* p78

verschütten *to spill v* p21
verschwinden *to disappear
v* p24
verschwommen *blurry
adj* p170
versenden *to ship v* p21
die Versicherung f *insurance
n* p174
die Unfallversicherung f
collision insurance
die Haftpflichtversicherung
liability insurance
die Version f *version n* p127
die Verspätung f *delay n*
p34, 37
verstehen *to understand v*
p24
Ich verstehe nicht. *I don't
understand.*
Verstanden? *Do you
understand?*
verstopft *constipated adj*
die Verstopfung f
*congestion, constipation
n* p166
versuchen *to try (attempt)
v* p21
der Verwandte m, die
Verwandte f *relative n*
verwenden *to use v* p21
verwirrt *confused adj*
verzollen (customs) *to
declare v* p21
das Video g n *video n*
der Videorekorder m *VCR n*
viel *a lot n*
viel *much adj* p11

viel Spaß *have fun* pviii

viele *many adj* p11

vier *four adj* p8

vierter *fourth adj* p10

ein Viertel *one quarter, one fourth*

vierzehn *fourteen adj* p8

vierzig *forty adj*

das Vinyl *gn vinyl n* p43

violett *purple adj*

das Visum *gn visa n*

der Vogel *m bird n*

voll *full adj* p85

vorbereitet *prepared adj*

Vorder- *front adj* p35

vorgestern *the day before yesterday adv* p4

die letzten paar Tage *these last few days*

vorstellen *to introduce v* p21

die Vorstellung *f show (performance) n*

vorwärts *forward adj* p6

W

der Wachmann *m guard n*

der Sicherheitsbeamte *security guard* p31

wachsen *to grow (get larger) v* p24

Wo sind Sie (formal) / bist du (informal) aufgewachsen? *Where did you grow up?*

die Wahl *f election n* p112

wählen *to dial (a phone number) v* p21

wählen *to vote v* p21

wandern *to hike v* p21

wenig *little*

wann *when adv* p3

der Wartebereich *m waiting area n* p31

die Warze *f wart n*

was *what adv* p3

Was gibt's? *What's up?*

das Waschbecken *gn sink n*

das Wasser *gn water n* p40

das heiße Wasser *hot water*

das kalte Wasser *cold water*

der Wasserhahn *m faucet n*

der Webdesigner *m Web designer n* p111

das Wechselgeld *gn change (money) n*

der Wechselkurs *m exchange rate n* p121

wechseln *to change (money) v / to change (clothes) v* p21

der Wecker *m alarm clock* p68

Weckruf *wake-up call n* p68

der Weg *m trail n*

weiß *white adj*

weich *soft adj*

der Wein *m wine n* p41, 77

das Weingut *gn vineyard n*

welcher / welche / welches *which adv* p3

weniger *See* wenig

wer *who adv* p3

Wem gehört ____? *Whose is ____?*

der Western *western n (movie)*

westlich, abendländisch *western adj*

die Wette f bet n
Ich gehe mit. I'll see your bet. p164
wetten to bet v p21
der Wetterbericht m weather forecast n
wie how adv p3, 12
Wie viel? How much?
Für wie lange? For how long?
wie (viele) how (many) adv
wiedergutmachen to make up (apologize, compensate) v p21
wiederholen to repeat v p21
Könnten Sie das bitte wiederholen? Would you please repeat that? p2, 50
Auf Wiedersehen m goodbye n p101
wiegen to weigh v p24
das Wi-Fi gn wi-fi n
willkommen welcome adj
Gern geschehen. You're welcome.
die Wimper f eyelash n
die Windel f diaper n
die Stoffwindel cloth diaper
die Wegwerfwindel disposable diaper
windig windy adj p111
windsurfen to windsurf v
der Winter m winter n p14
wir we pron pl
wirklich really adj
die Wirtschaft f economy n

das Wischerblatt gn wiper blade n
wissen to know (something) v p27
die Witwe f widow n p105
der Witwer m widower n p105
WLAN n Wi-Fi n p61
wo where adv p3
Wo ist ____? Where is ____?
die Woche f week n p4, 46
diese Woche this week
letzte Woche last week
nächste Woche next week
eine Woche one week
in einer Woche a week from now
der Wodka m vodka n
das Wohnmobil (van) / der Wohnwagen (trailer) gn / m camper n
wollen to want v p25
das Wörterbuch gn dictionary n

X
XL- extra-large adj

Z
der Zahn m tooth n p173
der Zahnarzt m dentist n p167
die Zahnpasta f toothpaste n p67
die Zahnprotese f dentures, denture plate n p173
zehn ten adj p8

zehnter tenth adj p10

zeichnen drawing (activity) v
  p21, 115

die Zeichnung f drawing
  (work of art) n

zeigen to point v **p21**

  **Könnten Sie mir das bitte
  zeigen?** Would you
  show me?

die Zeit f time n

die Zeitschrift f magazine n

die Zeitung f newspaper n

der Zeitungsstand m
  newsstand n p32, 140

das Zelt gn tent n

zelten to camp v **p21**

der Zentimeter m
  centimeter n

(zer-)brechen to break v **p24**

zerbrechlich fragile adj p128

zerkocht overcooked adj

zerkratzt scratched adj

die Ziege f goat n

ziehen to pull v **p24**

das Ziel gn destination n

die Zigarette f cigarette n

  die Schachtel Zigaretten
  pack of cigarettes

die Zigarre f cigar n

das Zimmer gn room (hotel) n

das Zimmermädchen gn
  maid (hotel) n

der Zinssatz m interest rate n

Zoll inch

der Zoll m customs n p33

der Zoo m zoo n p118

zu too (excessively) adv

zu toward prep

der Zug m train n p53

  der Expresszug express
  train

  der Nahverkehrszug local
  train

das Zuhause gn home n

zurückgeben to return
  (something) v **p24**

zurückkehren to return (to a
  place) v **p21**

zusätzlich extra adj p67

zusehen to watch v **p24**

der Zustand m condition n

  **in gutem / schlechtem
  Zustand** in good / bad
  condition

zuvorkommend courteous
  adj p72

zwanzig twenty adj p8

zwei two adj p8

zweisprachig bilingual adj

zweiter second adj p10

zwölf twelve adj p8